Climbing Higher

Climbing Higher

Mountaintop Meditations for
Each Day of the Year

COMPILED BY

AL BRYANT

Bethany Fellowship INC.
MINNEAPOLIS, MINNESOTA 55438

To
Mom and Dad Carlson
who had enough faith in
me to give me their
daughter

Published by Bethany Fellowship, Inc.
6820 Auto Club Road, Minneapolis, Minnesota 55438

Printed in the United States of America

Library of Congress Cataloging in Publication Data:

Main entry under title:

Climbing higher.

    1. Devotional calendars. I. Bryant, Al, 1926-
BV4810.C535   242'.2   77-24978
ISBN 0-87123-052-6
ISBN 0-87123-054-2 pbk.

Preface

Climbing Higher follows in the tradition of its predecessor, *Climbing the Heights*, which has become a favorite among thousands of readers. Well established in the ranks of best-loved daily devotional books, it is rapidly gaining the status of a classic since its release more than twenty years ago. In a sense, *Climbing Higher* has been twenty years in the making, for its compiler/author has been learning and growing throughout these years, and he shares some of his spiritual (and practical) insights thus gained in this new volume.

The arrangement of these devotionals reflects that theme of growth, following a distinct progression of thought through the months of the year. Each month's theme represents a step in that growth, commencing with the logical theme of "Beginnings" in January; February's emphasis is structured around the idea of "Learning to Love" (God, myself, and others); in March the "Winds of the Spirit" are the thread running through the month, with the development of a mature faith the underlying truth. So the child of God will progress through the year until he arrives in the "School of Discipleship" in September; graduates into the "Halls of Holiness" in November; and moves into the crowning celebration of Advent and the Second Coming of Christ in December.

The purpose and central theme of *Climbing Higher* is beautifully illustrated in some thoughts from J. R. Miller: "Men do not fly up mountains; they go up slowly, step by step. True Christian life is always mountain-climbing. Heaven is above us, and ever keeps above us. It never gets easy to go heavenward. It is a slow and painful process to grow better. No one leaps to sainthood at a bound. No one gets the victory once for all over his faults and sins. It is a struggle of years, and every day must have its victories if we are ever to be final and complete overcomers. Yet while we cannot expect to reach the radiant mountaintop at one bound, we certainly ought to be climbing at least step by step. We ought not to sit on the same little terrace, part way up the mountain day by day. Higher and higher should be our unresting aim."

These thoughts remind the reader that the Christian life is not to be static or stagnant, a sterile resting upon a plateau of complacency. Rather, it is supposed to be a growing process. Sometimes as you read these mountaintop meditations, you will be in the valley looking up. But you won't stay there! The next day you may be on one mountaintop looking across to another spiritual peak. However, the general trend of your life will be upward as you wend your way toward the heavenly places, always *Climbing Higher!*

In His love,
Al Bryant

Acknowledgments

In a book such as this, it would be impossible to adequately thank those to whom I am indebted. Even those unsigned meditations, which are my own expressions of love for my Savior and trust in Him, reflect the insights and convictions of those whose writings have been my devotional (and study) companions down through the years. However, the men and women whose names are listed below, all of them now with the Lord, are the ones to whom I am most indebted:

Phillips Brooks   G. Campbell Morgan
Oswald Chambers   Andrew Murray
Theodore Cuyler   John Roberts
S. D. Gordon   A. B. Simpson
Evan H. Hopkins   Hannah Whitall Smith
J. H. Jowett   C. H. Spurgeon
Alexander Maclaren   R. A. Torrey
F. B. Meyer   Oliver G. Wilson
J. R. Miller

I especially want to thank the widow of the late Mr. Wilson, Mrs. Marion Wilson, for permission to quote from her husband's editorials in *The Wesleyan Methodist.* I also want to thank Larry Christenson for permission to quote from his excellent book, *The Christian Family*, published by Bethany Fellowship, Inc.

January 1

In the beginning God created the heavens and the earth.
—Genesis 1:1

These are the first words of the Bible, and they express the key note of this marvelous Book—God *first*. There are a number of wonderful revelations made to us in this first chapter of Genesis. The origin of all things is briefly and wonderfully described. But God is mentioned first, and for this reason He *is* first.

He is at "the beginning." The first page of the Bible may indeed be called "God's own page," for it is full of God. It tells us that God created... moved... said... saw... divided ...called... made... set... blessed... finished... and rested. God's name occurs no less than 46 times in the first two chapters of Genesis; and as we thus find God at the opening of the Bible, so we should find Him at the opening of the year; we should begin the new year with God first.

He should be first in our thoughts and first in our words; then all through the year it should be still the same—God first. If we seek first His kingdom and His righteousness, He will see that all other necessary things are added unto us. Put God first in everything and we shall know the meaning, through receiving the fulfillment of that promise to the Philippians (4: 19), "My God shall supply all your need according to his riches in glory by Christ Jesus."   —*John Roberts*

January 2

In the beginning was the Word, and the Word was with God, and the Word was God. He was in the beginning with God.—John 1:1, 2 (RSV)

We are still at the beginning of the year. Yesterday we looked at the Old Testament counterpart of this passage, Genesis 1:1, and were reminded that the only way to "begin the new year right" was to put God first, in the very center of our lives. John is writing the same truth here at the beginning of his Gospel. He is telling us who Jesus is, who God is—and why He must be central in our lives if we are to have a "Happy New Year."

Just a week ago we celebrated the incarnation of Christ by setting aside Christmas Day as a day commemorating His birth. We might sum up the reason for the incarnation in this brief sentence: "He came to become what we are, so that we could become what He is." This says it all—and bears our deepest contemplation and meditation.

Who is Jesus? First of all, He is God in the flesh. Jesus said, "He who has seen me has seen the Father." John tells us that His chief characteristic is "life" and this very *life* becomes the *light* of men. This is where we must begin the new year—and where we must begin the new life as well. Apart from Him we cannot see, we cannot know, what life is all about. "But in him was life," Jesus goes on to say, "and the *life* was the *light* of men." In John 9:15, Jesus said: "As long as I am in the world, I am the light of the world." He is still here. His incarnation is basic to man's knowledge of God. "I have come as light into the world, that whoever believes in me may not remain in darkness" (John 12:46).

One of the most noticeable characteristics of the Christian faith is the joy it brings to the believer—a joy pictured for us in the basic idea of light. Somehow sadness and light do not mix. Sadness belongs to darkness, while joy is always symbolized by light. "Joy cometh in the morning," says the Psalmist—and morning brings light. In the same way, light and life seem to belong together, to walk hand in hand.

This, then, is the secret of the joyous Christian life—a vital connection to the life-giving source, the One who is both life and light. The One about whom John wrote elsewhere: "We are writing this that your joy may be complete" (1 John 1).

January 3

Remember ye not the former things, neither consider the things of old. Behold, I will do a new thing; now it shall spring forth; shall ye not know it? I will even make a way in the wilderness, and rivers in the desert.—Isaiah 43:18, 19

This new year is our new opportunity, but it is also our serious responsibility. No one knows what it will bring, but all can know how they will meet the coming days—they can be met under the protecting hand of God.

God's riches are within reach of all who call upon Him. His power is available every moment of every twenty-four hours in the year ahead. As I enter this year:

I resolve to choose God—to follow as, where, and when He leads.

I would make my days joyous even when clouds hide the sun's bright shining—joyous with the joy born not of earthly things or possessions, but of divine relationship.

I would fill every day with purposeful endeavor—not for selfish ends, but for sacred accomplishments.

I would live for others—for their physical and spiritual welfare.

I would aim to be great according to Christ's measure: "He that would be great among you let him be servant of all."

I would aim to adjust myself to whatever circumstances

may surround me, and not try to force everything to surrender to my desires.

I would keep my heart clean—unscarred by dishonesty, meanness, smallness, or selfishness.

I would gain new visions of God—of His truth, His justice, His holiness, His hatred for sin, His undying love for man.

I would be a cup of strength to suffering souls, a reassuring voice to straying souls, and a helping hand to faltering souls.

In the Name of our Strong Deliverer, our Lord and Saviour Jesus Christ, I would live every day of this coming year victoriously, joyously, faithfully. —*O. G. Wilson*

January 4

He led them forth by the right way, that they might go to a city of habitation.—Psalm 107:7

Nothing is more important at the beginning of a journey than that we should make a right start. To be in the right way we must follow the right Guide: "*He* led them forth." When a man is in a pit, it is not safe leading he needs first, but a complete deliverance. God takes us out of the horrible pit and sets our feet upon the rock before He establishes our ways.

We sometimes fail to know and follow His guidance because we allow too great a space to come between. The beginning of a new year is a good time to draw close to the Guide. The guidance that is not only safe, but also happy and blessed, is the guidance of God's eye. In Psalm 32:8, David shares God's promise to His people, "I will instruct thee and teach thee in the way which thou shalt go: I will guide thee with mine eye."

But none who follow Him afar off know what that guidance is. "The right way" means not the right way in the abstract, but the right way for *me*. It is not written, they went in the right way; but, "He led them." They could never have found it, much less continued in it, without His leading. The right way is always His way. "Teach me Thy way, O Lord."

—*Evan H. Hopkins*

January 5

Ye have not passed this way heretofore.—Joshua 3:4

It is good for a man to come to a future which he does not know, for then he will be completely dependent upon his Guide. It is good for you if God brings you to the borders of some promised land. Do not hesitate at any experience because it is unknown, untried. Do not draw back from any way because you never have passed that way before. The truth, the task, the joy, the suffering, on whose border you are standing, oh, my friend—go into it without fear; only go into it with God, the God who has always been with you.

Let the past give up to you all assurance of Him which it contains. Set that assurance before you. Follow that, and the new life to which it leads you shall open its best richness to you.

Only we know that with a world which needs so much, and with a God who knows its needs and who loves it and pities it so tenderly, there must be in the long year ahead some approach of its life to His life, some coming of the Lord!

—Phillips Brooks

January 6

Let the word of Christ dwell in you richly.—Colossians 3:16
Be filled with the Spirit.—Ephesians 5:18

The life of the Christian is the Christ life. So far as *our* will and responsibility are concerned there must be *personal* feeding on Christ, and in order to do this we must live in the atmosphere of the Spirit exclusively. As there must be no neglect in providing the bread of heaven, so also must there be no descent to the malarial valleys. Life must be lived on the mountain heights in unceasing relation to the Spirit, who is the one and only interpreter of Christ.

Some years ago I met in England a dear friend, and looking at him was filled with sorrow as I saw that he was in the grasp of an insidious disease which with deadly erosion saps away the life. After a long interval, when I was in Colorado I saw him again, and hardly knew him. The rare air of the mountains had given him back his old strength, and had made impossible the spread of his disease. He told me, however, that while feeling perfectly well, it was necessary for him to stay upon those mountain heights, or the old trouble would return.

Let us keep ever in the mountain air. If we descend into the old valleys, the paralysis of the past will come again. We must live in the atmosphere of the Spirit, high on the mountains of vision, and there the appetite for the bread of heaven will be strong, and, feeding upon Christ, we will "grow up into him in all things."

—G. Campbell Morgan

January 7

Whosoever drinketh of the water that I shall give him shall never thirst; but the water that I shall give him shall be in him a well of water springing up into everlasting life.
—John 4:14

The soul was made for God, and when it returns to God it finds peace and contentment. It is not meant here, of course, that the Christian has no more desires; for longing is the very condition of more blessedness. "Blessed are they who hunger and thirst after righteousness: for they shall be filled." If there is no thirst there really is no life. The dove that flew away from the ark went on weary wings everywhere, but found only a wide waste of desolate waters, with no place to alight. Then she flew back to the ark, and was gently drawn inside, where she found warmth, safety, and rest.

The story of the dove illustrates the history of the soul that wanders everywhere seeking rest, at last returning to God. How much better if men believed this truth of universal experience and went at once to God! An immortal soul, from its very nature, cannot find what it needs anywhere save in God himself. This word of Christ tells us also what true religion is. It begins in the heart. It is not something outside—a mere set of rules to be obeyed, an example to be copied. It is new spiritual life in the soul; it is Christ coming into the heart and dwelling there. It is a *fountain* of life—not a mere cistern, but a living spring open and ever flowing. Since it is fed from heaven, this living fountain in the heart shall never be exhausted, no matter how dry this world may be. Its connection is with the river of life, which flows from under God's throne.

If we are true Christians, we have our religion with us wherever we go. We are not dependent upon circumstances. Trouble does not destroy a Christian, because the fountain of his joy is within. This new fountain of life when opened in the soul is the beginning of eternal life. —*J. R. Miller*

January 8

I am the good shepherd: The good shepherd giveth his life for the sheep. —John 10:11

The wonderful fact about the Christian life is that the Good Shepherd, the Lord Jesus Christ, is involved intimately and creatively in every aspect of our lives, the small things as well as the momentous. There are some who would deny this intimate experience of Christ. As a practicing Christian, however, I can testify that such negative and so-called "realistic" thinking causes the Christian to miss the truth and the abundance of joy that comes with it. The "tough" Christian who tries to go it alone, and independently, hoping someday to meet Christ in heaven, needs to hear the good news that he doesn't have to wait 'til then.

In the daily newspapers in many cities, churches cooperate

in placing a large ad on Saturday evening urging people to go to church on Sunday. One such headline read: "Whatever the path you tread, let that path lead to God." This philosophy takes all the excitement out of being in Christ right now—in the present. We are on that path today—it's not a "whatever" situation. Either we are fellow travelers with Jesus at this moment—under His divine direction and in His divine company—or we are on another and false path entirely.

It seems easy to know God and exult in His presence at the high moments of life. But we can also know Jesus in the routine events of our everyday journey. Many Christians miss this discovery, because being fairly successful they act as though their lives were their own responsibility. But those who have come to desolate places in life, who realize that they cannot control every situation that arises, know that God must be in control (He is, whether we acknowledge it or not) and that He will provide as only He can.

January 9

The angel of the Lord encampeth round about them that fear him, and delivereth them.—Psalm 34:7

As I read this verse, a picture forms in my mind. I see a campfire set in a basin of land, surrounded by low hills. As I gaze around the horizon for a full 360 degrees, I see a mist arising on the ridges surrounding me, so that I am hemmed in as if by a protective shield brandished by the bright and shining "angel of the Lord."

As a child of God, wherever I go I am surrounded by this comforting presence. This surrounding presence is not fitful or fleeting. It is permanent. When David was in the wilderness of Judah, despite his hardships he sang, "Thou hast been my help, therefore in the shadow of thy wings will I rejoice" (Ps. 63:7). Later on in Psalm 34 (v. 17) David reiterates this theme: "The righteous cry, and the Lord heareth, and delivereth them out of all their troubles."

A greater than David has entered our world, this sphere so filled with wars and rumors of wars, unrest and confusion. In telling the first Christmas story, Luke has this word of comfort for us: "The dayspring from on high hath visited us, to give light to them that sit in darkness, to guide our feet into the way of peace" (1:78, 79). Some Bible students feel that the "angel of the Lord" mentioned so frequently in the Old Testament is the Lord Jesus Christ in preincarnate form. If this is true, Luke's promise of guidance and peace from the "dayspring" is a continuation of David's theme of protection expressed in Psalm 34.

The angel of the Lord is mentioned many times in the Scriptures, expressing both judgment and protection. He is the One with whom we have to do. He "delivers" the believer—but He sits in judgment on the unbeliever. How thankful I am to be the recipient of His protection rather than His wrath!

January 10

A man shall be as an hiding place from the wind, and a covert from the tempest.—Isaiah 32:2

"A Man." Who is this man? It is "the second man—the Lord from heaven" (1 Cor. 15:47). This man is our hiding place.

Jesus, Refuge of my soul,
Let me hide myself in Thee.

There we are sheltered and safe from the storm of the law's condemnation, as well as from the assaults of Satan.

"Thou art my hiding place; thou shalt preserve me from trouble; thou shalt compass me about with songs of deliverance" (Ps. 32:7). For every conceivable trial or trouble the Lord Jesus is the believer's refuge.

"There shall be a tabernacle for a shadow in the daytime from the heat, and for a place of refuge, and for a covert from storm and from rain" (Isa. 4:6). It is the Lord's will that we should under all circumstances avail ourselves of this refuge.

"He that dwelleth"—that is, he that "sitteth down," takes up his permanent abode, and does not merely use God as a *temporary* refuge. "He that sitteth down in the secret place of the Most High shall abide under the shadow of the Almighty." —*Evan H. Hopkins*

January 11

Mount up with wings as eagles.—Isaiah 40:31

To put it concisely, we Christians are to be like eagles. And I always picture the eagle as *soaring* effortlessly high in the sky, twisting and turning, wheeling and whirling above the mundane work-a-day world. He *uses* the air currents which are his natural habitat, instead of struggling *against* them. He uses them to rise even higher, rather than allowing them to buffet and baffle him, keeping him on the low level of the other birds around him. He builds his nest at the highest possible point so that he can maintain this lofty perspective, this "high view" that is his inheritance. From the heights he is able to see things hidden from the view of those who dwell on the lower levels of life.

There is a striking lesson here for the Christian who would live *his* life on the victorious level pictured for us as the "heights." There is something in the *perspective* and *position* of the eagle that you and I need to emulate. He is king of the birds as the lion is "king of beasts" in the jungle which is his habitat. The eagle, regal bird that he is, takes the highest view—the larger view, the broad perspective—whereas the lower species of birds tend to see life on a lower level, taking the narrow view, the victim of that limiting disease known as "tunnel vision."

From his low view of life the defeated Christian, too, misses God's best, experiences depression and discouragement, because he fails to see God's big plan for his life. Christian, listen to Isaiah's admonition. First, fulfill God's conditional command to "wait upon the Lord." Then, from the renewed strength thus gained, go on to "mount up with wings as eagles." Discover that you "shall run, and not be weary . . . walk, and not faint." The victorious Christian life is available to you. God's power is there—you can "soar" as a Christian if you allow His power to operate in your life!

January 12

Come ye, and let us go up to the mountain of the Lord.
—Isaiah 2:3

It is exceedingly beneficial to our souls to mount above this present evil world to something nobler and better. The cares of this world and the deceitfulness of riches are apt to choke everything good within us, and we grow fretful, desponding, perhaps proud and carnal. It is well for us to cut down these thorns and briers, for heavenly seed sown among them is not likely to yield a harvest; and where shall we find a better sickle with which to cut them down than communion with God?

May the Spirit of God assist us to leave the mists of fear and the fevers of anxiety, and all the ills which gather in this valley of earth, and to ascend the mountains of anticipated joy and blessedness. May God the Holy Spirit cut the cords that keep us here below, and assist us to mount! We sit too often like chained eagles fastened to the rock, only that, unlike the eagle, we begin to love our chain, and would, perhaps, if it came really to the test, be loath to have it snapped. May God now grant us grace, if we cannot escape from the chain as to our flesh, yet to do so as to our spirits; and leaving the body, like a servant, at the foot of the hill, may our soul, like Abraham, attain the top of the mountain, there to indulge in communion with the Most High.   —*C. H. Spurgeon*

January 13

O my God, I trust in thee; let me not be ashamed, let not mine enemies triumph over me. —Psalm 25:2

In an "experience" meeting on the frontier, those present were asked to stand and recite their favorite scripture portion. One after another arose and quoted promises from the Bible. Finally a lady with a serene face stood and said: "My favorite promise is that one where the Master said, 'It came, to pass.' When things become unbearable and it seems I cannot stand it any longer, I remember that Christ promised, 'It came, to pass.' It came by divine appointment and it will pass by divine appointment."

We may not agree with her exposition, but her philosophy is worth close study. "Life is ten percent what we make it," someone has said, "and ninety percent how we take it." One man is crushed by the adversities of life, while another keeps the flag of courage flying while he tightens his belt a little more and adds a few hours to his working day. The difference is not in the difficulty but in the determination of the individuals.

Ability to meet trouble is the supreme test of every human being. To whine or bemoan our fate is the mark of a weakling. To look certain disaster in the face with head unbowed, and plan to begin the removal of the rubble tomorrow of what were once our fondest hopes, is manhood at its highest, supported by a faith anchored to something bigger than ourselves.

A crisis is an opportunity to prove that we are men. For those who will climb, opportunity is the ladder which leads from the commonplace to the stars. He who keeps his windows open toward heaven cannot be whipped. As the years pass, and we view the things we considered most trying, they appear in a wholly different light. We can smile at our tears and fears, and rejoice over the things that made life most difficult.

The woman at the meeting was right: "It came, to pass." It will not be with us always. We will get through the mountain. We will top the mountain, "not somehow, but triumphantly."

—O. G. Wilson

January 14

Jesus said unto them, Verily, verily, I say unto you, Before Abraham was, I am. —John 8:58

Think for a moment upon the implications of what Jesus is saying here. God himself is the only One who was pre-existent before Abraham—and still lived 2000 years later—and still lives today, another 2000 years later. Since Jesus is God, He, too, is eternal. He always *was*, He always *is*, and He always *will be*. Past, present and future are the same to Him— He sees all the tenses of life from a perspective high above them, the perspective of the One who created all things.

Just think—the Jesus who walked around Palestine 2000 years ago with His disciples is the same Jesus we know today. The One we can walk with daily and turn to on a moment's notice. We don't even have to give voice to our petitions, for He fathoms our thoughts before they are exposed. He knows us as we are, so we don't have to hide ourselves from Him as we often do from our fellowmen.

And think about the awe-inspiring power and authority wrapped up in this Savior of ours! He was present at, and party to, the creation of the world and everything in it. This Almighty One is the One with whom we have to do! The Almighty One took the time to come to earth to "enflesh" God to man, to make God discoverable to man, indeed to give His very life that man might recover the relationship which he lost at Eden.

This is the One who goes with us in every experience of life—the happy as well as the heartbroken—for it is His business to heal broken hearts and restore relationships shattered by sin and all the sorrows life can bring.

January 15

This God is our God for ever and ever; he will be our guide even unto death.—Psalm 48:14

It is strengthening to our faith to declare to ourselves and to others what God declares to us. He has said, "I am thy God" (Isa. 41:10). Let our souls respond, "This God is our God for ever and ever."

It is an important step forward in the faith-life to rise from the prayer "Be thou" to the assurance "Thou art." It is thus that we step out and advance in the spiritual life. Many for years have been *seeking*, when they should have been *resting*, as to their soul's attitude toward God. When God declares to us a *fact*, it is for us to accept it and rest on it. When He gives us a *promise*, it is for us to plead it and expect its fulfillment.

The apprehension of the fact that God is our God, our covenant God—our everlasting portion—removes all difficulty in the way of trusting Him as our guide. "He himself will lead us," as Dr. Kay renders it, "over death—across the gulf of death." Death is not our destination. We walk "through the valley," not merely into it, as if it were a place where there is no "thoroughfare" (Ps. 23:4; 138:7).   —*Evan H. Hopkins*

January 16

Do things in such a way that everyone can see you are honest clear through.—Romans 12:17 (TLB)

Some Christians seem to think that all the requirements of a good life are met when there is active and successful Christian work: and because they do much for the Lord in public, they feel at liberty to be cross and ugly and un-Christlike in private. But if we are to walk as Christ walked, it must be in private as well as public, at home as well as abroad; and it must be every hour all day long, and not at stated periods or on certain fixed occasions. We must be just as Christlike to our employees as to our minister, and just as good in the bank as we are at prayer meeting. It is in the day-by-day routine of life, indeed, that practical piety can best show itself, and we may well question any professions that fail under this test of daily life.

A cross Christian, an anxious Christian, a discouraged, gloomy, exacting Christian, a doubting, complaining Christian, a selfish, cruel, hard-hearted Christian, a Christian with a sharp tongue or bitter spirit—all these may be earnest in their work, and may have honorable places in the church; but they are not Christlike Christians, and they know nothing of the realities with which the Bible deals, no matter how loud their professions may be. The life hid with Christ in God is a hidden life as to its source, but it must not be hidden as to its practical results. People must see that we walk as Christ walked if we say that we are abiding in Him.

We must prove that we possess what we profess. In short, we must be real followers of Christ and not theoretical ones only. And this means that we must really turn our backs on everything not pleasing to God, "as the servants of Christ, doing the will of God from the heart." —*Hannah Whitall Smith*

January 17

As I was with Moses, so I will be with you; I will not fail you nor forsake you.—Joshua 1:5

"As I was . . . so I will be" sums up God's promise to Joshua, and to us. Whatever He has been, He will continue to be. What is our guarantee? To name only one: past performance. Has He ever failed or forsaken you before? Joshua certainly knew about God's faithfulness firsthand. Even his name was a reminder. Originally it was Hoshea, meaning "salvation" (Num. 13:8), but Moses changed it, expanding on the original. He became Joshua (Num. 13:16), "Yahweh is salvation." And God had shone His faithfulness, His salvation, to Joshua, who had dared to bring a good report upon his return from the spying mission into Canaan. The entire book that bears his name is the story of Israel's success and God's faithfulness as they occupied the Promised Land. One further thought: the name of Jesus is the Septuagint spelling of Joshua, so our Savior's very name is another reminder of God's faithfulness.

One of the psalmists, Asaph, asks a pertinent question here, "Will the Lord cast off for ever? and will he be favourable no more? Is his mercy clean gone for ever? doth his promise fail for evermore?" (Ps. 77:7, 8). He answers his own question by looking back upon God's past performance: "I will remember the works of the Lord: surely I will remember thy wonders of old" (v. 11).

Are you convinced now of God's faithfulness? Remember how He has cared for you in the past, how His goodness has been your portion, how your prayers have been answered, how His guidance has come when the path was dim before you. If He did it before, He will do it again! You serve the very same God Joshua served. He will lead you into the Promised Land too. You can count on it!

January 18

Enoch walked with God.—Genesis 5:22, 24

Enoch was a family man. He lived many years after the birth of his eldest child and had both "sons and daughters." But during the whole of this period he "walked with God." He not only *walked* with God, but he also *pleased* God, and had the testimony or witness of the Spirit that he did so, "for before his translation he had this testimony, that he pleased God" (Heb. 11:5).

He must, therefore, have been saved from all sin and kept by the power of God from sinning. Now, if Enoch was thus kept thousands of years ago, and long before the dispensation of the Holy Spirit, then surely we may have the same experience today, for God, and Christ, and faith are still the same.

Walking peacefully with a friend implies union, fellowship, and progress by interchange of thought. "Can two walk together, except they be agreed?" (Amos 3:3). We are exhorted in Romans 6:13 to "yield ourselves unto God as those that are alive from the dead," and by doing so we manifest our oneness with Him. We live in fellowship with Him and so make real and continual progress in the divine life. Oh, that we may this day and every day of this year thus "walk with God."   —*John Roberts*

January 19

Sing unto the Lord a new song. —Isaiah 42:10

None can sing the new song who has not the new life. But many who have the life seem to have lost the song. The first thing that goes when we begin to backslide is the joy of the Lord. We cease to sing the new song. We are like Israel, who, though they had come out of Egypt, and had actually been established in the land, were not in a state of captivity, as Isaiah writes these words to them. Their answer might well have been, "How shall we sing the Lord's song in a strange land?"

If we would be joyous Christians, attracting others by the brightness of our lives, as well as the soundness of our views, we must learn how to abide in the land. It is not difficult to sing when we are abundantly satisfied with God's goodness to us, and are finding our needs met from the fullness of the grace of Christ. It is the soul that abides in Christ that continues to rejoice.

My song shall be of Jesus:
   His mercy crowns my days,
He fills my cup with blessings,
   And tunes my heart to praise!

My song shall be of Jesus,
   The precious Lamb of God,
Who gave Himself my ransom,
   And bought me with His blood.
—*Evan H. Hopkins*

January 20

He took the blind man by the hand, and led him out of the town. —Mark 8:23

That was a very gentle thing to do. Look closely at the picture—Jesus leading a poor man along the street. What thoughts does it start in our minds? The blind man represents each one of us in our sinful state—in the midst of a world of beauty, but seeing nothing; groping in the gloom, unable to find the way alone, doomed to perish forever in the darkness unless Someone takes us by the hand and leads us. As Jesus came to this man in his blindness, so He comes to each one of us, offering to take us by the hand and be our Guide, to lead us, through the gloom and the dangers, home to light and glory. We can never stumble in the darkness if He leads us.

The blind man entrusting himself, without fear or question, to be led by this Stranger, and quietly and confidently going with Him, is a picture of what true faith in Christ always does. It is in this way that we are to commit ourselves to Christ. It is not enough to lay our sins on Him; we must entrust our whole life to His guidance. We can never find the way ourselves in this world's paths, but we may entrust ourselves with unquestioning confidence to Christ's leading.

I do not try to see my way,
    Before, behind, or left, or right;
I cannot tell what dangers gray
    Do haunt my steps, nor at what height
Above the sea my path doth wind:
    For I am blind.

Yet not without a guide I wend
    My unseen way, by day, by night;
Close by my side there walks a Friend—
    Strong, tender, true: I trust His sight.
He sees my way before, behind,
    Though I am blind.
                                    —*J. R. Miller*

January 21

Have no anxiety about anything, but in everything by prayer and supplication with thanksgiving let your requests be made known to God.—Philippians 4:6 (RSV)

A twofold law controls the operation of God's peace: "In *nothing* be anxious; but in *everything*, by prayer and supplication with thanksgiving, let your requests be made known unto God" (KJV). It is not enough to say, "Don't worry, don't fret"; we must give them something better. Not a bare negative, but a blessed positive. It is not that we are to spend our days in long, entreating prayers; but in the simplest, plainest words, and about everything, however trivial and insignificant it might seem, *we are to make our requests known.*

Prayer and thanksgiving, mingled with the fragrance of thanksgiving, must tell out the story of need and desire into the ear of the great Father. Spread that heartbreaking letter before Him; take to Him the broken fragments of a shattered dream; open to Him the wounds from which the bandages have just been torn. It is no use worrying. Do not go about with a melancholy face and whining voice as if God were dealing more hardly with you than you deserve. Do not sit down in despair as if the joy of your life had fled forever.

Just tell Him how things are with you: what you had hoped; what you want; what is needed to complete your life; then leave it there. You have committed your cause to the wisest and most tender, to the strongest and truest friend. Then go forth to think and practice whatsoever things are true, honorable, just, pure, lovely, gracious, and the peace of God will open the way to the God of peace himself. Upon the heels of His messenger the King will come. When the palace is permeated by the atmosphere of heaven, the presence that makes heaven will shed its glory through every apartment of the soul.

These truths pass understanding. The attribute of the Person leads to the Person himself. We no longer just receive some gift of His ineffable nature; but we have found Him, we possess Him, we are possessed by Him, in whom love, joy, peace, longsuffering, gentleness, and goodness have their home. —*F. B. Meyer*

January 22

He knoweth the way that I take.—Job 23:10

"He knoweth the way that is with me" (margin). To the child of God this fact is a source of comfort. God knows all the circumstances of my life, every detail of my daily path. He knows, too, the weakness and frailty of our nature (Ps. 103:14). This gives no excuse for our sinning, but it is a ground for His compassion.

If we admit and face up to our helplessness and dependency, He will undertake for us. He will be our wisdom in the matter of guidance. He will be our strength in the matter of duty and difficulty. He will be everything to us that our circumstances demand.

But if, on the other hand, we are self-complacent as to the uprightness of the way that we take, we shut ourselves off from all the provisions of His grace. The ruling principle of our life is then self rather than Christ. God has not called us to himself that we should be our own guides or our own masters. The true life is the life of self-abnegation and self-renunciation—the life that hangs entirely upon God and expects Him to supply every need. It is in the sphere of our conscious weakness that divine strength is perfected.

—*Evan H. Hopkins*

January 23

He that dwelleth in the secret place of the most High shall abide under the shadow of the Almighty.—Psalm 91:1

To abide under the shadow of the Almighty reminds us of our Lord's words: "How often would I have gathered thy children together, even as a hen gathereth her children under her wings, and ye would not!" (Matt. 23:37). John Bunyan says that the hen has four calls: the call when night is near; the call for food; the call of peril; and the call of brooding love when she wants to feel her chicks under her wings. Today God is calling to each of us, saying: "Come, My children, make the secret place of My presence, of My environment, of My constant keeping, your home; for he that dwelleth in the secret place of the most High shall abide under the wings of God." When night is near, when money and food are scarce, when the hawk is ready to pounce on us, when loneliness and desolation oppress, let us hear the brooding cry of God our Father, and nestle beneath His shadow.

God is prepared to keep us in *all* our ways. Many of us expect God to bring us out at last, but we have no thought of His keeping us in purity of soul; we expect to be brought to heaven—battered, beaten, and contaminated on the way. But our God surely does better for us than that! He can keep us from yielding to temper, jealousy, hatred, pride and envy as well as to the grosser forms of sin. The promise is clear: "He shall give his angels charge over thee, to keep thee in *all* thy ways"—business ways, social ways, the ways of service into which God may lead us forth, the ways of sacrifice or suffering. Let us simply and humbly ask for the fulfillment of the promises in this Psalm. He will answer your prayers. He will be with you in trouble. He will satisfy you with many years of life, or with living much in a short time, and He will show you the wonders of His salvation. —*F. B. Meyer*

January 24

The Lord will provide.—Genesis 22:14

This was what Abraham learned in the most trying hour of his life. He learned it in the line of implicit obedience. He learned it in the trial of his faith. Could he ever forget this great truth?

It is the great fact that runs through the whole history of divine redemption. Whatever man's need has been or can be, God has *seen before* and made full provision.

The fact that our wants as sinners, guilty and lost, have been amply provided for—that we can stand before God acquitted of every charge, pardoned, reconciled, justified, and accepted—encourages us to believe that all our future necessities will be met in the same gracious and omnipotent Savior.

Let this quiet our every fear and silence each rising note of anxious foreboding. "The Lord will provide" is a golden sentence to be written on the portal of each new day. Let us show by our restful attitude and steady step that we believe the divine assurance.

How truly the apostle Paul proved the reality of it in his own life! And so he could say to those Philippian converts, "My God shall supply all your need according to his riches in glory by Christ Jesus" (Phil. 4:19). —*Evan H. Hopkins*

January 25

For he knows our frame; he remembers that we are dust.
—Psalm 103:14 (RSV)

"He knows our frame." The Bible is full of such gracious and tender words. "He remembereth us in our low estate." "I have many things to say unto you, but ye cannot bear them now." "He will not permit you to be tempted above that ye are able."

The burden is suited to our strength. The revelation is determined by our experience. The pace is regulated by our years.

"He carries the lambs in his arms." He "leads on softly." Nothing is done in ignorance. "The Lord is mindful of his own. He remembers his children."

And so I must practice the belief in God's compassionate nearness. In my childhood I used to sing: "There's a friend for little children, above the bright blue sky." I know better now. He is nearer to me than I can dream. I used to sing: "There is a happy land, far, far away." Now I sing: "There is a happy land, *not* far away."

The good Father and His home are not in some remote realm. There is no great distance between us. He is very, very near me, and He knows all about me.

"He knows our frame." —*J. H. Jowett*

January 26

But the very hairs of your head are all numbered.—Matthew 10:30

What meticulous care on God's part—not a hair but is registered with God. I might not have pulled my little sister's hair so vigorously when I was a little boy had I thought of God numbering the hairs.

Some sophisticated fellow, wise in the ways of doing things, asks: "But what sense is there to all this—our hairs numbered?" I'm sorry I can't satisfy your curiosity, but it occurs to me that if my hairs are all numbered, certainly my arms and legs and eyes and ears are as well. If God will not spoil a hair needlessly, it seems pretty certain to me that I am not in danger of losing a hand unless by His permission.

Some of us have lost so many of our hairs that God need not take much time looking after those that are left, but our other needs grow greater with each passing year. Do not forget, He'll be around all the year—all the *years!*

We need to hear Him say, "Come ye apart and rest awhile." We have tangled the threads in the great loom of life and are doing a good job of working ourselves into nervous collapse.

He cares about the hair, so He cares for me—"Rest in the Lord." Air and water, food and clothing—all are considered the basic essentials of life. Yet it seems to me that other things are also essential. It is essential that we—

Live so that we have nothing to hide from God.
Be tender with others and tough with ourselves.
Serenely face unpleasant situations.
Give more to the world than we take from it.
Work for God, not for money.
Look for beauty, and plant flowers wherever possible.

Since God has numbered my hairs, He has also numbered my needs. Everything essential to build holy character will be allotted to me by the love of God my Father and to the exact measure of my need. I do not know why He said, "The very hairs of your head are all numbered," but I'm glad He did!

—O. G. Wilson

January 27

And will be a Father unto you....—2 Corinthians 6:18

What a warm and wonderful feeling is generated by this word, "Father." What does it mean in this context? That God, Creator and Sustainer of the universe, is willing to adopt me into His family, to accept me, rebellious child that I am, back into His fellowship. My share of His inheritance awaits me; my place at the family table is reserved for me.

The timeless story of the Prodigal Son inevitably comes to my mind as I read these words and ponder their meaning. The rebellious son turned his back on his father, his family, and his true inheritance when he demanded immediate payment of what was his "due," and went off to a far country to "live it up" (or perhaps we should use the term "down" to describe his life-style). His attitude and actions are so typical of the one without Christ who wants to "live his own life" and not be bothered with any allegiance to God or the precepts and principles laid down in His Word. But what is God's attitude toward this headstrong individual? Does God turn His back?

A look at the end of the parable will answer that question. In fact, the answer is summed up in my nomination for a new title for this parable: "The Welcoming Father" rather than "The Prodigal Son." God, as pictured by the father in the story, is not just passively waiting for his son to come to his senses and return. He is actively involved in watching for him, and when he sees his son approaching the family home, he rushes out to welcome him with open arms and heart.

This is a graphic portrayal of our heavenly Father's attitude toward His children—even those rebels who deny His existence and trample on His love. If they will "come to themselves" as the Prodigal Son did, He will come to them with His forgiveness and His bountiful supply. And He "will be a Father unto you." Blessed thought and blessed relationship.

January 28

And when he saw the fig tree in the way, he came to it, and found nothing thereon, but leaves only, and said unto it, Let no fruit grow on thee.... And presently the fig tree withered away.—Matthew 21:19

Remember that there is an atheism, a "leaves-only" kind of belief that still repeats the creed. There is a "head" belief in God which does not let Him come, which does not bring Him into close contact with our daily life. The very reverence with which we honor God may make us shut Him out from the hard tasks and puzzling problems with which we have to do. Unfortunately, many so-called believers are like the savages who, in the desire to honor the wonderful sun dial which had been given them, built a roof over it.

Break down the roof; let God into your life!

—Phillips Brooks

January 29

The Lord thy God in the midst of thee....—Zephaniah 3:15

This fact is repeated in the seventeenth verse with some additions: "The Lord thy God in the midst of thee is mighty." Two facts stand out here: what He is and where He is. He is the Lord thy God. He is mighty. This implies covenant relationship. He is *thy* God. And this mighty One takes up His abode in the midst of His people—and in the heart of each believer. All things are therefore possible to him who is thus possessed. The Lord himself dwells in them to save and to keep.

Can we say that we have thus enthroned Him in our hearts? The Holy Spirit strengthens us to this end: that Christ may dwell in our hearts by faith (Eph. 3:17); that He might take up His permanent abode in our hearts. Thus enshrined He controls the whole being and transforms the outer life as well as the inner experience. That refers to a daily and continuous salvation—a perpetual deliverance from sin's power and service.

It is in this salvation that we find the fullest joy, because we are being preserved blameless and kept continually in the light of God's countenance. *—Evan H. Hopkins*

January 30

Ye are complete in him.—Colossians 2:10

The nature of the Christian life is Christ's life taking hold upon all the inner life of a man, changing, dominating, pulsating. It is seen therefore, and I do not think we can be too careful in emphasizing this, that Christian life is neither human imitation of Christ, nor correct intellectual positions concerning Christ. Neither is it a cult nor a system of thought. I may attempt to imitate Christ sincerely through long years, and yet never be a Christian. I may hold absolutely correct intellectual views concerning Christ as a person and His power, and yet never be a Christian. It is possible for me to admire Him, and attempt with all the power of my life to imitate Him, and yet never realize Him. It is quite possible for a person to believe most sincerely in His deity and in the fact of His atoning work, and moreover, in the necessity for regeneration, and yet never be submitted to His lordship, never to have personal share in the work of His atonement, never to be born again.

Nothing short of Christ himself coming into the life of the individual constitutes a Christian. If Jesus Christ is external to your life, there will be times when the world will not see Him and hear Him, and will not know you belong to Him. But if Christ be in you, living, reigning there absolutely, and you are obeying Him, there never will be a moment when the truth will not be evident. You cannot hide Christ if once He comes within. If the light is there, it simply must shine.

—*G. Campbell Morgan*

January 31

Finally, be ye all of one mind. . . .—1 Peter 3:8

This is not union: this is harmony. When an orchestra produces some great musical masterpiece, the instruments are all of one mind, but each makes its own individual contribution. There is variety with concordance: each one serves every other, and the result is glorious harmony. "By love serve one another." It is love that converts membership into fraternity; it is love that binds sons and daughters into a family.

Look at a field of wild flowers. What a harmony of color! And yet what a variety of hues. Nothing out of place, but no sameness. All drawing sustenance from the same soil, and all breathing the vitalizing substance from the same air!

"And ye, being rooted and grounded in love," Paul says in Ephesians 3:17, will grow up, a holy family in the Lord. If love is the common ground the varieties in God's family may be infinite!

So the unity which the apostle seeks is a unity of mood and

disposition. It is not a unity which repeats the exact syllables of a common creed, but a unity which is built of common trust, and love, and hope. It is not sameness upon the outer lips, but fellowship in the secret place. —*J. H. Jowett*

February 1

Deal gently with the young man. . . .—2 Samuel 18:5

A great battle was about to be fought between David and his servants and Absalom and his followers. But David's servants would not hear of his going out with them, so, in compliance with their wishes, he consented to stand "by the gateside." But as he saw them marching off he revealed to them the feeling of his heart by saying: "Deal gently with the young man, even with Absalom."

But, you may ask, was not Absalom David's sworn enemy? Was he not doing his utmost to destroy David and to take his throne? Yes, he was. Nevertheless, this was David's request: "Deal gently" with him.

As we ponder over this Christlike utterance, may we catch the same spirit and become filled with pity and compassion for the greatest of enemies or the worst of sinners. It is not likely we will ever have such an enemy as David had in his wicked son, and yet we see in our meditation today how his heart was full of love for him. David had never read the apostle's words in Romans 12:19-21 ("Avenge not yourselves, but rather give place unto wrath; for vengeance is mine; I will repay, saith the Lord. Therefore if thine enemy hunger, feed him; if he thirst, give him drink: for in so doing thou shalt heap coals of fire upon his head"), but by the power of God in him he was able to exhibit that same spirit. We, too, may receive power from God that will enable us to do likewise, to "deal gently" and "bless" all those who "persecute" or oppose us, and thus be able to "heap coals of fire upon their heads" and "to overcome evil with good."

Jesus, now our hearts inspire	Purify our faith like gold;
With that pure love of Thine;	All the dross of sin remove;
Kindle now the heavenly fire,	Melt our spirits down, and mould
To brighten and refine.	Into Thy perfect love.

—*John Roberts*

February 2

O thou of little faith, wherefore didst thou doubt? —Matthew 14:31

Another thing which can block prayer is doubt. The whole basis for prayer is believing and trusting God's Word. The key is just this: *What has God said?* Not, what has man said, or what do I think, but what has God said? Martin Luther prayed like this: "Not the merits of my prayer but the certainty of Thy truth." Here we have to re-educate the subconscious mind because that is where many of our doubts are rooted down. We may say with our conscious mind, "Oh, I believe! I have all the faith in the world!" But the subconscious mind says, "Oh, yeah?" In the subconscious are buried all the fears, doubts, uncertainties that have been shoved down there from childhood. And they don't change overnight. You only change them through a process of re-education and re-experience.

This is where the whole school of so-called positive thinking has its proper place. The deep mind reacts to positive thoughts, positive suggestions. You begin telling yourself, through prayer, meditation, reading the Scripture (reading it out loud!) that God "can be trusted—you can bank on God!" If you keep feeding that into the computer of your subconscious mind, sooner or later it's going to begin feeding back answers of faith. It's just about as simple as that—but *it takes time!* It doesn't happen overnight. *Faith does not grow in a day.*

—*Larry Christenson*

February 3

He that believeth shall not make haste.—Isaiah 28:16

According to one lexicographer the meaning of haste is to "hurry hither and thither as a person in confusion." A great and good man paraphrased this passage: "He that believeth shall not flutter to and fro"—as a bird in distress or badly frightened. Here is expressed the very essence of faith. It is resting on God and asking no questions.

"Rest in the Lord, and wait patiently for him: fret not" (Ps. 37:7). The individual described here is through with inward tensions. He has found a stabilizer, a tranquilizer, amid the distressing experiences of life.

Such a soul has built his house on the Rock and need not fear when the storm strikes. He may not be saved from the bone-piercing, tortuous winds, the pitiless rain and the devastating flood, but he will not flutter to and fro, for he built his house on the sure foundation, the tried stone (see first part of v. 16).

The time is not far away when the heavens shall pass away with a great noise and the earth and its works shall be burned up, but the one who does the will of God will abide forever. Perplexing situations will arise. Trouble may well come upon us. Adversity, slander and scorn may crowd in our door—yet—

Fear not, I am with thee; O be not dismayed;

For I am thy God and will still give thee aid;
I'll strengthen thee, help thee, and cause thee to stand,
Upheld by my gracious, omnipotent hand.

The unbeliever is distraught, dismayed, and fearful. He has no security. The things on which he has been taught to lean suddenly lose their sufficiency. He does not know where to turn; he "flutters to and fro"—from one cult to another perhaps— only to again be disappointed. To such troubled hearts the Master stands in the midst of the ages and cries: "Come unto me, all ye that labor and are heavy laden, and I will give thee rest." Bow before the King of kings, then follow His will to tranquillity and rest.

"Commit thy way unto the Lord." "Be still and know that I am God." "Be not anxious." Our living Lord will not fail! He will not fail you! His mercy is from everlasting and His blood covers all sin. Trust Him now and be at rest.

—*O. G. Wilson*

February 4

Samuel took a stone and set it up . . . and called its name Ebenezer, for he said, "Hitherto the Lord has helped us."
—I Samuel 7:12 (RSV)

Hear my cry, O God. . . . From the end of the earth will I cry unto thee, when my heart is overwhelmed: lead me to the rock that is higher than I.—Psalm 61:1, 2

There is strength and a stability about stones that make them symbolic of solidarity and trustworthiness. A solid native stone foundation under a lofty building gives the builder assurance that the building will withstand weather, heavy storms, even earthquakes and other unusual stresses. The Empire State Building has withstood many tests because of its design and deep underpinning of solid rock.

The stones or rocks in our meditation for today are somewhat different from the foundation under a building, however. The first stone would be classified as a "memorial stone." It was a reminder to Samuel and the children of Israel of God's faithfulness and His leading from the time Abraham left Ur right up to the present moment. The same God who led Israel also leads His children today—and will continue to lead you tomorrow. You can count on Him. He will be faithful to His promise.

I receive a real personal thrill from David's words in Psalm 61, because there are times when I really feel that my heart is about to be overwhelmed. Circumstances close in on me, the bottom falls out of some pet project, and down I go into the depths of despair, "the end of the earth," it seems. But there is Someone to whom I can go—Someone who is higher than I. Someone who can take my petty problems and put them into proper perspective, who can remove them, or solve them, or show me the way around them. All things are known to Him, and His children may be assured that He hears their cry. "Hitherto the Lord has helped us"—and, bless God, He will do so again!

February 5

Give us this day our daily bread.—Matthew 6:11

This seems a very small thing to ask—only bread for a day. Why are we not taught to pray for bread enough to last for a week, or a month, or a year? For one thing, Jesus wanted to teach us a lesson of continual dependence. He taught us to come each morning with a request simply for the day's food, that we might never feel we can get along without our Father. The manna in the wilderness taught the same lesson. Another lesson He wanted to teach us was that the true way to live is by the day. We are not to be anxious even about the supply of tomorrow's needs. When tomorrow comes it will be right for us to take up its cares. The poet says:

> Make a little fence of trust
> Around today;
> Fill the space with loving work,
> And therein stay.
> Look not through the sheltering bars
> Upon tomorrow;
> God will help thee bear what comes
> Of joy or sorrow.

We should not overlook the word "us." It is plural, and bids us send thought beyond our own individual needs and remember God's other children. This should always be a prayer for daily bread for our neighbor as well as for ourselves. Then while we thus enjoy our own plenty, we must share with those who have need.

> This crust is My body broken for thee,
> This water His blood that died on the tree;
> The holy Supper is kept, indeed,
> In whatso we share with another's need—
> Not that which we give, but what we share—
> For the gift without the giver is bare;
> Who bestows himself with his alms feeds three—
> Himself, his hungering neighbor, and Me.

—J. R. Miller

February 6

As the Father knoweth me, even so know I the Father: and I lay down my life for the sheep. —John 10:15

"The Father knoweth me." That means, "God has a will for every act of mine." What then can "I know the Father" mean except "In every act of mine I do the Father's will"? Obedience becomes the organ and utterance, or it becomes the substance and reality of knowledge on the side of him who is aware that in this more special sense God knows him.

I think of Jesus on that day when He called Lazarus back from the dead to life. He travels all the way from Galilee to Bethany. As last He stands beside the tomb. His soul is full of sympathy. The dreadfulness of death oppresses Him. Then He becomes aware of a will of God. He lifts His head. His face shines like the sun! The gloom is gone! He stretches out His hand. He opens His lips with the cry of life, "Lazarus, come forth!" "And he that was dead came forth, bound hand and foot with grave clothes."

God's will and Christ's obedience! Here, then, there is the perfect mutualness, the absolute understanding and harmony of the Father and the Son. If it were not the morning of the miracle at Bethany, but the awful morning of the cross, it would still be the same.

"Father, into thy hands I commend my spirit." There, in those words of completed obedience, the mutual knowledge of Father and Son is perfect, and being blends with being; the veil and barrier of the human flesh no longer hangs between.

—*Phillips Brooks*

February 7

Forgive us our debts, as we forgive our debtors.. —Matthew 6:12

To be able to write forgiveness in the Bible was God's most costly venture: "In whom we have redemption through his blood, the forgiveness of sins" (Eph. 1:7).

Love is more "than whole burnt offerings and sacrifice" (Mark 12:33). Forgive for the sake of the love debt you owe to Him. Calvary love seeks mercy for the erring one, and puts the kindest construction on the actions of others. It seeks forgiveness for the offender and forgives fully all wrongs against it.

Forgiveness flows from mercy and love. Were it not for mercy there would not be a glorified saint in heaven and not one disciple on earth. Mercy is the door through which all must enter the kingdom. How inappropriate, then, for a soul naming the name of Christ to be unmerciful, to harbor an unforgiving spirit.

"Be ye kind one to another, tenderhearted, forgiving one another, even as God for Christ's sake hath forgiven you" (Eph. 4:32). "I'll forgive but I'll not forget." Is that the way God for Christ's sake forgave you?

"He does not deserve forgiveness!" Did you deserve forgiveness? No, you were forgiven not because you deserved it, but because of Christ's sacrifice.

"I'll forgive, but from now on I want him to stay away from me." Christ did not say that to you. He said, "Come unto me."

"If ye do not forgive, neither will your Father which is in heaven forgive your trespasses" (Mark 11:26). Unforgiveness is rebellion against God. Unforgiveness stops the channel of answered prayer. Prayer from an unforgiving heart is blasphemy. The quantity of malice, bitterness, and party-spirit among Christians is fearfully great. No wonder prayer power is gone!

Do we know what it is to be of a forgiving spirit? Can we overlook the injuries we receive from time to time? Can we pardon an offense? If not, where is our Calvary love? Let us forgive as we hope to be forgiven. God's free forgiveness of sins is our highest privilege in this world. Our forgiveness of those who sin against us is the most God-like act we can perform. —*O. G. Wilson*

February 8

If ye forgive not men their trespasses, neither will your Father forgive your trespasses. —Matthew 6:15

A woman came to John Wesley and said, "Mr. Wesley, my talent is to speak my mind!"

Looking into the face of the woman, Mr. Wesley said, "I am certain that God wouldn't care at all if you buried that talent!"

When some people unhinge their tongues and give others a piece of their mind, they have no peace of mind left.

When Leonardo da Vinci was painting his great masterpiece, "The Last Supper," he became quite angry with a friend. He lashed out at him with hot, bitter words. Then he threatened the friend with vengeance. Returning to his canvas, he began to paint the face of Jesus. He found, however, that he was so perturbed and upset that he could not compose himself sufficiently to do the delicate work before him.

He went out immediately, sought his hurt friend, and humbly asked forgiveness for the tongue-lashing he had given him. Then he was in possession of that inner calm which enabled him to give the Master's face the tender and delicate expression he so well knew it must have. —*The War Cry*

February 9

Walk in love. —Ephesians 5:2

Love is the power that has drawn us as sinners unto God, that has melted the hardness of our hearts, and that now constrains us to live for Him and to Him. Love is the sphere of the Christian's activity.

"God is love; and he that dwelleth in love dwelleth in God, and God in him" (1 John 4:16). We are called to be followers, imitators of God. Therefore we have to "walk in love."

"God for Christ's sake hath forgiven you." If we imitate God in this respect, we shall forgive one another. The apostle makes no distinction between our being the objects of God's love and our being the objects of the love of Christ. It is one and the same love. This love we have is not only to contemplate and rejoice in, but we have to "walk" in it. That is, we have to show it practically; we have to exemplify it.

Walking is the phrase which the apostle uses to bring out the practical side of Christianity. As with our bodies so with our souls, we need exercise to reach the full development of the life. We cannot remain in health unless we are carrying out into practice that which we have received as the cardinal truths of our faith. —*Evan H. Hopkins*

February 10

Because thou hast put thy trust in me.... —Jeremiah 39:18

God loves to be trusted. Again and again throughout His Word He teaches and illustrates that those who do so will never be confounded. Here was a man of whom, perhaps, we should have never heard had it not been for the part he took on behalf of Jeremiah when he was thrown into the deep, dark, and dirty dungeon.

Now we see why he was such a friend to Jeremiah, because, though one of the king's servants, he was also a servant of the living God, and though he was in the city that was about to be destroyed, a message reached him from the God of heaven that he should be delivered. Why? Because he had put his trust in the Lord. Oh, how God loves to be trusted! and how He rewards those who put their trust in Him.

The three Hebrew children were delivered from the burning, fiery furnace because they "trusted in God." Daniel was taken up out of the lions' den, and no "manner of hurt was found upon him" "because he believed in his God," and it is positively asserted in God's Word that He shall deliver the righteous from the wicked and save them "because they trust in him." For this reason we are not surprised to hear God speaking to a man of whom we have heard but little: "I will deliver thee . . . because thou hast put thy trust in me." Oh, for a strong and perpetual faith in our living, loving Lord!

> Now I have found the ground wherein
> Sure my soul's anchor may remain;
> The wounds of Jesus, for my sin
> Before the world's foundation slain;
> Whose mercy shall unshaken stay
> When heaven and earth are fled away.
> —*John Roberts*

February 11

The Lord is good, a stronghold in the day of trouble; and he knoweth them that trust in him.—Nahum 1:7

What does it mean to be known of God? The Living Bible has a captivating lilt to it in its version of this verse: "The Lord is good. When trouble comes, He is the place to go! And He knows everyone that trusts in Him!" To be known of God means, in one sense at least, that He is my shelter and protection. In John 10:14, Jesus says: "I am the good Shepherd, and know my sheep. . . ." This is a vivid representation of one aspect of God's knowledge of His children, His sheep.

But there is a negative side to His knowledge as well. All things are known to Him—and He knows us as we are. What about the one who has no knowledge of God, the one who has no room for God in his life? By implication, this verse (both the Old Testament expression and the New Testament) teaches that those who deny His existence, those who live as though He did not exist, are in turn not known of Him, in the sense of having received His shelter and protection. In one sense, when we Christians live our lives anxiously, uptight about those things that happen to us, or seem threatening to happen, we are denying God His rightful place of prominence in our lives. What blessings we miss by thus ignoring the place of safety and shelter He wants to give us.

"God is our refuge and strength, a very present help in trouble," says the Psalmist (46:1). If, however, we are trying to make it "on our own," we pass by this refuge and fail to tap into His strength. We live like spiritual paupers because of that failure. God *knows* me, but I can limit His blessing in my life by my failure to really *know* Him, and all His fullness and adequacy for my needs.

February 12

He [poured] water into a bason, and began to wash the disciples' feet, and to wipe them with the towel wherewith he was girded.... Ye also ought to wash one another's feet.—John 13:5, 14

If I seek to bless others, it must be in the humble, loving readiness with which I serve them, not caring for my own honor or interest, if I can but be a blessing to them. I must follow Christ's example in washing the disciples' feet. A servant counts it no humiliation, and is not ashamed to be counted an inferior; it is his place and work to serve others. If we first learned from our Lord to associate with others in the blessed spirit of a servant, what a blessing we should become to the world.

The spirit which will enable one to live such a life of loving service can be learned from Jesus alone. Love never speaks of sacrifice. For love nothing is too hard. It was love that made Jesus a servant. It is love alone that will make the servant's place and work such blessedness to us that we shall persevere in it at all costs. Only love, a heavenly, unquenchable love, gives the patience, the courage, and the wisdom for this great work the Lord has set before us in His holy example: wash one another's feet.   —*Andrew Murray*

"From that time forth began Jesus to shew unto his disciples, how that he must go unto Jerusalem, and suffer many things... and be killed... Peter... began to rebuke him, saying... Lord: this shall not be unto thee" (Matt. 16:21, 22). The question continually before us is, are we to spend our time and strength simply for our own enrichment, or are we always praying and working with an eye to the divine service that lies before us? Are we among those who say, "I must go to Jerusalem, suffer, sacrifice, die"; or among those who say, "I must take care of myself, spare myself"? If we take Peter's attitude, we shall lose our own life and never save others. But if we choose Christ's way, we shall find our lives and help others.   —*G. Campbell Morgan*

February 13

I am poor and needy; yet the Lord thinketh upon me; thou art my help and my deliverer.—Psalm 40:17

Many feel as did the Psalmist, "I am poor and needy," because they have lost what they held dear. Many souls are surrounded by trouble and sorrow, frustrated by loss and failure, plagued by a feeling that life is a dead-end street. One of the first steps out of the fog and confusion of such a life is to admit your inability and acknowledge your utter dependence upon God.

The Psalmist had the answer, "The Lord thinketh upon me." And He is perfectly acquainted with your situation, your dangers, your wants. He knows all your problems and is familiar with the great wilderness through which you pass, and He is able and willing to offer seasonable help. Whatever help is needed, whenever help is needed, wherever help is needed, He stands ready to supply that need.

The God who thinks on you is the God at hand. Not afar off. Not unreachable off in eternity somewhere. But nigh you, even within you. All the events of life are under His control. He is the God of all grace, the God of all comfort, the God of all power. Therefore, when His purpose is worked out in your life, He will immediately deliver you.

Our difficulty is that in the hour of great trial we turn our attention to the trial. We look at the dark clouds and are overwhelmed. We look at the loss and failure of our plans and feel despair creeping in upon us. We must turn our eyes from every other thing and think upon God, look to God, talk with God, and let Him talk with us. Let us never forget: "The Lord thinketh upon me." He is thinking about me even now!

—O. G. Wilson

February 14

It shall be given you in that same hour what ye shall speak.—Matthew 10:19

And so I am not to worry about the coming crisis! "God never is before His time, and never is behind!" When the hour is come, I shall find that the great Host has made "all things ready."

When the crisis comes *He will tell me how to rest.* It is a great matter to know just how to rest—how to be quiet when "all without tumultuous seems." We irritate and excite our souls about the coming emergency, and we approach it with worn and feverish spirits, and so mar our Master's purpose and work.

When the crisis comes *He will tell me what to do.* The orders are not given until the appointed day. Why should I fume and fret and worry as to what the sealed envelope contains? "It is enough that He knows all," and when the hour strikes the secrets shall be revealed.

And when the crisis comes *He will tell me what to say.* I need not begin to prepare my retorts and my responses. What shall I say when death comes, to me or to my loved one? Never mind, He will tell me. And what when sorrow or persecution comes? Never mind, He will tell me.

—J. H. Jowett

February 15

And they brought him hastily out of the dungeon.— Genesis 41:14

How often is the remark made that "all things come to them that wait." But while there may be much truth in this little proverb, it does not contain the whole truth. If, however, we are prepared to add this: "If they wait patiently and believingly upon the Lord Jesus Christ," then the saying may be quite correct.

Joseph had pleaded, and earnestly too: "Bring me out of this . . . dungeon." But he was not delivered the moment he prayed. "Two full years" had to pass away, and still poor Joseph was in his prison. But God had not forgotten him, and Joseph kept believing, and in God's own time and way he was gloriously delivered and brought "hastily out of the dungeon."

Now, Joseph's God is our God, and nothing honors Him more than unbounded confidence in Him. In all times of darkness and trial "commit thy way unto the Lord, trust also in him, and he shall bring it to pass," for He is the same to those who trust Him, "yesterday, today, and forever."

> Commit thou all thy griefs
> And ways into His hands,
> To His sure trust and tender care
> Who in heaven and earth commands.
>
> Who points the clouds their course,
> Whom winds and seas obey.
> He shall direct thy wandering feet,
> He shall prepare thy way.
>
> Thou on the Lord rely,
> So safe shalt thou go on;
> Fix on His work thy steadfast eye,
> So shall thy work be done.
>
> *—John Roberts*

February 16

Humble yourselves under the mighty hand of God.— 1 Peter 5:6

The first step toward faith is a humble admission of need. The next step is a humble acceptance of the help which is offered. It is this thing called *surrender*. It is letting God take charge. Writing to Christians in his day, who also faced perilous times, the apostle Peter put it this way: "Humble yourselves under the mighty hand of God" (1 Pet. 5:6). Let Him come in and take charge. Let our private wills and hopes and plans and opinions be surrendered to His sovereign presence.

What does it mean for Jesus to "take charge"? Assuming that we recognize the need, assuming that we raise the cry for help, assuming that we make this initial step of surrender—what may we expect to follow in terms of practical results?

The apostle Peter suggests that when we humble ourselves under the sovereign hand of God, He takes charge of three basic concerns of our life. He takes charge of our sense of personal *worth*, our quest for personal identity. He takes charge of our *worries*, the practical problems that press in on us in everyday life. He takes charge of our *warfare*, the spiritual struggle against the powers of destruction and evil. These three concerns, seen as a whole, demonstrate the comprehensiveness of His care for those who surrender to His lordship. He pays attention to the most intimate yearning of the heart, the most immediate pressure of circumstance, yet He never loses sight of the ultimate destiny which He has appointed for those whom He names as His own.

—Larry Christenson

February 17

That we through patience and comfort of the scriptures might have hope.—Romans 15:4

The apostle Paul is alluding to a tremendous spiritual principle in this "comfort" passage, and verse 5 begins to open up a concept probably not often associated with Pauline writings—that of acceptance by believers of one another, regardless of denominational background. Verse 5 in the Living Bible reads, "May God who gives patience, steadiness, and encouragement, help you to live in complete harmony with each other—each with the attitude of Christ toward the other."

True, Paul was writing to a specific congregation of Christians, a diverse group of believers drawn together by a common love for Christ. But, in a wider sense, doesn't that description apply to the Christian church as a broad body of believers? Shouldn't all Christians be able to "praise the Lord together with one voice, giving glory to God, the Father of our Lord Jesus Christ," as Paul exhorts in verse 6 of this same chapter?

Paul is scratching the surface of a vast truth in this passage. He goes on to say in verse 7 of the same chapter, "In a word, *accept* one another as Christ accepted us, to the glory of God" (New English Bible). I wonder what would happen if in the Christian church all Christians, with their diversities of interpretation but their oneness at the cross of Christ, would follow this admonition. Would the church be stronger or weaker? Would the gospel be spread more effectively—or less effectively?

Think about the implications of that word, "accepted." Elsewhere Paul tells us that we are "accepted in the beloved" (Eph. 1:6). What a thrilling thought it is to know ourselves accepted by Christ—and accepted by our fellow Christians. And what a tragedy that this acceptance is sometimes clouded by trivial disagreements and differing doctrinal interpretations among Christians.

The ground is level at the cross of Christ, but unfortunately we Christians are merely human and sometimes build our ladders of prejudice and pettiness to raise ourselves above our brethren. Instead, let us "accept one another as Christ accepted us."

February 18

As one whom his mother comforteth, so will I comfort you.—Isaiah 66:13

In chapter 12 of Isaiah, the prophet says, "O Lord . . . thou comfortedst me," and in this passage we are able to see the tender way in which God comforts those who are His. "As one whom his mother comforteth, so will I comfort you." The Psalmist has assured us that "like as a father pitieth his children, so the Lord pitieth them that fear him." Our Lord has, therefore, taken the place of both father and mother. Even more than this, for in chapter 6 He says: "Can a woman forget her child, that she should not have compassion on her own son?" This is well-nigh impossible, yet it might be so in one case out of a thousand. God's love, however, is beyond and far deeper than even that of a mother. Therefore He declares: "I will never forget thee."

He also tells us that we shall be His in that day when He makes up His jewels. "I will spare them as a man spareth his own son that serveth him." And then we have the words of Jesus: "If ye, being evil, know how to give good gifts unto your children, how much more shall your Father which is in heaven give good things to them that ask him?"

Can we wonder, then, at God saying to the prophet, "Comfort ye my people," when we see how He is to them more than a father and mother combined? Let us learn from this passage what our God is to us, and how He owns, remembers, pities, and comforts, and undertakes, as an almighty parent, to provide for all our needs. —*John Roberts*

February 19

He that is mighty hath done to me great things. . . . He careth for you. —Luke 1:49; 1 Peter 5:7

Is it not wonderful that the mighty God, so great, so holy, should ever think of a poor, lowly sinner on this earth? But does He really? It scarcely seems possible. Only consider how many billion people there are in this world. Can it be that the glorious God ever gives a separate, special thought to any one person among so many? He may give thought to a few great people—to kings and rulers, and to certain very good men and women; but surely He does not think of anyone so small and obscure as I.

Ah, yes! He does. Remember Ishmael, that child of Abraham, once dying of thirst in the desert. God heard his mother's cries amid all the noise in the world, and sent an angel to point out a spring of water and thus save the child's life.

Remember, too, the story of Moses. His mother could no longer shelter her baby son from the wrath of the Pharaoh. So she hid him in an ark laid near the banks of the Nile; you recall how God cared for that helpless infant and provided for him in a marvelous way.

Jesus said our heavenly Father cares for a sparrow and feeds it, and that He even clothes each little flower in the field. If there is not a bird or flower that He does not think of and care for, surely He gives thought and care to us, His crowning creation! We are better than a sparrow, better than a flower. We have immortal souls; we are God's own children; and was there ever a true father who did not think of, and love and care for, his children?

He calls each one of us by name. He hears our prayers. He knows when anything is going wrong for us, or when we are in any trouble. He watches over us and sends blessings to us every day. What a wonderful thought, that God, this great and mighty God, thinks of each one of us, and does *great things* for us! —*J. R. Miller*

February 20

Whom having not seen, ye love. —1 Peter 1:8

The religion of Christ is a religion of love. It is a revelation of life, and a manifestation of light; but, above all, it is a religion of love. Love needs a person as its object. You cannot love an abstraction. That person is Christ, who is the brightness of the Father's glory.

We have never seen with our natural eyes that risen Lord. But we are sure of His existence; we believe in the reality and completeness of His work; we have trusted in His grace and favor. And more than this, we *love* Him—because He first loved us (1 John 4:19).

Those who love Him have joy in His presence. "Whom have I in heaven but thee? and there is none upon earth that I desire in comparison of thee." They delight in His presence and service. They are in sympathy with Him who has come to seek and to save that which was lost, and who says to us, "Rejoice *with* me" (Luke 15:6). They feast on His Word. It is not only duty that impels them, it is also desire that draws them.

Those who know Him love Him; and to love Him is to follow on to know Him better.   —*Evan H. Hopkins*

February 21

Holding forth the word of life; that I may rejoice in the day of Christ.—Philippians 2:16

Keep things in proper relation to their respective importance. One reason we become discouraged is that we form distorted pictures of the experiences that affect us. When a friend supposedly slights us (intentionally or otherwise), we are in danger of considering all friends unworthy. When we fail at some undertaking—singing a solo, driving a car, applying for a job—we often go home and, in a despairing mental state, decide: "I'm no good; I'll not try again."

Suppose you did fail to pass your driver's test, there is another day coming and perhaps a more sympathetic examiner. Life is not made up of a single event, but a long series of occurrences. The failure today may be the preparation needed for tomorrow's effort. Rewards come from difficulties conquered. No one achievement is the apex of success. Always there are more mountains to climb and more hurdles to surmount.

Don't lose life's perspective; keep things properly related. If you must be overwhelmed let it be in an ocean, not in a bath tub! The old mill, driven by water power, useful in its day, is now idle and obsolete. The watering trough at the side of the road to refresh weary horses is no longer necessary. The pony express, an example of tough horseflesh and equally tough men, has passed into history. We may stand at the old mill and lament its passing. Or we may go out and grow grain, grind it in the electric-powered plant, and feed the world.

We may long for the good old days when men were men and women were housewives and mothers, and miss the challenge of this our day. There is no road to yesterday. Today is our opportunity, our responsibility.

This is a frightening day because men do not hold life in true perspective. We have looked at *things* and are confused, alarmed. Take a look at God—supreme, just, holy, good. Nothing is too hard for Him. Out of the chaos and degradation of this generation Christ is gathering a band of holy people who will go out in the rapture. Live for this event and life's little annoyances will be held in proper perspective.   —O. G. Wilson

February 22

My soul, wait thou only upon God; for my expectation is from him.—Psalm 62:5

The solemn question comes to us, "Is the God I have a God who is to me above all circumstances, nearer to me than any circumstance can be?" Christian friend, have you learned to live your life having God so genuinely with you every moment that in the most difficult circumstances He is always more present and nearer than any difficulty? All our knowledge of God's Word will be of little or no help to us if we cannot answer that question affirmatively.

Why do so many of God's beloved children complain continually, "My circumstances separate me from God; my trials, my temptations, my character, my temper, my friends, my enemies, anything can come between my God and me"? Is God not able to so take possession that He can be nearer to me than anything in the world? Must riches or poverty, joy or sorrow, have a power over me that my God does not have? No. But why, then, do God's children so often complain that they feel separated from God by their circumstances?

There can be but one answer: "They do not know their God." If there is trouble or feebleness in the church of God, it is because of this. We do not really know the God we have. That is why, in addition to the promise, "I will be their God," the promise is so often added, "And ye shall know that I am your God." If I know that, not through man's teaching, not with my mind or my imagination; but if I know that, in the living evidence which God gives in my heart, then I know that the divine presence of my God will be so wonderful, and my God himself will be so beautiful, and so near, that I can live my days and years a conqueror through Him who loved me and gave himself for me. Is not that the life we need?

—*Andrew Murray*

February 23

Surely the Lord is in this place; and I knew it not.—Genesis 28:16

That was the first time for many a day that Jacob had named the name of God. In all the dark story of his wicked intrigue the name of God is never mentioned. Jacob wanted to forget God! God would be a disturbing presence! But here he encounters Him in a dream, and in the most unlikely place. "And he was afraid, and said, How dreadful is this place!" Jacob had yet to learn that there is everywhere "a ladder set up on the earth and the top of it reaches to heaven." There was a ladder from the very tent in which he wore his deceptive skin. There was a ladder from the secret place where he and his mother wove their mischievous plot. There is no corner of the earth which is cut away from the divine vigilance. God gets at us everywhere.

But there is a merciful side to all this. If the ladder be everywhere, and God can get at us, then also everywhere we can get at God. There are "ascending angels" who will carry our confessions, our prayers, our sighs and mournings, to the very heart of the eternally gracious God. —*J. H. Jowett*

February 24

Cast all your anxieties on him, for he cares about you.
—1 Peter 5:7 (RSV)

A person or a family plagued by worry can hardly be an effective witness for Jesus. He makes us His witness precisely by delivering us from worry—by taking our anxieties upon himself.

But how? How does Jesus take charge of our worries? Or, to see it from the other end of the stick, how do we cast our anxieties on Him? This involves more than a mental act. For even though worry is a psychological state, it is related to factors outside one's mind. And God does not invite us to cast merely our mental attitude on Jesus, but to cast on Him that which brings on our mental attitude. There are practical ways in which to convey our worry to Jesus. According to the nature of the worry, you will convey it in a particular way. Whenever a worry comes up, one must pray for the wisdom to see just how to convey it over to Jesus.

What about those worries which are more generalized—a low mood, a sense of frustration or discontent, even downright depression? One might call them emotional worries, worries centered around one's own personality and feelings. Here, too, we must look for the practical steps by which we can convey these worries over to Jesus.

Jesus has provided a way. Your emotions are tied to your whole being. When you become a Christian, you are mystically yet truly related to other Christians in what the Bible calls "the body of Christ" (Rom. 12:5). This is more than an interesting metaphor. It is a mystical reality. Your emotional health depends on what you can receive and give within the body of Christ. When you are down, some other member of the body of Christ is going to be up. When someone else is down, you may be up, and able to help him. We depend upon one another. ... This is the way we convey our emotional worries to Jesus: We live as functioning members of His body, in which the individual members have a care for one another.

—Larry Christenson

February 25

He ... rebuked the wind, and said unto the sea, Peace, be still.—Mark 4:39

He spoke to the storm and to the tossing sea as if they were intelligent creatures—just as a man would speak to his servants. The truth we learn here is that He is Lord of nature; that the elements recognize His voice and obey Him even in their wildest moods. If we only fully believed this, it would bring a great deal of peace to our lives. No tempest ever breaks beyond the control of Him who is our Lord and Redeemer. No wave ever rolls any farther than He permits. There is nothing in this world that is not under the control of that Hand nailed to a cross.

A story is told of a Christian army officer at sea with his family in a storm. There was great terror among the passengers, but he was calm. His wife, in her terror, scolded him for his serenity, saying he ought to be concerned for her and the children, if not for himself, in such danger. He made no reply, but soon came to her with his pistol drawn, and with an angry scowl, pointed it at her heart. She was not the least alarmed, but looked up into his face with a smile. "What!" said he, "are you not afraid when a drawn revolver is at your heart?" "No," she replied, "not when it is in the hands of one who loves me." "And would you have me," he asked, "to be afraid of this storm when I know it is in the hand of my heavenly Father, who loves me?"

Thus even in the wildest tumults of nature or circumstance, we should be at peace since our Savior is Lord of all. Someone tells of being at sea in a terrible cyclone, and of seeing a little bird fly down, when the storm was at its height, and light on the crest of a wave, there to sit serenely as if it had been perching on a branch in some quiet forest. So should the believer in Christ repose in quietness and confidence in the wildest storm.

—J. R. Miller

February 26

For the mountains shall depart, and the hills be removed; but my kindness shall not depart from thee, neither shall the covenant of my peace be removed, saith the Lord.
—Isaiah 54:10

In today's unstable world, we see all around us evidences of the truth of Isaiah's prophecy. Mountains and hills are indeed fragile in the face of earthquakes and man-made upheavals. What happened to Hiroshima at the end of World War II could happen to an entire country or continent with the sophisticated weapons of war that exist today. But our God is like the Rock of Gibraltar which cannot be moved. If God could fail, then all creation could be obliterated. His children can know that God will never leave them nor forsake them, for His love is without end and His "kindness shall not depart from thee."

There is a phrase in the Psalms that emphasizes this truth even better than does the prophet Isaiah. In Psalm 72:17 Solomon says, "His name shall endure for ever." The words, "endureth forever," occur more than ten times in the Psalms alone —always in relation to the Lord, His name, His righteousness, His praise, His truth, and His judgments. In other books of the Bible, His mercy and His word are described as enduring forever. The One who endures forever is our God, our Lord, our Savior! We may know with a certainty set down indelibly in God's record book that eternity is ours in His company! Along with all these other attributes, we know that His kindness will be ours forever!

February 27

And one [sparrow] shall not fall on the ground without your Father.—Matthew 10:29

The door of our garage was left partly open. A sick sparrow crept in at one side, behind a bundle of newspapers, and died alone. No, it was not alone. God was there.

G. Campbell Morgan says of this passage: "Do not spoil this quotation by saying that Jesus meant that not one of them shall fall to the ground without the Father's knowledge. He did not say that. The King said that God is *with* the dying sparrow."

I felt a sense of awe as I carried the dead sparrow to a place of burial—God was present. Jesus is showing that the smallest details of life are in God's knowledge and under His matchless care. He who feeds the sparrow will not starve the saint. Nothing can come to the trusting child of God except as God permits it. From the dungeon comes a *Pilgrim's Progress*, and from the hours of perpetual darkness comes the soul-inspiring music of Fanny Crosby. "Fear ye not, therefore."

Your very hairs are numbered; not just counted, but numbered. Your standing in eternity is assured, for "whosoever will confess me before men, him will I confess also before my Father which is in heaven."

We are inclined to think that Christ's confession quoted here means that at sometime, someplace in the remote future, He will confess our name before the Father and the holy angels. Of course, that will be true, but when we confess Christ now, present tense, before men, He then confesses our name before the Father.

Bear in mind, the Master did not say we would have things easy, that we would be honored and loved by all. Quite the contrary. Do not expect to fare better than the Master. But in the midst of your opposition, in the hour of your blackest trial, remember God is present. Since He is present at the funeral of the sparrow, He will be present at the suffering of His saints!

—*O. G. Wilson*

February 28

As the sufferings of Christ abound in us, so our consolation also aboundeth by Christ.—2 Corinthians 1:5

What were the sufferings to which the apostle here refers? They were the sufferings endured, "whether by himself, or by His Church with which He identified himself." Christ calls His people's sufferings His own: "Because of the sympathy and mystical union between Him and us (Rom. 8:17; 1 Cor. 4:10; Heb. 2:17, 18), Christ's own sufferings are revived in His people's." "They are borne for His sake. They tend to His glory (Eph. 4:1; 1 Peter 4:14, 16)."

But though the sufferings are many, the consolation exceeds them. The apostle continually dwells, in his epistles, on the subject of comfort. He shows us how each person of the Trinity ministers to the consolation of the people of God, and that a restful heart is as essential to our work and progress as a strong and courageous heart. In fact, comfort is the secret of strength and courage. Joy and suffering are often in the apostle's mind and writings as the paradox of the Christian life.

"As sorrowful, yet always rejoicing." —*Evan H. Hopkins*

February 29

To another faith by the same Spirit. . . .—I Corinthians 12:9

Now God does have a "gift of faith." This is a sudden penetration of the deep mind by the faith of God himself. It is for a specific situation. It is not an everyday experience. It is a special gift from God. The faith we are talking about here is the kind that abides, that grows slowly like a fruit, and comes more and more to trust God.

Psalm 16:7 has a wonderful promise for us when it comes to the activity of God upon the deeper levels of our consciousness. It says, "I bless the Lord who gives me counsel; in the night also my heart instructs me." Your conscious mind never sleeps. If you enter into this seriously, the way every Christian should—the way a scientist or any specialist spends time and dedicates himself to his specialty—you will find yourself waking up praying; you realize that you were in a state of prayer before you woke. That has been taking place in the depths of your mind as you slept.

So faith must be learned, not only in our conscious mind where we say, "I believe." It must also be learned in the depths of our being. One man has said, "If we would believe the Apostles' Creed, every word of it, there would be miracles happening in every single worship service." That is literally true—if we believed the Creed from our toenails to the top of our head. But we do not. We have deep levels of doubt within us. That is not a word of condemnation, but simply of fact. To know that fact gives us a starting point, so that we can be aware of it and enter into a program of growth.

—*Larry Christenson*

March 1

Faith is the substance of things hoped for, the evidence of things not seen.—Hebrews 11:1

If this may be called a definition, it is the only definition of faith we have in the Bible. Before he gives us its working, and its results in the lives of men the inspired writer puts before us its nature.

He thus describes it: "Faith is the substance [or confidence] of things hoped for." It substantiates the *promises* of God; and not the promises only, but the *present facts* or realities of revelation, which are to sight, for the most part, unseen.

What we cannot see with the natural eye, what we cannot touch and realize with physical sense, faith enables us to grasp as actually present and true.

Faith must not be confused with fancy. God does not say, "*Imagine* these blessings in your heart, and believe them, *as if* they were really true." No, God begins by declaring their actual existence, that they are already true, and *because* they are true, commands us to believe. He never bids us believe without providing a foundation of *promise* or of *fact* on which to rest our faith.

And so faith becomes to us "the evidence" or demonstration —the convincing proof—of things not seen. It is not a matter of trusting in the dark what we cannot see in the light, but of accepting God at His word, for this is evidence enough for the child of God. —*Evan H. Hopkins*

March 2

Great peace have they which love thy law.—Psalm 119:165

Statesmen know that an armament race eventually and almost inevitably leads to war. They know that the only road to peace is through disarmament, but they also know that, world round, there is so much distrust, fear, and hate that to disarm would be suicidal. David Lloyd George, former prime minister of England, said: "You are not going to get peace with millions of armed men. The chariot of peace cannot advance over a road littered with cannon." How, then, can the nations of the world turn from the road of inevitable war to the road of universal peace? What does God's Word say?

"When a man's ways please the Lord, he maketh even his enemies to be at peace with him. Better is a little with righteousness than great revenues without right" (Prov. 16:7, 8). "Aquaint now thyself with him, and be at peace" (Job 22:21). The first step toward universal peace is an adjusted relationship with God. Let every man make peace with God, on God's terms, and peace will come. Men of good will must be the instruments and agents of Him who yearns over all the families of the earth. When man is out of fellowship with his God, he is distrustful, fearful, and filled with revenge. "There is no peace, saith the Lord, unto the wicked" (Isa. 48:22).

When the soul surrenders to Christ, and the inner drives are purified, man is at peace with himself and with God. There is a promised future state of peace and prosperity for the world: "They shall beat their swords into plowshares; and their spears into pruninghooks; nation shall not lift up a sword against nation, neither shall they learn war any more" (Micah 4:3). This golden age, this yearning hope, is to be brought in by the Christ. It may be entered now in personal experience, and it will spread over the whole earth when the Lord Jesus Christ establishes His everlasting kingdom over all earthly kingdoms.

He comes to reign in peace, to fulfill the divinely implanted longing for peace. The road to peace, then, is to make Christ known to the nations. Carry the gospel to every tribe and people, lift up the standard, declare His righteousness with the Holy Ghost power sent from heaven. This is the path to peace. —*O. G. Wilson*

March 3

The fruit of the spirit is love. . . .—Galatians 5:22

We may have the Spirit within us, and yet there may be a sad lack of fruit in our lives. The Holy Spirit may be grieved. And when He is grieved He ceases to fill us with His fruit. It is not by strain and effort that we become fruitful. As with growth, so with fruitfulness, it is not energy that is needed so much as a healthy condition of soul. Then we must keep clearly before us: it is not the fruit of the Christian but the fruit of the Holy Spirit which is being considered here. The Christian *bears* the fruit, but the Spirit *produces* it.

The fruit of the Spirit consists of one cluster of nine different virtues. In no sense have we to manufacture them.

What, then, is the secret of divine fruitfulness? The indwelling and fellowship of the Holy Spirit. Let Christ be recognized as Lord within the soul; let Him be honored and obeyed, and the Holy Spirit will not fail to shed abroad in our hearts the love of God (Rom. 5:5). He will not fail to fill us "with all joy and peace in believing" (Rom. 15:13).

Fruitfulness is brought about not by *imitation* so much as by *manifestation*. It is the outcome of that which dwells within. —*Evan H. Hopkins*

March 4

The fruit of the Spirit is . . . joy.—Galatians 5:22

Joy does not come alone. It comes between "love" and "peace." Those are three things we cannot bring about in ourselves by any direct efforts of our own, however earnestly and feverishly we may try. We cannot make ourselves "love," or rejoice, or be peaceful. These are the fruits of the Spirit.

In relation to these inner conditions of mind we are to be passive. It is the Holy Spirit who produces this fruit and fills our hearts with such emotions. The active virtues follow as the necessary outcome of this inner condition. It is when divine "love, joy, and peace" are graciously filling our hearts that our actions will be characterized by longsuffering, gentleness, goodness, faithfulness, etc.

Let us recognize the Holy Spirit's personality and presence, as One dwelling within us. If we are grieving Him, how can He comfort us? He is then our Reprover. But it is emphatically His office or capacity to comfort. When we honor Him, and yield to His gracious sovereign sway, then He not only ceases to reprove—He begins at once to fill our hearts with His fruit. —*Evan H. Hopkins*

March 5

The fruit of the Spirit is longsuffering, gentleness.—Galatians 5:22

If "love, joy, peace" describe the inner condition, "longsuffering, gentleness, goodness" would seem to point to the outward conduct. " 'Longsuffering' is *passive,* 'patient endurance under injuries inflicted by others'; 'gentleness' is *neutral,* a 'kindly disposition towards one's neighbours,' not necessarily taking a kindly form; 'goodness' is *active* as an energetic principle" (Lightfoot).

We must not confound "longsuffering" with a dogged endurance, which is often the result of indifference and obstinacy, and in which there is neither meekness nor love. Nor, again, is "gentleness" to be confounded with weakness or an easygoing disposition which lacks decision and strength of character. "Gentleness," which is the fruit of the Holy Spirit, has nothing of timidity in it. Some of the most courageous spirits have been remarkable for their gentleness. But the point to remember is this: These are not virtues to be manufactured by the Christian. They are fruit to be brought forth by the Spirit. The Christian is a *branch*, not the *root.*

—*Evan H. Hopkins*

March 6

Stand fast in one spirit, with one mind striving together for the faith of the gospel. . . . I press toward the mark for the prize of the high calling of God in Christ Jesus.
—Philippians 1:27; 3:14

Thank God for goals! To quit trying is to stagnate, to become obese and sluggish physically, dull and lethargic mentally. If we think we've arrived spiritually as well, and "lean back on our laurels," we'll find the same thing happening to our souls that I have described as happening to our bodies and minds.

The apostle Paul was very goal-conscious. He never felt he had arrived spiritually, but he went on striving for mastery of the inner man until the day of his death, if we are to judge by his writings which apparently continued almost to the day of his martyrdom. We know that he wrote some of his most victorious and unforgettable epistles in prison. And at that time in his life when he was literally behind bars, his constant theme was victory and freedom (see the book of Galatians). So Paul didn't believe in rest and relaxation. He believed in constant exercise, taking his cue from the successful athlete who steadfastly pressed forward seeking the prize, never slacking in his effort to be first.

And what Paul practiced in his personal life, he urged upon the Philippian Christians as well. He admonished them to strive "together for the faith of the gospel." Does faith come by striving? In the sense Paul is writing about it does. He considered the gospel, and unity in it, a worthy goal for his spiritual children, and for Christians today. Don't "ease up" just because you may have reached a certain goal previously established. Set new goals! And don't be afraid to reach a little. If your goals are too easy, you may find yourself slowing to a walk, then sitting down in the shade while the rest of the church passes you by. Ask God to give you a goal to strive for—then count on Him for strength to reach it.

March 7

And he came . . . into the temple. —Luke 2:27

Notice the three words I have omitted in the text above—"by the Spirit." What a wealth of meaning lies wrapped up in those words, "He came by the Spirit into the temple"! Ordinary men would have said "by chance." Many Christians would have thought, *How fortunate!* or *How unusual!* But Luke, the beloved physician and evangelist, said: "He came by the Spirit."

We are told first that "the Holy Ghost was upon him" (v. 25); next, "That it was revealed to him by the Holy Ghost" that he would see "the Lord's Christ"; and then that "he came by the Spirit into the temple" at just the moment Mary and Joseph "brought in the child Jesus."

How given up to and led by the Spirit good old Simeon must have been. But the Holy Spirit is just as willing to lead consecrated men today as He was then. Romans 8 is full of the work of the Holy Spirit, and teaches that "the sons of God" are "led by the Spirit." Therefore, if while using my own understanding, I do not lean upon it, but in all my ways acknowledge Him, He will direct my paths even as He did Simeon's. And I shall experience the blessedness of going here and there, or of doing this and that, "by the Spirit."

—*John Roberts*

March 8

He led them on safely. —Psalm 78:53

Before we are ready to consider the "way," we must be sure as to the destination. "Where am I going?" That is the first question. Then comes the inquiry as to the road we are traveling.

The destination is not a place merely, but a Person. He died, "the just for the unjust, that he might *bring us to God*" (1 Pet. 3:18). The right way is the way that leads to God. He brings us now into God's presence. We have access through the Lord Jesus Christ into the Holiest. And He will hereafter present us "faultless before the presence of his glory with exceeding joy" (Jude 24). "He led them forth by the right way, that they might go to a city of habitation" (Ps. 107:7).

The perpetual presence of Christ as the guide of His people is a great and blessed reality. *"He* led them." Though pardoned and redeemed, quickened and set free, they are not able to guide themselves. They are as helpless in the journey as they were in the "horrible pit." *"He* brought me up also out of an horrible pit, out of the miry clay, and set my feet upon a rock, and established my goings."

"Thou has delivered my soul from death: wilt not *thou* deliver my feet from falling?" (Ps. 56:13).   —*Evan H. Hopkins*

March 9

But ye shall receive power, after that the Holy Ghost is come upon you: and ye shall be witnesses unto me. —Acts 1:8

Someone comes in when the door swings wide to Jesus. We call that someone the "Holy Spirit." He kindles a soft but intense fire inside. You find yourself instinctively doing things for others, and telling them of Jesus. And as you do there's a something—a gentle, winsome, burning something—that wings its way into people's hearts like morning sunlight into a room. The word used for it is "power." But the thing is more than the word ever tells.

Jesus let all the way in, and then let all the way out—that's the message for all the world. His blood cleanses; His presence changes heart and habits. Then He pushes His way out through the new light in the eye, the new gentleness of the tongue, the new earnestness of the life, out through word and glad and ready feet. His coming in brings life. *His getting out makes you know better that He's in.*   —*S. D. Gordon*

March 10

I will put my spirit within you . . . a new spirit I will put within you. —Ezekiel 36:27, 26

God's child, Israel, had been a naughty child—she (or, in this day of women's lib, should I write "it"?) had fallen far short of God's plan and gone deeply into idolatry. This is the burden of Ezekiel's message to his fellow Israelites, the message he was delivering for God. In Ezekiel 11:19 God says, "I will give them one heart, and I will put a new spirit within you; and I will take the stony heart out of their flesh, that they may walk in my statutes, and keep mine ordinances and do them; and they shall be my people, and I will be their God."

Thank God, He does not condemn us even though we deserve His condemnation because of our sinfulness. No, He offers us a "new spirit," an opportunity for a changed life, a new life, a new beginning, a new start. Paul must have had this blessed biblical truth in mind when he wrote, "For the law of the Spirit of life in Christ Jesus hath made me free from the law of sin and death." This new Spirit God offers is a spirit of freedom, not the bondage of fear that was a part of Israel's idolatrous worship.

Oh, the glorious freedom of the Christian who abides in Christ, who has His Spirit indwelling him! Long ago the poet John Newton wrote:

> Joy is a fruit that will not grow
> In nature's barren soil;
> All we can boast, till Christ we know,
> Is vanity and toil.
> But where the Lord hath planted grace,
> And made His glories known,
> These fruits of heavenly joy and peace
> Are found, and there alone.

And that is just the song my heart sings as I reflect on the glorious truth of this often overlooked passage in Ezekiel. Help me, Father, to be a student of your whole Word—and to apply it to my whole life!

March 11

Hereby know we that we dwell in him, and he in us, because he hath given us of his Spirit. —1 John 4:13

A great Bible teacher of another generation often said that the secret of grasping the meaning of a particular portion of scripture lay in one simple practice which any Bible student, great theologian or beginner, could follow: whenever you see a "therefore" in the Bible, check back to see what it's *there for.* I'd like to apply that same principle to our verse for today, but to a different word—"hereby." Instead of looking back for the reason it is there, I look ahead in the same verse where I'm told that the reason I can know I dwell in Christ is that I have His Spirit. How do I know I have His Spirit? Verse 12 tells me, "If we love one another, God dwelleth in us, and his love is perfected [made complete] in us." Think of it, I as an obedient, Spirit-filled believer, have a small part in presenting a "complete" picture of God's love!

But there's a greater truth here. As a believer, I am *in Christ*, so I am under His protection from anything *outside* of me. Christ is *in me*, so I have *inside* might and power to withstand any outward force of evil. I am completely impregnable in Him!

Paul, too, gives us a solid checkpoint for determining the Spirit's ministry in our lives: "But ye are not in the flesh, but in the Spirit, if so be that the Spirit of God dwelleth in you." What part of you has the ascendancy in your life—the flesh or the spirit? Do not give place to the devil and fleshly pursuits. Rather, yield to His Spirit that the glorious fruit of that presence may be shown in your life—and that will result in spiritual fruit for you as you let your light shine before men, glorifying God in all that you do.

March 12

For the Spirit searcheth all things, yea, the deep things of God.—1 Corinthians 2:10

The deep things of God cannot be discovered by unaided reason. "Eye has not seen": they are not to be discerned by the artistic vision. "Ear has not heard": they are not unveiled in the discussion of the philosophic schools. "Neither hath entered into the heart of man": even poetic insight cannot uncover them. All the common lights fail in this realm. We need another illumination—that provided by the Holy Spirit. And the Spirit is offered to us "that we might know the things that are freely given to us by God."

Here we have the reason why so many so-called "common" or uncultured people are spiritually wiser than many who are learned and even erudite. They lack talent, but they have grace. They lack accomplishments in the scholarly realm, but they have the Holy Spirit. They lack the telescope and the microscope, but they have the sunlight. They are not scholars, but they *are* saints. They may not be theologians, but they have true religion. And so they have "the open vision." They "walk with God," and "the deep things of God" are made known to their souls.

We must put first things first. We may be busy polishing our lenses when our primary and fundamental need is light. It is not a gift we require, but a Friend.   —*J. H. Jowett*

March 13

The Comforter, which is the Holy Ghost, whom the Father will send in my name.—John 14:26

"The Comforter" is one of the names of the third person of the Trinity. It is found only in John's Gospel and First Epistle (14:16, 26; 16:7, 1 John 2:1). The meaning of the word is "one who is called to another's side to aid him," as an advocate in a court of law.

The Holy Spirit is, therefore, represented as an Advocate or Counsel, "who suggests true reasonings to our minds and true courses of action for our lives, who convicts our adversary, the world, of wrong, and pleads our cause before God our Father. It is to be noted that *Jesus*, as well as the Holy Spirit, is represented as Paraclete. The Holy Spirit is to be *another* Paraclete, and this falls in with the statement in the First Epistle: 'We have an *Advocate* with the Father, Jesus Christ the righteous' " (Vincent).

Christ has not ceased to be our Comforter because He has sent "another Comforter." Nor is He an absent Advocate because His visible presence is withdrawn. The Holy Spirit fulfills His office of Comforter in many ways, but chiefly in revealing the fact that the risen Lord is truly *with*, and *in*, us.

—*Evan H. Hopkins*

March 14

Therefore, being justified. . . .—Romans 5:1

We come now to the first great aspect of "the gospel of Christ"—justification. In verse 1 we have justification and reconciliation: "justified by faith" and "peace with God." In verse 2 we have divine acceptance and unspeakable joy, and all this through "our Lord Jesus Christ." Then comes "glorying in "tribulations"; not, of course, in the tribulations themselves, but in the effects.

Every sorrow is appointed by the Father, and so appointed that they are the means of producing patience, experience, hope, and love; and thus we learn to glory in them.

The words "much more" occur in five different places in this justification chapter, after which we are led into chapter 6 to receive entire cleansing from all inward defilement. "Shall we continue in sin?" is now the question, and the answer is: "Nay, certainly not!" We shall seek for the Fountain that cleanses and for the Power that keeps us.

Yielding and reckoning are the key words of this chapter, the word "yield" occurring five times, teaching justified souls to "yield themselves unto God." Chapter 7 teaches the weakness of self. It is full of me's and we's and I's and my's. There are 33 capital I's in this short chapter, and altogether 60 references to self, without any reference whatever to the Holy Spirit.

Then we are led into chapter 7 to learn how the sanctified walk with and live for the glory of God. In this chapter we find only two capital I's: one is buried "with the glory" and the other swallowed up in "the love of God." The Holy Spirit takes the place of self and is mentioned 19 times, being called the Spirit—of God, of Christ, of Adoption, and of Life. He is in us to deliver, help, and instruct, and we are in Him and led by Him. Therefore, instead of living in Romans 7, full of self and defeat, I will seek to live in Romans 8 to be kept, used, and controlled by the Holy Spirit. —*John Roberts*

March 15

I, even I, am he that comforteth you.—Isaiah 51:12

God's dealings with Israel are a sample of His dealings not only with the Church, but with the individual believer. The fact of His condescension is the thought that underlies the form of the expression, "I, even I." Let your soul ponder that fact. It is the God of heaven and earth, the Creator and Sustainer of all things, who thus stoops tenderly to soothe the sorrowing and cast-down soul.

And when He gives comfort, who then can give trouble? It is a comfort that is superior to all outward surroundings. It is God's own peace in the heart, a peace, therefore, that passes all understanding (Phil. 4:7).

This comfort is no mere question of the emotions—it is intelligent. He gives us a reason for the comfort He administers. He shows us the ground on which our consolation rests. This reason and this ground are found in His revealed character, in His unchanging faithfulness, His all-sufficient power, His infinite resources, and in the exceeding greatness of His love.

"Let not your hearts be troubled; ye believe in God, believe also in me" (John 14:1). —*Evan H. Hopkins*

March 16

Be not far from me; for trouble is near.—Psalm 22:11

It is in the hour of trouble that the believer realizes the value and preciousness of the promises of God. God's promises are not intended to dispense with our prayers. It is true God does not need information; nor does He need to be persuaded to be merciful. But He has so ordered it, that if we would know the fulfillment of His promises, we must make our requests known unto Him (Phil. 4:6); and so He has said, "He shall call upon me, and I will answer him: I will be with him in trouble; I will deliver him, and honour him" (Ps. 91:15). The presence of the Lord—as a fact revealed to the soul—includes every possible spiritual blessing. "Salvation belongeth unto the Lord: thy blessing is upon thy people" (Ps. 3:8).

To cry unto God, and to seek His presence, is not to doubt the truth of His promise. It is to plead it. It is like bringing the banknote to the bank to be cashed. As David prayed, "Say unto my soul, I am thy salvation" (Ps. 35:3), so we may say, "Say unto my soul, 'I am with thee.' Tell me, down in the depths of my heart, that which I know in my head."—*Evan H. Hopkins*

March 17

I have given you authority . . . over all the power of the enemy.—Luke 10:19
Yes, ask anything, *using my name, and I will do it!*—John 14:14 (TLB)

You remember that in the Lord's Prayer, the Master taught us to say, "Deliver us from evil." A modern rendering of that would read, "Rescue us from the evil one (Satan)." Christ has given us "authority . . . over all the power of the enemy," and we are rescued from the evil one by using that authority *in Jesus' name.*

But not everyone can use the Master's name. Some men in Ephesus tried to use it, to cast out evil spirits by speaking His name as they had heard the disciples do. But the demons knew full well who had a right to use that name, and they caused the men in whom they dwelt to jump upon the offenders and tear them and leave them bleeding. They did not have the right to use that name. Obedience is the requirement for the Lord Jesus' name, and with obedience always goes "faith." And faith is this: knowing that Jesus *is* the Victor. That scarred Jesus, that crowned Jesus—it is to have no doubt about *Him!*

A missionary from Tunis told me of an Arab woman, a Mohammedan with all the fanaticism, ignorance, and superstition that marks that strange belief. She was won to Christ, and her family did everything in their power to force her to recant, but failed. So they secretly and characteristically put poison in her food. After the woman had eaten it, she knew immediately what had happened. Greatly alarmed, she did not know what to do. Unconsciously at first she began to repeat the name of Jesus, the great name above every name; not aloud, but now with all the intensity of one who felt the sentence of death in her body, she kept repeating that marvelous name: "Jesus! Jesus! Jesus!" For several days that went on until at last she was completely restored. That was only a physical rescue, but to each true and obedient believer Christ has given "authority . . . over *all* the power of the enemy"—in His glorious name!
—*S. D. Gordon*

March 18

He is a shield unto them that put their trust [take refuge] in him. —Proverbs 30:5b

Webster classifies a shield as "a piece of protective armor," and gives the additional meaning of "any person or thing that guards, protects, or defends." How descriptive this is of God's work in the lives of His children. The Holy Spirit is God's presence in the world today, and we Christians can walk in confidence that He is with us as our Protector and Shield. God, in the person of the Holy Spirit, is our Defender! He is our Shield from the onslaughts of the enemy, Satan.

What confidence this should give us as we go about our daily tasks! Almighty God, Creator of the universe, is my Sustainer. Before Satan or any other harm can reach me, it must first defeat and destroy God. I know that is impossible, so I can have confidence as I face the world with all its evils and potential for harm. These words in Proverbs are credited to Agur, a writer unknown to us. But David, the Psalmist, whose name is famous in the annals of faith, frequently uses this same term to describe the "shielding" ministry of the Holy Spirit in our lives:

"For thou, Lord, wilt bless the righteous; with favour wilt thou compass him as with a shield" (Ps. 5:12).

"But thou, O Lord, art a shield for me" (Ps. 3:3), David cried out when he was fleeing from his rebellious son, Absalom.

"The word of the Lord is tried: he is a buckler [shield] to all those that trust in him" (Ps. 18:30b).

Somehow, as I read passages like these, I am reminded of the "comforting" work of the Holy Spirit in my life. So often we speak, and rightly, of His convicting power. We Christians need that aspect of His presence, too, when we stray from the path He has marked out for us. But I fear we sometimes neglect the "comfort" of His presence by overemphasizing His convicting power. As we think of Him today, let us remind ourselves that He is our Captain, that He goes before us. He is our Shield who surrounds us with His care. Not only can we trust Him, but, as the RSV translates it, we can "take refuge" in Him, confident that He will guard, protect, and defend us.

March 19

The Lord is good, a strong hold in the day of trouble; and he knoweth them that trust in him. —Nahum 1:7

These words appear in the very midst of a description of the terrible majesty of God. They set forth His *goodness* to His people. They declare ringingly what He is to them "in the day of trouble." He is a *stronghold* to them at such a time.

"The name of the Lord is a strong tower: the righteous runneth into it, and is safe" (Prov. 18:10). "Them that trust in him" (see Nahum 1:7), taken literally, means "take shelter or refuge in Him." Scholars point out that the words in the original express that which is habitual and permanent, an established way of life. It is the habit of such people to put their trust in the Lord and to abide under the shadow of the Almighty. It is just the way they live from day to day!

Days of trouble are often turned into days of blessing, because these days teach us what God can be to us in a way that days of ease or prosperity could not reveal.

"The Lord . . . knoweth them that trust in him." Not a single act of childlike faith, however secret, escapes His holy notice. He knows each trustful gaze, each step of faith, each act of confidence we place in Him. —*Evan H. Hopkins*

March 20

And God heard . . . and said unto [Hagar], . . . Fear not. . . . And God opened her eyes. —Genesis 21:17, 19

Every day we move among people who are troubled. They are going about with masks covering heartaches; worries and disappointments are piling up inside them. A great author has said: "Everyone is fighting a hard, lonely battle."

Recall for a moment the story of Hagar—the long, bitter story of an outcast. The victim of a pitiless social order, she was caught in a mighty maelstrom of sorrow. But God knew and cared, and when Hagar in her heart gave herself up to die, the majestic presence of His infinite love hailed her— "Fear not!" Though she was cast out penniless and alone, God was near and "God opened her eyes."

When the child of God stands confused and stunned, it is well to remember that God knows, and Satan can bring nothing upon us but what our heavenly Father has anticipated. Christ is ready to share every man's burden. He will enter into the sorrow of every woman. He has promised, "I will not leave you comfortless: I will come to you." With the burdens comes the Christ. Even when the soul seems shrouded in sorrow, through which not a ray of light can penetrate, Christ will enfold the soul in the promises of His love.

God knows every heart so intimately that nothing can surprise Him. His glorious omnipotence rubs shoulders with us in the affairs of life. His almightiness supplants our weakness. His understanding love appreciates how hard we have tried even when we failed, and looks upon our intention, not upon our accomplishment.

The patriarch Job expressed his faith in these words: "Though he slay me, yet will I trust him. . . . I shall come forth as gold" (Job 13:15; 23:10). Yes, the night of suffering may be long, but the day will dawn. We shall come forth to full and complete understanding of the workings of God with us. "I will trust and not be afraid." —*O. G. Wilson*

March 21

O God, my heart is fixed.—Psalm 108:1

What is a fixed heart? Not a heart that is full of confidence or of faith merely, but a heart whose faith is centered upon God. It is not faith that is the secret of the heart's fixedness (or stability), but the rock Christ Jesus, on whom faith reposes its confidence.

There is only one center that is absolutely immovable and unchangeable. And that is God. The strength or stability of the believer is not due to the tenacity of his grasp, so much as to the firmness of the Rock on which he rests. We must not look at our faith, but at Him on whom our faith depends. This condition of rest being reached, all fear vanishes.

"The Lord is my light and my salvation; whom shall I fear? the Lord is the strength of my life; of whom shall I be afraid?" (Ps. 27:1).

"He shall not be afraid of evil tidings; his heart is fixed, trusting in the Lord. His heart is established, he shall not be afraid" (Ps. 112:7, 8).

A fixed heart is a praising heart. "I will sing and give praise, even with my glory" (Ps. 108:1). By his "glory" the poet David means his soul, and all the capacities and faculties which belonged to him as an intelligent being, created in the divine image. —*Evan H. Hopkins*

March 22

That the trial of your faith, being much more precious than of gold that perisheth, though it be tried with fire, might be found unto praise and honour and glory at the appearing of Jesus Christ.—1 Peter 1:7

Trials test, but they also deepen and intensify the spiritual temper of the believer just as the furnace strengthens steel, and the fire purifies gold.

Testing inevitably produces a better person—or a bitter person. In a sense, the outcome is up to the individual and his attitude toward testing.

The courageous quadriplegic girl, Joni Eareckson, contrasts the individual reactions to pressure as taking one of two courses. One person, under pressure, can react as does a marble—splintering into sharp pieces of glass, hurting anyone with whom he comes in contact. Or one can handle pressure as does the grape—yielding sweet and refreshing wine as the pressure is applied.

In our scripture today, Peter goes on to give the secret of reacting like the grape. In verse 8, referring to Jesus Christ, he says, "Whom having not seen, ye love; in whom, though now you see him not, yet believing, ye rejoice with joy unspeakable and full of glory." This is the secret of being a "grape" Christian. If we can rejoice under trial, if we can yield submissively under pressure, we can give forth the sweetest fragrance and the sweetest wine.

This is not a call to compromise or lack of conviction. It is a call to submissiveness and yieldedness to whatever the heavenly Father allows to come into your life. Dare the clay say to the sculptor, "Don't touch me"? If the shapeless lump of clay is to be made into something beautiful and meaningful, it must yield to the sculptor's pressure and shaping.

May God help each one of us as His children to praise Him through the trials of life as well as in the high places.

March 23

John calling unto him two of his disciples, sent them to Jesus. —Luke 7:19

John was perplexed about certain things. There were some matters that were worrying him, that he could not figure out for himself, and he sent to Christ to ask Him about them. That is just what every one of us should do when we encounter perplexities and problems in our lives. We should carry them straight to Jesus. Even the children have their disappointments and trials. They have discouragements. Now, they should not worry about these matters. Of course they cannot always understand them; how could they expect to understand everything in such a vast world as this? But is it not a comfort to know that Jesus understands it all? He knows what He is doing.

So the wise way for us is just to do what John did—tell Jesus about our doubts and perplexities. That is the rule Paul gives for keeping free from anxiety. "Be careful [or anxious] for nothing; but in everything by prayer and supplication with thanksgiving let your requests be made known unto God" (Phil. 4:6). Then He promises that if we do this, we will never have to worry: "The peace of God . . . shall keep your hearts and minds" (Phil. 4:7).

The meaning of all this is that we should never carry a worry of any kind even for a moment, but whenever we begin to entertain doubts, we should go instantly and tell Jesus all about it, and leave it in His hands, that He may manage it for us.

The leaving is the hardest part. We can easily take it to Him, but we are so apt to pick it up again and carry it back with us, and keep it, just as if we had not taken it to Him. We should learn to tell Jesus our perplexities and sorrows, and then commit it to Him without further anxiety. This is faith and the path to true peace. —*J. R. Miller*

March 24

Prepare ye the way of the Lord.—Isaiah 40:3

These were the words of "the voice of him that crieth in the wilderness." When 700 years afterward, John the Baptist was preaching repentance "in the wilderness of Judea," the evangelist Matthew said that "this is he that was spoken of by the prophet."

Now, nearly 2,000 years have passed since the Baptist's voice was heard saying, "Repent" and "Prepare ye the way of the Lord," and yet this preparation is not fully completed. Thank God it has been completed in the hearts and lives of millions! But there are millions more to whom we still must cry: "Prepare ye the way of the Lord!" He is anxious not merely to come *to* us, but to come *in* us—to come in the fullness of His grace into our hearts and lives. But He cannot do this until we have "prepared the way." We must put away and lay aside everything which is of the nature of a stumbling block in His way.

"Prepare ye the way of the Lord," so that He may come triumphantly right into the heart, and there set up His throne and reign with undisputed sway. This is His desire; may it, too, be mine.

When He's within and has control,
He saves and sanctifies the soul.

He will not begin without and work within, but will begin within and work without. First, the "spirit," next, the "soul," and then, the "body" (1 Thess. 5:24). "If any man hear my voice, and will open the door, I will come in." Let me, then, today see that "the way" is prepared for the incoming of my Lord and King.

Love and help us, blessed Jesus;
Help us to be wholly Thine,
Every idol and enchantment
For Thy glory to resign.

Love and keep us, blessed Jesus;
Keep us from denying Thee;
Keep our wayward feet from straying
Into paths of vanity.
—*John Roberts*

March 25

And straightway the father of the child cried out, and said with tears, Lord, I believe; help thou mine unbelief.— Mark 9:24

I hear men praying everywhere for more faith, but when I listen to them carefully and get at the real heart of their prayers, very often it is not more faith at all that they are wanting, but a change from faith to sight.

Faith says not, "I see that it is good for me, and so God must have sent it," but "God sent it, and so it must be good for me." Faith walking in the dark with God only prays Him to clasp its hand more closely, does not even ask Him for the lifting of the darkness so that the man may find the way himself. —*Phillips Brooks*

March 26

For ye shall not go out with haste, nor go by flight: for the Lord will go before you; and the God of Israel will be your rearward [rear guard].—Isaiah 52:12

If you have ever watched an important personage such as a president in a parade or other public appearance, you have seen how he was literally surrounded by a burly bodyguard. That is an imperfect picture of what Isaiah is talking about here. That infamous day in Dallas, Texas, saw the late President Kennedy guarded before and behind by Secret Service and even Dallas police—but the assassin's bullet found its mark anyway, despite the careful precautions taken. Our Protector, however, is the Lord God of Israel himself, and His protection is perfect, completely trustworthy.

The Psalmist provides an equally dramatic promise of protection: "The Lord shall preserve thee from all evil; he shall preserve thy soul." Talk about protection and preservation! This promise covers the entire spectrum of life—even eternal life. The Lord does not promise exemption or immunity from evil, but He does promise to protect you in the evil day. The Living Bible puts it this way: "He keeps you from all evil, and preserves your life" (Ps. 121:7).

With His promise of safekeeping, the child of God is equipped for every experience that life can send his way. Conscious that life even for the Christian can be complex and even dangerous, the Christian can rest in the assurance that nothing can happen to him outside the Father's view, for His love and care surrounds His child "fore and aft." No need of haste or panic on his part, knowing that the Lord will go before him and be his rear guard. No need for fear and frustration when he knows "the Lord shall preserve thee." What better guarantee of safety can he ask for than that!

March 27

We look not at the things which are seen . . . for the things which are seen are temporal; but the things which are not seen are eternal.—2 Corinthians 4:18

We see from the context that the main thought of the passage is the spiritual transformation of our character. The outward man perishing—the inward man daily being renewed. This should go on continually. But it is conditional. It is "whilst we are looking not at the things which are seen, but at the things which are not seen." In other words, it is while we are living and walking by faith—while we continue to see Him who is invisible. The believer lives in two worlds at once.

There is an outward world of sense. Of course, the believer is not unconscious of the things that are seen. And there is the invisible world of faith. The unseen is as real as the seen—no, because the things which are seen are temporal, and the things which are not seen are eternal. It is the unseen world that is the true and the real; the visible is but the shadow.

As we live surrounded by the things that are seen, let us not look *at* them but *through* them!   *—Evan H. Hopkins*

March 28

He went out, not knowing whither he went.—Hebrews 11:8

Abraham began his journey without any knowledge of his ultimate destination. He obeyed a noble impulse without any discernment of its consequences. He took "one step," and he did not ask to see "the distant scene." That is faith, to do God's will here and now, quietly leaving the results with Him. Faith is not concerned with the entire chain; its devoted attention is fixed upon the immediate link. Faith is not knowledge of a moral process; it is fidelity in a moral act. Faith leaves something to the Lord; it obeys His immediate commandment and leaves to Him direction and destiny.

And so faith is accompanied by serenity. "He that believeth shall not make haste"—or more literally, "shall not get into an anxious fuss." He shall not get into a panic, neither remembering fears from his yesterdays, nor borrowing fears from his tomorrows. Concerning his yesterdays, faith says, "You have beset (protected) me behind." Concerning his tomorrows, faith says, "You have protected me before." Concerning his today, faith says, "You have placed your hand upon me." That is enough, just to feel the pressure of His guiding hand.   *—J. H. Jowett*

March 29

At the commandment of the Lord they rested in the tents, and at the commandment of the Lord they journeyed.—Numbers 9:23

This is the secret of peace and calm elevation. If an Israelite, in the desert, had taken it into his head to make some movement independent of Jehovah; if he took it upon him to move when the crowd was at rest, or to halt while the crowd was moving, we can easily see what the result would have been. And so it will ever be with us. If we move when we ought to rest, or rest when we ought to move, we shall not have the divine presence with us.   —*C. H. MacIntosh*

By faith Abraham, when he was called to go out into a place which he should after receive for an inheritance, obeyed (Heb. 11:8).

Whither he went, he knew not; it was enough for him to know that he went with God. He leaned not so much upon the promises as upon the Promiser. He looked not on the difficulties of his lot, but on the King—eternal, immortal, invisible, the only wise God, who had deigned to appoint his course, and would certainly vindicate Himself. O glorious faith! This is thy work, these are thy possibilities: contentment to sail with sealed orders, because of unwavering confidence in the love and wisdom of the Lord High Admiral: willing to rise up, leave all, and follow Christ because of the glad assurance that earth's best cannot bear comparison with heaven's least.   —*F. B. Meyer*

March 30

Sanctify them through thy truth; thy word is truth.—John 17:17

Christ is our Sanctification. The Holy Spirit is our Sanctifier. And the truth, or Word of God, is the instrument the Holy Spirit uses in sanctifying us.

We are sanctified by the truth in proportion as the powers and faculties of our being are brought under the sway of that truth. There are forces and qualities of our nature that may be used either for good or evil: reason, imagination, prudence or wisdom, endurance, courage, etc. Now the truth sanctifies us when it appropriates these qualities and consecrates them to the service of God.

The truth is called the "engrafted word" (James 1:21), because just as a graft appropriates these qualities, such as the life of the tree, and brings it into contribution to itself, so the Word which has found an entrance into our innermost being has the power of drawing out all that is excellent in the natural character, and transforming it into Christian virtue.

The wild rose on the bramble becomes the beautifully developed and fragrant flower on the graft; so these moral qualities, which may exist in a pagan, become transfigured by the engrafted word, and the life of the indwelling Holy Spirit, into the graces of the Spirit (Col. 3:16).

—Evan H. Hopkins

March 31

He that is spiritual judgeth all things, yet he himself is judged of no man.—1 Corinthians 2:15

Earthly judgment is woefully inadequate in our modern day. Men make heroes of criminals and belittle Christians for their Christlikeness. This is not surprising, for the natural man does not understand things of the Spirit, and therefore cannot be expected to evidence spiritual discernment.

But what about the spiritual man? Without his spiritual dimension he, too, would be inadequate for the demands made upon him. Solomon knew that without God's enablement, he would lack the wisdom to wisely rule his people—so he implored God for wisdom above every other attribute.

In our day it is the Holy Spirit who is the Source of all wisdom. We need His perspective in order to cope with the complexities of modern living. One who is Spirit-filled will find it possible to discern the proper path and walk in it.

This results in ultimate recognition by his fellowmen. Reluctantly, perhaps, they will admit the godly man's additional dimension. He has something they do not have, and they are aware of an unvoiced longing for something to fill "the God-shaped vacuum" in their lives. This awareness provides the Christian with an open door to witness and show what Christ means to him—and if our lives are not creating opportunity for witness, they are somehow lacking.

May the two aspects of this verse operate in my life—that I have deep spiritual perception and in my "spirituality" let me not "turn off" my friend in his walk toward Christ. May I be a clear channel and a useful tool in my Master's hand, a tool that does not twist and turn as He uses it, but follows His every command.

April 1

Thou art Peter, and upon this rock I will build my church; and the gates of hell shall not prevail against it.—Matthew 16:18

For centuries, a tremendous controversy has raged around this verse and its meaning. The RSV notes on the words for

"Peter" and "rock" hint at the problem of identifying what or who Jesus meant by the word "rock." The original Greek for "Peter" is "Petros" and the Greek for "rock" is "petra." Based on these differing words in the original Greek, one interpretation, the one most acceptable among the Protestant branch of Christendom, is that the rock referred to here is not Peter but his faith in Christ (see v. 16), which is representative of the faith of all Christians in the fact of Christ's resurrection. What was Peter's confession in verse 16? "Thou art the Christ, the Son of the living God." This is the foundation upon which the church is built.

A look at a more recent translation of the words "gates of hell" in this verse may give us even more insight into the meaning of the passage. Usually we think of gates as shutting one in, but here again the RSV sheds new light: "Powers of death shall not prevail against it." The gates of "hell" are the "powers of death." Prevail against what?—the resurrection of Christ. Death could not hold Him, and it cannot hold us as His followers.

This is the victorious message of our verse for today. There is no controversy here—Satan and death have been defeated by Jesus Christ and His abundant life. And His life becomes ours the moment we believe. In Him we have already conquered death, and it holds no sting for us—it has no power over us! The church is not buildings and mortar; it is redeemed people living for their Redeemer in every nook and cranny of the world. Despite the apparent inroads made by the world into the organized church, Christ's church, His people, will prevail. We have Christ's Word for it.

April 2

God was in Christ, reconciling the world unto himself, not imputing their trespasses unto them. —2 Corinthians 5:19

The death of Christ was no mere example of self-sacrifice. It was the divinely appointed method of removing the guilt of sin, and of bringing the sinner to God in peace. It was not an experiment by One who was merely a sinless Man.

"But all things" were of God, who reconciled us to himself through Christ. God was in Christ. We have no room now for doubt as to whether that work was sufficient or acceptable. Reconciliation of God's side is already effected. His law has been vindicated and His name magnified by that work of atonement. And now the service He commits to His servants here upon earth is called "the ministry of reconciliation."

"We are ambassadors on behalf of Christ, as though God were intreating by us; we beseech you on behalf of Christ, be ye reconciled to God" (2 Cor. 5:20, R.V.).

To know God in Christ is to know that He is the God of our salvation and to be at peace. Think not that you have to make your peace with Him. That you could never do. Christ has accomplished this through His blood. —*Evan H. Hopkins*

April 3

Ye are dead, and your life is hid with Christ in God.
—Colossians 3:3

More literally it is, "For he died." The words do not describe a *condition of deadness*, as many have assumed, but they point to the fact that death, as a crisis, has been passed through. And if we recognize the principle that all the great *facts* of redemption find their accomplishment first of all in Christ rather than in our individual experience, then we see that the death referred to took place on the cross.

"For ye died" with Christ when He died. You were identified with Him in His death. This is the meaning of your baptism. "Know ye not, that so many of us as were baptized into Jesus Christ were baptized into his death?" "Into *His* death," remember, not into *your* death.

The fact with which faith is concerned is not something which finds its center in yourself, but in Christ. "For ye died." When? When you were baptized? No. When you experienced that wonderful blessing? No. But when *Christ* died, and you, in the eye of God, died with Him. This is the foundation of all experimental knowledge. We must begin with the judicial fact, or we shall have no solid basis upon which to rest.

—*Evan H. Hopkins*

April 4

I am he that liveth, and was dead; and, behold, I am alive for evermore.—Revelation 1:18

That word "liveth" is a word of continuous, perpetual life. It describes the eternal existence which has no beginning and no end; which, considered in its purity and perfectness, has no present and no past, but one eternal and unbroken present— one eternal now.

It is the "I Am" of the Jehovah who spoke to Moses. "He that liveth" is the living One; He whose life is the life, complete in itself, and including all other lives within itself.

My dear friends, if anything has come to us to make us feel what a fragmentary thing our human life is, I think there is no greater knowledge for us to win than that the life of One who loves us as Christ loves us is an eternal life, with the continuance and the unchangeableness of eternity.

—*Phillips Brooks*

April 5

But where sin abounded, grace did much more abound.
—Romans 5:20

Justification means two things: first, that God's law is just, and second, that every sinner is unjust; therefore if God is to justify a man He can do it only by vindicating the law and by destroying the sinner out of him. We put it that Jesus Christ came to save sinners; He did not say so, He said, "I came to call *sinners to repentance*" (Matt. 10:13). This phrase, "God loves the man, but hates the sinner," although not scriptural, conveys the idea. When God saves a sinner, profoundly speaking, He does not save the sinner: He saves the man who is a sinner by removing the sinner out of him. When once he receives the humiliating conviction that he has broken God's law, and is willing to accept on God's terms the gift of forgiveness and of a new life, he will find he is brought to the place he can live a holy life in order to vindicate God in forgiving him. This is evangelical repentance, and it is fundamentally different from the reformation which springs from remorse awakened by an overweening self-respect.

A sinner can never stand in the presence of God; there is no justification whatever for sin in His presence; that is why a man convicted of sin has such a desperate time. He realizes with the Psalmist, "Against thee, thee only, have I sinned, and done this evil in thy sight." Beware of attempting to deal with sin apart from a complete reliance on the Redemption, and when you see men sinning, remember, your heart should be filled with compassion, because if you have ever had the slightest dose of conviction of sin yourself, you will know what awaits them when the recognition of sin comes home.

Bear in mind that what makes Christ's glory is His severity, i.e., His love for God's holy law rather than His love for man: Jesus Christ stood on God's side against man. On the cross men crucified the Son of God—and God forgave them while they did it. It is blasphemy to make little of sin. The final issue in every life is—God must kill sin in me, or sin will kill God out of me. —*Oswald Chambers*

April 6

For as the Father hath life in himself; so hath he given to the Son to have life in himself.—John 5:26

This is my reservoir! *The Son has life in himself!* All vitality has its source in Him. He is the enemy of death and the deadly. I can paint the dead to look like life; I can use rouge for blood, and make the white lips red, but the body remains clammy and cold. I can "cosmeticize," but I cannot vitalize. I can "break the ball of nard" and make perfume. "But the sleeper still sleeps." Only in Him is life. "In Christ shall all be made alive."

And here is my hope: "the Son gives life to whom he will" (John 5:21, RSV). He is not only a reservoir, He is also a river. He is the "river of the water of life." And His blessed purpose is to flow into desolate places, converting deserts into gardens, and making wildernesses to blossom as the rose.

This final blessed thought stirs my soul. He will come my way if only I will "hear" and "believe." There is a flippant hearing which, while it listens, laughs Him to scorn. There is a cheap hearing which will venture nothing on His counsel. And there is the hearing of faith, which simply "takes Him at His word," and in the glorious venture experiences the unsealing of the fountain of eternal life. "Whosoever will, let him take of the water of life freely." —*J. H. Jowett*

April 7

I am crucified with Christ.—Galatians 2:20

What are the marks of a crucified man? The first is, deep, absolute humility. Christ humbled himself and became obedient unto death, even the death of the cross. When the death to sin begins to work mightily, that is one of its chief and most blessed proofs. It breaks a man down, down, and the great longing of his heart is, "Oh, that I could get deeper down before my God, and be nothing at all, that the life of Christ might be exalted! I deserve nothing but the cursed cross; I give myself over to it." Humility is one of the great marks of a crucified man. He knows he deserves nothing but to be crucified, and he is ashamed of himself.

Another mark is impotence, helplessness. When a man hangs on a cross, he is utterly helpless, he can do nothing. As long as we Christians are strong, and can work, or struggle, we do not get into the blessed life of Christ; but when a man says, "I am a crucified man, I am utterly helpless, every breath of life and strength must come from my Jesus," then we learn what it is to sink into our own impotence and say, "I am nothing."

Still another mark of crucifixion is restfulness. Yes, Christ was crucified and went down into the grave, and we are crucified and buried with Him. There is no place of rest like the grave; a man can do nothing there. "My flesh shall rest in hope," said David, and said the Messiah. Yes, and when a man goes down into the grave of Jesus, it means this: that he just cries out, "I have nothing but God, I trust God; I am waiting upon God; my flesh rests in hope; I have given up everything, that I may rest, waiting upon what God is to do to me."

Remember, the crucifixion, death, and burial are inseparably one. And remember, the grave is the place where the mighty resurrection power of God will be manifested. Also remember those words spoken by Jesus at the grave of Lazarus, "If thou believest thou shalt see the glory of God." Where shall we see the glory of God most brightly? Beside the grave. Go down into this death believing, and the glory of God will come upon you, and fill your heart. —*Andrew Murray*

April 8

The Lord God omnipotent reigneth. —Revelation 19:6

The tried believer has often to remind himself that the God of his salvation is the Lord omnipotent. Without giving way to open unbelief, the soul sometimes yields to the habit of limiting God's grace and power. This was the sin of God's people of old.

"They . . . limited the Holy One of Israel" (Ps. 78:41). That is, they set a mark to His power. They said He could do this and that, but can He spread a table in the wilderness? This was as much as to say that God was not omnipotent: to deny His omnipotence was to deny His deity.

Here, then, was Israel's sin. Alas! how often God's children are guilty of limiting God! We need ever to keep before us this divine attribute—"the Lord God omnipotent reigneth." He is Almighty to save and to keep. "All power is given unto me in heaven and in earth" (Matt. 28:18).

"Some trust in chariots, and some horses"; but we will remember who He is, and what He is. A view of His attributes will calm our fears and deliver us from the sin of unbelief. (See Luke 18:27; Psalm 9:10.) —*Evan H. Hopkins*

April 9

Every word of God is pure [proves true]. —Proverbs 30:5a

What is the world looking for today? What is lacking in modern life—what "bugs" people as they follow their routines, living their workaday lives? One of the most troublesome issues seems to lie in the area of real authority. People are looking for a "sure word" and they can't seem to find it.

God has the only "sure word." The writer of Proverbs states unequivocally that "every word of God proves true" (RSV). The Psalmist David is just as dogmatic. He says, "The words of the Lord are pure words; as silver tried in a furnace of earth, purified seven times." The RSV again gives it a slightly different flavor: "The promises of the Lord are promises that are pure," and the Jerusalem Bible says: "The words of Yahweh are without alloy."

In Psalm 18:30 David takes the analogy a step further: "As for God, his way is perfect: the word of the Lord is tried: he is a buckler to all those that trust in him."

In the modern vernacular we might say, "We can trust Him because He's been there!" God's Word can be trusted because it has proved itself over and over down through the centuries. David believed it; the writer of Proverbs believed it; Job believed it and cried out triumphantly, "I know that my Redeemer liveth!"

Paul told Timothy, "Nevertheless the foundation of God standeth sure, having this seal, the Lord knoweth them that are his" (2 Tim. 2:19). The writer to the Hebrews adds a further note, "That by two immutable things, in which it was impossible for God to lie, we might have a strong consolation, who have fled for refuge to lay hold upon the hope set before us: which hope we have as an anchor of the soul, both sure and steadfast" (Heb. 6:18, 19).

I'm glad that in a world without roots, I have the sure word of God for my root, my foundation. He's proved himself to me times without number. Should I begin to doubt Him now?

April 10

Reckon ye also yourselves to be dead indeed unto sin, but alive unto God. —Romans 6:11

Paul writes, "You *are dead* with Christ." On the strength of that he says, "Reckon yourselves dead unto sin." What does that mean? Dead to sin? We cannot see it more clearly than by referring to Adam. Christ was the second Adam. What happened in the first Adam? I died in the first Adam; I died to God; I died in sin. When I was born, I had in me the life of Adam, which had all the characteristics of the life of Adam after he had fallen. Adam died to God, and Adam died in sin, and I inherit the life of Adam, and so I am dead in sin as he was, and dead unto God.

However, at the very moment I begin to believe in Jesus, I become united to Christ, the second Adam, and as certainly as I am united by my birth to the first Adam, I am made partaker of the life of Christ. What life? That life which died unto sin at Calvary, and which rose again; therefore God by His apostle tells us, "Reckon ye also yourselves to be dead unto sin, but alive unto God through Christ Jesus." You are to reckon it as true because God says it and because it is so. Your new nature is indeed, in virtue of your vital union to Christ, actually and utterly dead to sin.

"But why, if I am dead to sin, do I commit so much sin?" you ask. The answer God's Word gives is simply this: You do not allow the power of that death to be applied by the Holy Spirit. What we need is to understand that the Holy Spirit came from heaven, from the glorified Jesus, to bring His death and His life into us. The two are inseparably connected. That Christ died, He died unto sin, and that He lives, He lives unto God. The death and the life in Him are inseparable; and even so in us the life to God in Christ is inseparably connected with the death to sin. And that is what the Holy Spirit will teach us and work in us. If I have accepted Christ in faith by the Holy Spirit, and yielded myself to Him, Christ every day keeps possession and reveals the full power of my fellowship in His death and life in my heart. —*Andrew Murray*

April 11

Reckon ye yourselves to be dead indeed unto sin, but alive unto God through Jesus Christ our Lord.—Romans 6:11

This is the divine command. It does not say, "Reckon sin to be dead," but, "Reckon yourself dead unto it." Sin was once our lord and master. He (Satan) claimed you as his slave. He demanded your service, and he is ready to pay his wages to those who serve him. "The wages of sin is death."

But Christ has set you free from this tyrant Sin. You need no longer recognize his claim. It is through death that your connection with him as your master has been broken. No master can compel obedience from his slave if death has come and broken the connection between them.

It is through death that we are freed from our old master, Sin. Not *our* death, but *Christ's* death, and *we died with Him.* That is true legally. In order for it to be true practically and experientially, "reckon ye yourselves"—not only to have died, but—"to be dead indeed unto sin." It is not a feeling of deadness to be realized. Because the same person is to be dead and alive at one and the same time—dead unto sin, and alive unto God.
—*Evan H. Hopkins*

April 12

And take up his cross, and follow me.—Matthew 17:24

The cross is to be *taken up*, not simply borne when laid upon the shoulder by someone else. This implies willing, cheerful suffering for Christ. Some people endure trials, but always with complaining. The spirit of these words requires cheerfulness in suffering for Christ. Half the trial is gone if we meet it in this glad spirit.

Notice again, it is *his* cross and not some other man's that each one is to take up. It is the particular cross that God lays at our own feet that we are to bear. We are never to make crosses for ourselves, but we are always to accept those which are allotted to us. Each one's own cross is the best for him. Sometimes we think our lot is unusually hard, and we compare it with the lot of this or that other person, and wish we had his cross instead of our own. But we do not know what other people's crosses really are. If we did we might not want to exchange. The cross that seems woven of flowers, if we put it on our shoulders we might find it filled with sharp thorns under the flowers. The cross of gold that seems so bright, we would find so heavy it would crush us. The easiest cross for each one to bear is his own.

There is a way to get the crosses out of our lives altogether. A father explained it to his child this way: Taking two pieces of wood, one longer than the other, he said, "Let the longer piece represent God's will; the shorter, your will. If I lay the two pieces side by side, parallel to each other, there is no cross; it is only when I lay the shorter piece across the longer that I can make a cross. So there can be a cross in my life only when my will falls across God's, when I cannot say, 'Thy will be done.' If my will falls into line with His, there is no cross." The way to take out the crosses is therefore always gladly to accept, through love to Him, whatever trial, pain, or loss God sends.
—*J. R. Miller*

April 13

Then said Jesus, Father, forgive them. . . . To day shalt thou be with me in Paradise. . . . Father, into thy hands I commend my spirit.—Luke 23:34, 43, 46

Look at our Lord in relation to His foes. "Father, forgive them; for they know not what they do!" Their bitterness had not embittered Him. The "milk of human kindness" was still sweet. Nothing could sour our Lord, or convert His good will into malice, His serene goodness into wild revenge. And how is it with me? Are my foes able to maim my spirit as well as my body? Do they win their end by making me a smaller man? Or am I generous even on my cross?

And look at our Lord in relation to the penitent thief. "To-day shalt thou be with me in paradise!" There was no self-centeredness in our Savior's grief. He was the good Physician, even when His body was mangled on the cross. He healed a broken heart even in the very pangs of death. When "there was darkness over all the earth," He let the light of the morning into the heart of the desolate thief. And, good Lord, graciously help me to do the same.

All this amazing graciousness is explained in our Lord's relationship to His Father. "Father, into thy hands I commend my spirit." Yes, everything is there. When I and my Father are one, my spirit will remain sweet as the violet and pure as the dew. —*J. H. Jowett*

April 14

The Lord hath made known his salvation: his righteousness hath he openly showed in the sight of the heathen.
—Psalm 98:2

Why do the crowds come out on Easter? It is not sufficient answer to say it is because of habit, that it is fashionable to go to church on that day. For that simply raises another question: Why has it become a habit and why is it fashionable? No, one has to go deeper than that. What is the supreme problem that confronts the individual and the race?

The supreme problem is the triumph of righteousness and truth. This is what the Resurrection stands for. Easter means that truth will triumph, that righteousness cannot be kept in the tomb. You may nail it to the tree, you may wrap it in graveclothes and seal it in the tomb, but truth and righteousness do not perish. Whenever truth and righteousness are crushed to earth on some black Friday, there dawns an Easter morning.

The Psalmist declared, "I was envious at the foolish, when I saw the prosperity of the wicked. There are no bands in their death: but their strength is firm. . . . When I thought to know this, it was too painful for me; until I went into the sanctuary of God; then understood I their end" (Ps. 73:3, 4, 16, 17).

Easter means that evil and sin and hypocrisy and oppression cannot ultimately win. And this is sound reasoning in these days of arrogant godlessness and unprincipled oppression. No one can cherish hate and unforgiveness while meditating on the Resurrection and the glories of immortality. He who would look scornfully on a brother knows nothing of the resurrection message.

A little child returned from the pre-Easter service to tell eagerly of the new song they had sung: "Christ has rhythm." It is the resurrected Christ who brings song into the daily life and rhythm and happiness to the souls of men. —*O. G. Wilson*

April 15

And they entered in, and found not the body of the Lord Jesus.—Luke 24:3

That empty tomb means the conquest of *death*. The Captive proved mightier than the captor. He emerged from the prison as the Lord of the prison, and death reeled at His going. In the risen Savior death is dethroned; he takes his place at the footstool to do the bidding of his sovereign Lord and King.

And that empty tomb means the conquest of sin. Sin had done its worst, and had failed. All the forces of hell had been rallied against the Lord, and above them all He rose triumphant and glorified.

Not long ago I discovered a spring. I tried to choke it. I heaped sand and gravel upon it; I piled stones above it! And through them all it emerged, noiselessly and irresistibly, a radiant resurrection!

So the empty tomb becomes the symbol of a thoroughfare between life in time and life in the unshadowed presence of our God. Death is now like a short tunnel near my home; I can look through it and see the other side! In the risen Lord death becomes transparent.

"O death, where is thy sting? O grave, where is thy victory?"
—J. H. Jowett

April 16

If ye be reproached for the name of Christ, happy are ye.
—1 Peter 4:14

This word *Christian* came to the early Church by a process. The multitude, curiously looking on from day to day at their worship, their testimony and teaching, their life and character, could see one feature predominating all else. One name was always on their lips; one Presence they were always invoking; one word they were always repeating—*Christ*. So they came to call His disciples *Christ ones*; for that is just what Christian means, a *Christ one*.

But, is our testimony, our worship, our life today such that it would lead the world, if it knew nothing of our religion, to call us *Christians*? Would there be so much of the name, the testimony, and the Spirit of Christ in our faces, our songs, our work, and our daily lives that the disciples should again be called *Christians* because they were Christ ones?

"What the world wants today is not more Christians, but more Christ ones." It is not the imitation of Christ, but it is identification with Christ that constitutes vital Christianity. It is not the human trying to copy the divine, but it is the divine coming into the human and lifting it to His level and making it second nature to be like God. "Christ liveth in me." "Your life is hid with Christ in God." Christianity is not primarily a new way of living, of believing, of worshipping, but Christianity is coming into a new relationship to a Person. It is meeting Jesus and going on with Him.
—A. B. Simpson

April 17

Thy gentleness hath made me great.—2 Samuel 22:36

What constitutes true greatness? Are not the godlike ones the great? Is long life greatness? But who can live so long as he who through faith in Christ has begun to live eternally? Is privilege greatness? Who is as privileged as he whose sins are washed away? Is character greatness? Whose character is comparable with that of him to whom has been imputed the righteousness of Christ? Are riches greatness? Who is so rich as an heir of glory? Is fame greatness? Who are more famous than those whose names are written in the Book of Life? Is power greatness? Can there be a greater exercise of power than that which overcomes the world? Is human family greatness? Whose kin takes precedence over the sons and daughters of the Almighty?   —*James M. Gray*

Man's standards of success are not God's standards. In the eyes of the world many men are successful who are failures in God's sight. Alexander the Great was a world conqueror —but he died in a drunken spree. Hitler conquered most of Europe—but he hated and persecuted God's ancient people, and he died a suicide. In the realm of business and politics many have sold their souls to grasp money, power or fame. On the other hand, many servants of God, because of faithfulness to God, like John the Baptist have had their "heads cut off," so to speak, by some Herod who despised the Gospel.
—*Christian Victory*

April 18

No man is able to pluck them out of my Father's hand.
—John 10:29

The safety of God's children does not rest on their own attainments, or even their own fidelity and decision, but on the power of God. However great may be the strength of our enemies, or however subtle their efforts to overcome the believer, it is our comfort to know that no man can pluck them out of the Father's hand. It implies that we are being held by God himself.

"Hold thou me up, and I shall be safe." "I will uphold thee with the right hand of my righteousness" (Isa. 41:10). Here is the secret of our comfort: not what we are or hope to become, but what God is.

"I know whom I have believed, and am persuaded that he is able to keep that which I have committed unto him against that day" (2 Tim. 1:12). The ability of our God is the ground of our confidence. Greater is He who is with us than all those who can be against us.

"I am persuaded," said the apostle, "that neither death, nor life, nor angels, nor principalities, nor powers, nor things present, nor things to come, nor height, nor depth, nor any other creature, shall be able to separate us from the love of God, which is in Christ Jesus our Lord" (Rom. 8:38, 39).

—*Evan H. Hopkins*

April 19

The Lord hath done great things for us.—Psalm 126:3

Such was the testimony given by the Jews after their return from Babylon to Jerusalem. Their experience appeared at first to be almost too good to be true; they felt "like them that dream." But as soon as they fully realized their perfect freedom their mouths became "filled with laughter" and their "tongue with singing."

In this situation they realized to some extent the truth of Bildad's statement in Job 8:20, 21: "God will not cast away a perfect man, neither will he help the evil doers: till he fill thy mouth with laughing, and the lips with rejoicing." They were thus filled, and their praise and thanksgiving astonished the nations around them, causing them to exclaim: "The Lord hath done great things for them."

To this the Jews replied: "The Lord hath done great things for us, whereof we are glad." Oh, how sad they had recently been! They had hung their harps upon the willows and "wept" as they "remembered Zion." But now, through coming back to Zion and to God, their tears had dried, and they were glad. The Lord had done "great things" for them.

But have I not cause for gladness too? Has He not done great things for me? He has brought me out of bondage into liberty, out of slavery to the Evil One, into the "arms of Jesus." Yes, indeed the Lord has done great things for me, whereof I, too, am glad!

—*John Roberts*

April 20

This God is our God for ever and ever: he will be our guide even unto death.—Psalm 48:14

It is strengthening to our faith to declare to ourselves and to others what God declares unto us. He has said, "I am thy God" (Isa. 41:10). Let our souls respond, "This God is our God for ever and ever."

It is an important step forward in the faith-life to rise from the prayer "Be thou" to the assurance "Thou art." It is thus we step out and advance in the spiritual life. For years, many have been *seeking* when they should have been *resting*, as to their souls' attitude toward God. When God declares to us a *fact*, it is for us to accept it and rest on it. When He gives us a promise, it is for us to plead it and expect its fulfillment.

The apprehension of the fact that God is our God, our Covenant God—our Everlasting Portion—removes all difficulty in the way of trusting Him as our Guide. "He himself will lead us," as Dr. Kay renders it, "over death—across the gulf of death." Death is not our destination. We walk "through the valley," not merely into it, as if it were a place where there is no "thoroughfare" (Ps. 78:52, 53; 23:4). —*Evan H. Hopkins*

April 21

The Lord is my helper, and I will not fear what man shall do unto me.—Hebrews 13:6

The writer to the Hebrews is expressing a vital spiritual truth here. Surprisingly enough, it does not receive too much attention elsewhere in the Scriptures, aside from the Psalms. A quick look at these verses helps to put the concept into perspective:

"Thou art the helper of the fatherless" (10:14).

"Lord, be thou my helper" (30:10).

"Behold, God is my helper" (54:4).

"For he shall deliver . . . him that hath no helper" (72:12). The first three of these Psalms are attributed to David, the last to his illustrious son, Solomon. David learned his lesson of dependence upon the Lord during his years as a shepherd and warrior, and his first-person expression reflects that personal experience. Solomon, on the other hand, seems to speak academically, in the third person. A glance at other passages in Psalms reveals that David often prayed to his God to "help" him and thanked Him for that help.

All of us know what it means to need help. When our work is piled mountain high around us, the only answer is prayer. Many great men of God, men who accomplished great things for Him, have written that the greater their responsibility, the more time they spent in prayer. David would echo a hearty "Amen" to that practice, for it was his practice, too.

Christian, remember these truths. If God is your Helper, you need not worry no matter how great the task, no matter how outspoken the opposition. When we pray, we release the floodgates of power from on high that will buoy us up and over the greatest obstacle, lift us above and beyond those difficulties and dangers that press in upon us. Thank God, He is our Helper, and we need not fear what man can do to us!

April 22

And we know that all things work together for good to them that love God. —Romans 8:28

It is about as common as breakfast to hear such expressions as: "If only I had done differently." "I wish I had followed your advice." And we feel that had we done differently life would have been abundant and full.

One of life's most useless occupations is to fill our days brooding over what cannot now be changed, and neglecting today's opportunities for self-improvement and service to others.

He who spends his days looking backward will either miss the glories of the sunrise or the beauty of an evening sunset. To be ever looking backward makes one feel that everything is slipping away and gives a sense of futility to life.

"It might have been" is the cry of defeat. It also may show a lack of trust in the greatness, goodness, and power of God. The apostle Paul could look back at life from apparent defeat and declare, "All things work together for good to them that love God." Yesterday is past; let it go. It was good while it was here, but now it is only a memory and cannot be recalled. Do not spoil today by weeping because you cannot live yesterday again. Live today!

Said Leo Bennett: "I am resolved that not one day shall pass that I do not experience some thrilling personal adventure which will elevate my spirit and bring color into my life." And the late William Stidger wrote: "One adventure each day will keep the blues of monotony away."

Live today as though you had met the risen Christ fresh from the tomb this morning. His presence will brighten dark places and bring cheer for lonely hours. It is today we are living. See nature's beauties around you, enjoy its loveliness, listen to its song, and speak kindly to all you meet. "All things *do* work together for good!" —*O. G. Wilson*

April 23

I have seen his ways, and will heal him. —Isaiah 57:18

Healing, in a spiritual sense, is often referred to in connection with the backslidings of His people whom God forgives. "Return, ye backsliding children, and I will heal your backslidings" (Jer. 3:22). The soul that seeks God's pardon truly is not content with mere forgiveness; it desires cleansing and healing. Not the guilt of sin only, but its defilement and power are sought when we are thoroughly in earnest about our soul's salvation. And it is this that God promises.

The cross of Christ is not the source of our pardon only; it is the place of our healing: "*With his stripes we are healed*"

(Isa. 53:5). As we received pardon, so we received healing. Both are the fruit of Christ's death and both are accepted by faith. "Thy faith hath made thee whole" (Mark 5:34).

It is the whole soul, the soul that lives in spiritual health, that is alone ready to meet temptation. We fall before the allurements of sin, because temptation too often finds us enfeebled by disease—spiritual weakness.

Let us seek and claim that which God has bestowed upon us in Christ.   —*Evan H. Hopkins*

April 24

He giveth to all life, and breath, and all things. —Acts 17:25

When the spring comes, the oak tree with its thousands upon thousands of leaves blossoms all over. The great heart of the oak tree remembers every remotest tip of every farthest branch, and sends to each the message and the power of new life. And yet we do not think of the heart of the oak tree as if it were burdened with such multitudinous remembrance. It is simply the thrill of the common life translated into these million forms.

Somewhat in that way it seems to me that we may think of God's remembrance of His millions of children. That patient sufferer, that toiling worker are far-off leaves on the great tree of His life; far off, and yet as near to the beating of His heart as any leaf on all the tree.

If any doubt about Him, issuing from them, stops up the channel so that He cannot get to them, He waits behind the hindrance, behind the doubt, and tries to get it away. He feels the withering of the unbelieving, unfed leaf as if a true part of himself were dying. And when the obstacle gives way, and the doubt is broken, and the path is once more open, it is almost with a shout that the lifeblood leaps to its work again, coursing out to the estranged one with new life and force.

—*Phillips Brooks*

April 25

His sisters sent unto him, saying, Lord, behold, he whom thou lovest is sick. —John 11:3

In their trouble the sisters' first thought was of Jesus, and they sent for Him at once. We should not overlook this lesson. No doubt they sent for the physician; but they also sent for Christ. We should never fail to send word to Christ when anything is wrong in our home. We should want Him always in our sickrooms when our loved ones are suffering.

We must notice also the message which the sisters sent to Christ. It was short and simple. They did not beg and plead with Him to come; indeed, they made no request whatever; they merely told Jesus that His friend Lazarus was ill, and left it to Him to decide what He would do. They knew that He would do the right thing from the prompting of His own heart. Notice also the plea. They did not say, "He who *loves you* is sick," but, "He whom *you love* is sick." They made their appeal to Christ's own heart rather than to any personal claim. This is always our best plea with Christ—His love for us, not our love for Him.

There is something also in this message which speaks of a deep feeling of peace in the midst of danger. Many persons in such experiences lose all their courage and often their faith; but these sisters, though in such deep distress, maintained their composure. They had learned lessons of peace from Christ in the bright, sunny days beforehand, and when the trouble came they were ready for it, and were not disturbed. If we could get Christ's sweet comfort when sorrow comes, we must welcome Him in the days of gladness. If this Bethany family had shut Christ out of their home when they were well and happy, they could not have expected His blessed comfort in their sore distress. We must take Christ in the bright days if we would have Him in the dark. —*J. R. Miller*

April 26

At Jesus' feet.—Luke 10:39

At Jesus' feet—that is our place of privilege and of blessing, and here it is that we are to be educated and fitted for the practical duties of life. Here we are to renew our strength while we wait on Him, and to learn how to mount on wings as eagles; and here we are to become possessed of that true knowledge which is power. Here we are to learn how real work is to be done, and to be armed with the true motive power to do it. Here we are to find solace amidst both the trials of work—and they are not few—and the trials of life in general. Here also we are to anticipate something of the blessedness of heaven amidst the days of earth, for to sit at His feet is indeed to be in heavenly places, and to gaze upon His glory is to do what we shall never tire of doing yonder. —*W. Hay Aitken*

Alone with Jesus! What a different front Christianity would present to the world if the Lord's people were more often there! What humility, and gentleness, and love would characterize all their dealings! What holiness stamped on the very brow that all might read! What few judgments passed on others; how many more on ourselves! What calmness and resignation and joyful submission to all the Lord's dealings!
—*F. Whitfield*

April 27

Let all those that put their trust in thee rejoice: .... let them also that love thy name be joyful in thee.—Psalm 5:11

He maketh me to lie down in green pastures.—Psalm 23:2

I can hear these violets chorus
To the sky's benediction above;
And we all are together lying
On the bosom of Infinite Love.

Oh, the peace at the heart of Nature!
Oh, the light that is not of day!
Why seek it afar forever,
When it cannot be lifted away?
—*W. C. Gannett*

What inexpressible joy for me to look up through the apple blossoms and the fluttering leaves and to see God's love there; to listen to the thrush that has built his nest among them and to feel God's love, who cares for the birds, in every note that swells his little throat; to look beyond to the bright blue depths of the sky and to feel they are a canopy of blessing—the roof of the house of my Father; that if the clouds pass over it, it is the unchangeable light they veil; that, even when the day itself passes, I shall see that the night itself only unveils new worlds of light; and to know that if I could unwrap fold after fold of God's universe, I should only unfold more and more blessing, and see deeper and deeper into the love which is at the heart of all. —*Elizabeth Charles*

Let God do with me what He will, anything He will; whatever it be, it will be either heaven itself or some beginning of it. —*Wm. Mountford*

April 28

Herein was the love of God manifested in us, that God has sent his only begotten Son into the world, that we might live through him.—1 John 4:9

What is the connection between God's love and Christ's death? How does any self-sacrifice on the part of Jesus demonstrate God's *love*? The relation between God and Christ must be singularly close for Christ's death to prove God's love.

Suppose it had been said, "*Paul's* death proves the love of God"? There would be no force in that fact. But when we read, "Christ's death proves it," does not the assertion "hold water," and is there common sense in it at all except the one supposition—that the man who said God's love was proved by Christ's death believed that the heart of Christ was the revelation of the heart of God? And that what Christ did, God did in His well-beloved Son?

If you believe, as I believe, that Jesus Christ was God manifested in flesh, then it is reasonable to say, "God commendeth *his own love* to us in that *Christ* died for us."

Remember, too, that God's love is all-embracing, because it embraces everyone. It can only be true that Christ died for us all if every man on earth has the right to say, "Christ died for me."

God does not deal with men in a crowd. Christ's death was not for men in a crowd. It was not for the abstraction, "humanity," "the world," "mankind." It was for men, one by one, singly, as if there had not been another human being in existence except just that one. I believe that we were all in Christ's heart, all in His purpose, when He gave himself up to death for us all. Therefore, His cross on which He yielded himself to the outward penalty of sin so that none of its inward penalty might ever fall upon those who trust in Him is the manifestation of the love of God to the whole world. Because Christ's death embraced in its purpose the whole world, and every unit that is in it, therefore He died for me! Do you believe that? —*Alexander McLaren*

April 29

For God so loved the world. —John 3:16

In John's first epistle we are told that God is love in essence, for verily "God *is* love," and in our meditation today we see how He is love in action, for He "so loved the world." But when we begin to meditate upon the love of God, we not only get into an ocean which is both boundless and fathomless, but altogether beyond our conception; yea—

Tis more than angel's tongue can tell,
Or angel's mind conceive.

There is only one Being who can comprehend it, and that is God himself.

God only knows the love of God!

I have heard of a man whose heart became filled with God's love, and he exclaimed: "Could I stand in a pulpit that reached the stars, with every man on earth my audience, and eternity as my day, the topic I would speak upon should be the boundless, wondrous love of God."

God's boundless love extends to sinful me: He "so loved the world," and proved it in the gift of His "only begotten Son." But what was the purpose of this unspeakable gift? The Lord Jesus "gave himself for us that he might redeem us from all iniquity," that He might turn useless, destructive, miserable, sinful slaves of Satan into useful, happy, holy children of God, that we "should not perish but have everlasting life."   —*John Roberts*

April 30

Blessed be the Lord, who daily loadeth us with benefits [bears up], even the God of our salvation. —Psalm 68:19

Jesus Christ is our great Benefactor. This should evoke from me a great burst of praise and thanksgiving as I contemplate His goodness to me. This gift He gives is much more than tangible and temporary. He actually "bears me up," according to a later translation of the passage (RSV). In Psalm 65:5, David extols Him as the God of our salvation and thanks Him for His deliverance, "who art the hope of all the ends of the earth, and of the farthest seas." In Psalm 55:22 David advises the believer to "cast thy burden upon the Lord, and he shall sustain thee: he shall never suffer [permit] the righteous to be moved."

Lest you think these promises are limited to Old Testament times, let me remind you that the apostle Paul quotes this verse immediately preceding (Ps. 68:18) where Christ is pictured for us as our great High Priest who "when he ascended on high he led a host of captives, and he gave gifts to men" (Eph. 4:8). This is the One who is bearing us up, the One who in himself is our salvation.

The apostle John also reminds his fellow Christians that they are the recipients of this divine bounty: "And of his fullness have all we received, and grace for [upon] grace" (John 1:16). Paul adds another dimension to this promise when he tells the Colossians, "For in him [Jesus] all the fullness of God was pleased to dwell" (1:19). Not only does He bear us up, but in Him we have, are literally part of, the very fullness of God himself!

Talk about your treasures. The Christian receives "grace upon grace" and happiness heaped upon happiness, divine favor upon divine favor. Oh, fellow Christian, how can we complain when we arc on the receiving end of such benefits? Let us join the saints of all ages in a great choir of praise to our God for all of His goodness to us!

May 1

He that doeth the will of God abideth forever. —1 John 2:17

These words imply, not so much dwelling, or persistence, or continuousness, during our earthly career, as much as they describe the absolute and unlimited permanence of the obedient life. Obedience will endure when all things else, "the world and the lusts thereof," have passed into obscurity and cease to be. It is true that Christian men, temples of Christ, are subject to the same law of decay as all created things are. It is true, on the other hand, that men whose lives are confined within the limits of the material and visible have only these lives as permanent. Their fruit continues, though it is fruitless fruit, inasmuch as they have to bear forever the responsibility of their past.

The lives that run parallel with God's will, last, and when everything contrary to that will, or negligent of it, is summed up, it comes to nought and is abolished, but the obedient lives continue. The life that is in conformity with the will of God lasts in another sense, since it persists through all changes, even the supreme change that is wrought by death, in the same direction and in substantially the same way. The man who is doing God's will here, in the midst of a busy life, will do God's will above, amid the glories of heaven. It will be the same life with the same abiding principles, so it will last forever.

If we grasp the throne of God, we shall be co-eternal with the throne that we grasp. We cannot die, nor our work pass and be utterly abolished as long as He lives. Some trees, like sturdy scotch firs, have strong trunks, and obstinate branches, and unfading foliage, as if they could defy any blast or decay. But their roots run along the surface, and down they go before the storm. Others, far more slender in appearance, strike their roots deep down and stand whatever winds blow. So strike your roots into God and Christ. "He that doeth the will of God abideth forever." "In my Father's house are many abiding-places." They who have dwelt in Christ, persistently seeking to have His truth dwell in them and wrought out by them, will pass into the permanences of the heavenly home. —*Alexander Maclaren*

May 2

If ye abide in me, and my words abide in you, ye shall ask what ye will, and it shall be done unto you. . . . The effectual fervent prayer of a righteous man availeth much.—John 15:7; James 5:16

Here on earth the influence of one who asks a favor of others depends entirely on his character and the relationship he bears to him with whom he is interceding. It is what he is that gives weight to what he asks.

It is not otherwise with God. Our power in prayer depends upon our life. Where our life is right we shall know how to pray so as to please God, and prayer will secure the answer. The texts quoted above point in this direction: "*If ye abide in me,*" says our Lord, ye shall ask and it shall be done unto you. It is the prayer of *a righteous man,* according to James, that availeth much.

In 1 John 3:22, John says: "Whatsoever we ask, we receive of him, *because* we keep his commandments, and do the things that are pleasing in his sight." All lack of power to pray properly and perseveringly, all lack of power in prayer with God, points to some lack in the Christian life. It is as we learn to live the life that pleases God that God will give what we ask.

Let us learn from our Lord Jesus, in the parable of the vine, what the healthy, vigorous life is that may ask and receive what it will. Hear His voice, "If ye abide in me, and my words abide in you, ye shall ask what ye will, and it shall be done unto you." And again at the close of the parable: "Ye did not choose me, but I chose you, and appointed you, that you should go and bear fruit, and that your fruit should remain: that whatsoever ye shall ask the Father in my name, he may give it you."

And what is now, according to the parable, the life that one must lead to bear fruit, and then ask and receive what we will? What is it we are to be or do that will enable us to pray as we should, and receive what we ask? The answer is in one word: it is the branch life that gives power for prayer. We are branches of Christ the living Vine. We must simply live like branches, abiding in Christ, then we shall ask what we will, and it shall be done unto us.   —*Andrew Murray*

May 3

The Lord shall reign. —Micah 4:7

This glorious fact fills the heart of every believer, every follower of the Lord Jesus Christ with joy. However great the power of Satan may appear to be, we may triumphantly exclaim that a time is coming when "the Lord shall reign." His reign shall be a reign of *peace.* He has been called "the Prince of Peace," and we are told that "He is our peace," so that His subjects will possess and enjoy peace, perfect peace, both with their king and with each other.

His reign shall also be *universal.* The words of Daniel are: "There was given him dominion, and glory, and a kingdom, that all people, nations, and languages should serve him."

Not only shall His reign of peace be universal, but it shall be *everlasting.* Gabriel said to Mary: "Of his kingdom there shall be no end." And in Revelation 11:15 we read: "There were great voices in heaven, saying, The kingdoms of this world are become the kingdoms of our Lord, and of his Christ; and he shall reign for ever and ever." What a glorious prospect we have, then, in anticipation!

> To Him shall endless prayer be made,
> And praises throng to crown His head;
> His name, like sweet perfume, shall rise
> With every morning sacrifice.

> People and realms of ev'ry tongue,
> Dwell on His love with sweetest song;
> And infant voices shall proclaim
> Their early blessings on His name.

> Let every creature rise and bring
> Peculiar honors to our King;
> Angels descend with songs again,
> And earth repeat the loud Amen.

Have I chosen Him as my King? Have I consented to allow Him perfect control over the whole of my life? Does He sit upon the throne of my heart and reign supreme over all my desires, tempers and works? Oh, that this ancient prophecy of Micah may be fulfilled to the fullest extent in my experience this day: "The Lord shall reign!" —*John Roberts*

May 4

If ye then, being evil, know how to give good gifts unto your children, how much more shall your Father which is in heaven give good things to them that ask him?
—Matthew 7:11

No father will answer his hungry child's cry for bread with a stone, or give the child a serpent if he asks for a fish. Even sinful parents have in their hearts something of the image of God's own fatherhood. If a true earthly father, with all his imperfection, will not mock a child's cry, but will respond lovingly, how much more will our Father in heaven do for us?

"How much more?" is a question none can answer. We can only say as much as the heavenly Father is more loving, and wiser, and more able to give than is the earthly father. Yet we must explain this promise also by other scriptures. The gate of prayer is set very wide open in this verse, yet those who would enter must come in the right way and seek "good" things.

While no one who asks for bread will receive a stone, neither will one who asks for a stone receive a stone. And many times we do come to God pleading with Him to let us have a stone. Of course we imagine it is bread and that it will be food for us. It is some earthly thing, some gift of honor or pleasure, some achievement of ambition, some object of heart desire. It looks like bread to our deluded vision. But

God knows it is only a cold stone, that it would leave us starving if we were to receive it; and He loves us too much to give in to our pleadings for it. When we ask for a stone He will give us bread. Thus it is that many requests for earthly things are not granted. Yet the prayers are not unanswered. Instead of the stone we wish, God gives us the bread we need. We do not always know what is bread and what is a stone, and we must leave with God the final decision in all our prayers. —*J. R. Miller*

May 5

In every thing by prayer and supplication with thanksgiving let your requests be made known unto God.—Philippians 4:6

The apostle warns them against anxiety. "Be careful for nothing." Be not anxious concerning anything, but "in every thing by prayer...." This is one of the means by which to guard against worry. Turn your trouble or anxiety into prayer. Let it be definite and specific. Let it be earnest and full of praise.

The remembrance of past mercies will not only strengthen our faith and lead us to expect future mercies and blessings; it will help us to be more real and childlike in prayer. A special promise belongs to this precept which follows it immediately: "And the peace of God, which passeth all understanding, shall keep your minds and hearts in Christ Jesus."

It is in vain we pray to be kept if we neglect to obey the Lord's direction. The burdens and cares that come upon us daily we must commit unto the Lord daily. It is as we fulfill the condition that we shall find the truth of the promise. God will surely fulfill His own undertaking, but He expects us to be obedient to His will. —*Evan H. Hopkins*

May 6

Pray one for another, that ye may be healed. The effectual fervent prayer of a righteous man availeth much.—James 5:16

Weymouth translates this verse even more strikingly: "The heartfelt supplication of a righteous man exerts a mighty influence." Prayer may be empty words, with no more power than empty shells. What is more foolish than to fire empty shells that have no effect when they land? Yet that is what many professed prayers really are; they have nothing in them, and they accomplish nothing. They are just forged upon the lips, and they drop useless to the ground as soon as they are spoken.

Effectual prayers are born deep in the heart; they are flooded with heart-treasure, with faith, with desire, with holy urgency. And they go out into a heedless world with power to shake and shatter.

What are my prayers like? *If I were God, would I listen to them?* Are they mere pretences at prayer, full of nothing but sound, signifying nothing? Is there any reasonable ground for assuming that they can accomplish anything? Or are my prayers weighted with sincere desire? Do they involve themselves with my brother's good as well as my own? Are they spoken in faith? Do they go forth in great expectancy?

Then do they surely exert "a mighty influence." Then do they become fellow laborers with all God's ministries of grace. The greatest thing I can do greatly is pray.   —*J. H. Jowett*

May 7

But he [Jesus] withdrew himself into the wilderness, and prayed.—Luke 5:16

If you enter into prayer and make a serious business of it, make it a part of your everyday life, you will begin to live no longer out of your human talents and resources. You will begin drawing on the power of God for your everyday life.

First of all, keep a daily quiet time with God. This is simply the discipline and training of the spiritual life which would be comparable to the training and practice of an athlete. When you see an athlete perform a perfectly executed maneuver on a field of contest, you are seeing him at an instant of action. Behind that instant of action is a whole program of discipline and training. He never would have had that instant of perfectly executed action if the discipline and training were not behind it. Nor will you have moments of real encounter with God and moments of answered prayer if you don't go through the discipline of a daily quiet time with God. This is an absolute essential. If you are not willing to do this, then you might as well forget about prayer. Prayer for you will always be something that you hear about rather than something that you experience.

Anything that you want to do is going to require some of your time. There is no better way to find out what you really put value on than to look at the way your calendar is arranged. What you give time to is what you really consider significant. As you evaluate how much time you give to God, you can pretty well tell how important you really consider Him to be. If you say, "Oh, I believe in God, and I'm going to serve God, but I'm just too busy for prayer," your subconscious says, "I get it. It's just a big cover-up. It doesn't mean a thing." When you really believe something is important, you make time for it. So that is the first rule, and if you keep that as faithfully as humanly possible, you will discover tremendous changes coming into your life. —*Larry Christenson*

May 8

Let us therefore come boldly unto the throne of grace, that we may obtain mercy, and find grace to help us in time of need. —Hebrews 4:16

Christ, the great High Priest, gives those whom He has redeemed direct access as priests to God. For them the veil of the temple is torn in two, and the holiest place open to their reverent entrance. He has done it by His revelation of God, through which He has brought the whole depth and tenderness of the Father's heart close to our hearts. He has done it by His death, which removes all obstacles to a sinful man's entrance into that holy presence, bringing us nearer through His blood. He does it by putting within our hearts the Spirit which cries, "Father," the new life set toward God as water rises to the level of its source. Thus every soul of man, however ignorant, guilty, or weak, may come into the presence of God, needing no priest, no hand to lead, no introducer. Trusting in Christ our forerunner, who is for us entered within the veil, we may come boldly to the throne, and may hold direct fellowship with the Father and the Son.

Every priest must have something to offer. And this great High Priest makes it possible that we should come, not empty-handed, but bringing the one sacrifice acceptable to God—the offering of hearts set on fire by His love. Christ has offered the one all-sufficient sacrifice for the sins of the whole world. On the basis of that offering, we can draw near with our thanksgiving and our sacrifices. Our offerings can never purge away sin: that has been done once and for all by our great High Priest. Whoever is freed from his sins by the blood of Christ is thereby made himself a priest, qualified to offer spiritual sacrifices of joyful thanksgiving. The sacrifices we have to offer are ourselves—yielding ourselves in the blessed self-surrender of love, and placing ourselves unreservedly in God's hands, to live to His praise, to be directed by His supreme will. With such sacrifices God is will pleased.

—*Alexander Maclaren*

May 9

This poor man cried, and the Lord heard him, and saved him out of all his troubles.—Psalm 34:6

David's ability to praise in the midst of problems should be an example to every Christian, showing us how to handle our difficulties creatively. This verse from Psalm 34 reveals his simple secret and gives us a formula for successful praying. First of all, David humbles himself and sees himself as he really is. He could have reminded God that he was in line for the throne of Israel, that he was the hero of the Israelite army, the slayer of Goliath. Instead, he calls himself a "poor man"—he acknowledges his need and puts himself in position to have that need met.

What ringing assurance David echoes when he adds, ". . . and the Lord heard him." He doesn't launch into a long dissertation or extensive analysis of prayer principles. He states simply and unequivocally that "God heard him." And we can confidently claim the same assurance. The Bible is full of examples of prayer heard and answered, but it also gives principles that must be followed. For example, in Psalm 66:18 the writer warns, "If I regard iniquity in my heart, the Lord will not hear me." James 4:3 points out that "You ask and do not receive, because you ask wrongly" (RSV), showing that improper motive and an impure heart can "ground" our prayers.

David's concluding phrase is a ringing declaration of his faith. Not only did God hear him, but He "saved him out of all his troubles." Not just the worst of his troubles, or the most troublesome of his troubles, but *all* his troubles. The God with whom we have to do is not a God of halfway measures. He even took David "*out* of all his troubles," to a place of serenity and security. This same promise of the presence of God can be ours as we follow the principles David has inscribed for us here in this precious and practical verse.

May 10

I seek not mine own will, but the will of the Father which hath sent me. —John 5:30
Thy will be done in earth, as it is in heaven.—Matthew 6:10

God's ways are not our ways. His plans often move right through our plans in their stately marches. We are not only to do the will of God in our busy activities, but we are to allow it to be done in us and respecting us.

We pray and the answer does not come. In our bitter disappointment we say, "Has God not promised that if we ask we shall receive?" Yes, but Jesus himself prayed that the cup of His agony—the betrayal, the trial, the ignominy, the crucifixion—might pass, but it did not pass. Paul prayed that his thorn in the flesh might be removed, but it was not removed. All along the centuries mothers have agonized in prayer over their dying babies, and yet the little hearts have grown still in death.

Are not prayers answered then at all? Certainly they are. Not a word that goes on wings of faith up to God fails to receive His attention and answer. But often the answer that comes is not relief but the spirit of acquiescence to God's will. The cup did not pass, but the will of Jesus was brought into such perfect accord with His Father's that His cries for relief died away in words of sweet, peaceful yielding. The thorn was not removed, but Paul was enabled to keep it and *forget* it in glad surrender to his Master's wish. The child did not recover, but the parents were helped to rise, and wash away their tears, and worship God.

We are to have desires, but they are to be subordinated to God's supreme desire, which is *far better and wiser than ours.* We are to make plans, but they are to be laid at God's feet that He may either take them up into His own plan, as parts thereof, or set them aside and give us better plans. —*J. R. Miller*

May 11

Oh that thou wouldest keep me from evil.—1 Chronicles 4:10

Jabez was a man of prayer. It was the habit of his life. This was the secret of his courage, his goodness, and his success.

Here is one petition from his prayer. It reminds one of another petition: "I pray not that thou shouldest take them out of the world, but that thou shouldest keep them from the evil" (John 17:15). After all, this is better than more territory, more power, more wealth. It is better than all temporal blessings "Keep me from evil."

Are there not many things we need to be kept from every day? There is evil without and evil within. It is not our vigilance that keeps us, but the Lord himself, though it is those who are watchful and prayerful whom He keeps. "Except the Lord keep the city, the watchman waketh but in vain" (Ps. 127:1). It is the soul that commits itself to God to be kept that knows the sufficiency of His keeping power. Many are trying to believe that the Lord will keep them without yielding themselves right over into His hands to be kept.

Am I honest in my prayer, "Keep me from evil"?
—*Evan H. Hopkins*

May 12

Men ought always to pray.—Luke 18:1

You shoot off a quick prayer because you are in the midst of your daily work. You don't have time to take off a half hour for prayer. You pray right now because a situation has come up.

Of course, arrow prayers are only successful, as a general rule, when they are well grounded in the life of prayer. It's the person who is schooled in prayer and praise as a regular thing who can draw upon prayer in situations of immediate need.

In Nehemiah 2:4, we see Nehemiah coming as the cupbearer to the king: "And the king said to me, 'What would you like to request?' So I prayed to the God of heaven." Now, Nehemiah didn't get down on his knees and have a half-hour prayer session there in front of the king. He shot off an arrow prayer to God right then, because he wanted God to be in his answer to the king. And God answered Nehemiah's arrow prayer.

You can't find God on the run. You have to be willing to take the time necessary to come into His presence. Arrow prayers, in the midst of daily activities, gain their power from the blocks of time set aside solely for prayer. People who live out of their pockets don't have an adequate diet. Neither do people find the power of God filling their prayers who try to exist spiritually on moments of prayer fleetingly flung toward heaven.

Prayer is a rich and varied experience. It takes time, effort, dedication, But no time is better spent, no dedication more wonderfully rewarded. The promises of God are as great as His boundless love: "*Whatsoever* you ask . . . " (Mark 11:24).

—*Larry Christenson*

May 13

Men ought always to pray, and not faint.—Luke 18:1

A great many people become discouraged in praying because the answer does not come at once. It should be settled in the mind, first, that God *always* hears the true prayer, and that He will always send *an* answer, though it may not always be the answer we desire. He never despises or disregards the cry of one of His children, but sometimes for wise reasons He delays the answer. Perhaps it cannot be prepared at once. God's plans reach out widely, and sometimes He works slowly. Look at Joseph in Egypt—a slave, then a prisoner. No doubt he was praying every day for release, and he may have thought at times the answer was long in coming.

But when it came, he could see that one reason for the delay was that all things might be made ready. It took years to prepare the answer that came at last with such blessing.

Or the reason for God's delay might be to draw out our faith, to increase our earnestness. The story of the Syrophenician woman illustrates this. At first Jesus "answered her not a word"; but it was for her sake that He kept her waiting. She received a far better answer at the last than she could have received at the first. Suppose she had "fainted" after her first apparent repulse from Jesus; think what she would have lost.

No doubt thousands of prayers are never answered because men faint at God's seeming delay. Perhaps you have lost many a joy and blessing because you gave up before the answer came. A little longer and patient perseverance would have brought you a great reward. After spending thousands of dollars drilling for oil, the operator became discouraged and sold out for a fraction of his investment. The purchaser started to drill, and in six hours found a flowing well. We see what "fainting" cost the first owner. Many Christians lose heart just when the answer is about to come. —*J. R. Miller*

May 14

He calleth his own sheep by name, and leadeth them out.
—John 10:3

These words suggest three precious thoughts: First, there is divine *possession.* We who believe in Him belong to the Good Shepherd. We are His own sheep. He has set His mark upon us. He distinguishes His own in a way that they can never be confounded in His sight with those that are of the world.

Then, second, there is divine *knowledge.* He says, "I *know* my sheep" (v. 14). He has intimate acquaintance with them, so that He can call each sheep by name.

Third, there is divine *guidance.* "He leadeth them out." He goes before them. Each day He leads them into fresh pastures, into new paths of service, into untrodden fields of patient following. If the Shepherd knows His sheep, it is that the sheep may know their Shepherd. "I know my sheep, and am known of mine." This mutual knowledge implies sympathy, love, community of nature (1 John 4:7; Gal. 4:9; 1 Cor. 8:3; John 17:3, 25).

Christ first took our nature that we might afterwards receive His. He who laid down His life for us, now gives His life to us. —*Evan H. Hopkins*

May 15

For what is our hope, or joy, or crown of rejoicing? Are not even ye in the presence of our Lord?—1 Thessalonians 2:10

Nothing else is so cleansing as the consciousness of God's presence. Things that we have long tolerated become intolerable when we bring them into the white light of the presence of the Holy One. How many things we do in the darkness of the night, yea, even in the broad light of day, that we could not for a moment think of doing if we realized God was right there by our side—*looking.* God is always present, whether we realize it or not; if we cultivate the consciousness of His presence, our lives and hearts will speedily whiten until they become as the very snow.

People wonder what Jesus would do in this relation or that, but the Bible tells us plainly what He actually did do—He spent much time in prayer. He would rise a great while before day and go out into the mountain to pray alone. He spent whole nights in prayer. If we are to walk as Jesus walked, we must lead a life of prayerfulness. The man who is not leading a life of prayer, no matter how many excellent things he may be doing, is not following his Lord. —*R. A. Torrey*

May 16

As he went out of Jericho with his disciples and a great number of people, blind Bartimaeus . . . sat by the highway side begging. —Mark 10:46

Our Lord hears the cry of need even when it rises from the center of a tumultuous crowd. A mother can hear the faint cry of her child in the bedroom above, even when the room resounds with the talk and laughter of her guests. So our Lord heard the cry of poor Bartimaeus. The lone, sorrowful cry, "Lord, have mercy on me" (see vv. 47, 48), pierced the clamor, "and Jesus stood still" (v. 49). My soul, cry to Him, for "Jesus of Nazareth passeth by."

Bartimaeus knew what he wanted. He merged all his petitions into one: "Lord, that I might receive my sight!" Let me, too, come to my Saviour with some great, dominant, all-commanding request. I'm afraid I trifle with the Master. I ask Him for toys, for petty things, while all the time He is waiting to give me "unsearchable wealth," "sight, riches, healing of the mind." "The Lord is great"; and shall I add, "and greatly to be *prayed*"!

How delicately gracious it is that our Lord should attribute the miracle to Bartimaeus himself. "Thy faith hath made thee whole!" As though the Lord had no share in the ministry! He makes so much of our faith, and our endeavor, and our obedience. "If ye had faith as a grain of mustard seed." That's all He wants, and miracles are accomplished. —*J. H. Jowett*

May 17

I will look unto the Lord; I will wait for the God of my salvation: my God will hear me.—Micah 7:7

The power of prayer rests in the faith that God hears it. In more than one sense this is true. It is this faith that gives a man courage to pray. It is this faith that gives him power to prevail with God. The moment I am assured that God hears *me*, too, I feel drawn to pray and to persevere in prayer. I feel strong to claim and to take in faith the answer God gives.

One great reason of lack of prayer is the absence of the living, joyous assurance in the believer: *My God will hear me.* If the believer had the vision of the living God waiting to grant his request, and bestow all the heavenly gifts he needs, for himself or those he is serving, how everything would be set aside to make time and room for this one and only power that can insure heavenly blessing—the prayer of faith!

When a man can, and does, say, in living faith, "My God will hear me!" surely nothing can keep him from prayer. He knows that what he cannot do or get done on earth can and will be done for him from heaven.

Shall we not all set ourselves to learn the lesson which will make prevailing prayer possible—the lesson of a faith that always sings, "My God will hear me"? Simple and elementary as it is, it requires practice and patience, time and heavenly teaching, to learn it as we should. Under the impression of a bright thought, or a blessed experience, it may look as if we knew the lesson perfectly. But ever again the need will recur of making this our first prayer—that God who hears prayer would teach us to believe it, and so to pray properly.

If we desire it we can count on Him. He who delights in hearing prayer and answering it, He who gave His Son that He might ever pray for us and with us, and His Holy Spirit to pray in us, we can be sure there is not a prayer He will hear more certainly than this: that He so reveal himself as the prayer-hearing God that our whole being may respond, "*My God will hear me!*" —*Andrew Murray*

May 18

Thus says the Lord God: This also I will let the house of Israel ask me to do for them: to increase their men like a flock. —Ezekiel 36:37 (RSV)

This passage shows the connection between promise and prayer—the promise that God gives and the prayer that it is His will we should offer. When God is about to pour out His blessings upon man, He prepares them to receive by drawing out their hearts in prayer unto Him.

Prayer is the forerunner of all spiritual mercies. It is God's own appointed way; it is His revealed will that we should "ask" if we would "receive." Not that He is unwilling to grant these mercies, nor that He needs to be moved by our importunity to be gracious unto us. But in order that we should not think His gifts as common things, and receive His blessings as if they came to us as a matter of course, He will for all these things be asked by His children.

One of the chief lessons we have to learn is the privilege of prayer. It forms a most important part of our spiritual training, to acquire the habit of constant contact with God in prayer. It is thus that an attitude of humble dependence is brought about in the soul, and a spirit of continual thankfulness is fostered. The promise calls to prayer, and prayer brings down the blessing, and the blessing calls forth the praise.

—Evan H. Hopkins

May 19

Pray without ceasing. —1 Thessalonians 5:17

We need to watch always that our prayers are real, fresh from the heart, and that they never degenerate into mere formalities, words without desires and without faith. True prayer is talking to God as one talks to a friend; mere words are empty mockery. As we grow in Christian life, prayer becomes more and more real to us, and we are conscious of a progression. From prayer merely as a recourse in emergencies, and then prayer at appointed times, we move on to prayer as a state of daily living. In this last and highest development, stated times of prayer are not abandoned, but the heart does not limit itself to these in communing with God. The spirit of devotion overflows the fixed hours of prayer and holds fellowship with God continuously. Even the busiest hours of work are brightened by many a moment of heavenly communion.

This is what is meant by walking with God. Men talk to Him at their work, in ejaculations of prayer. Thomas à Kempis says, "God alone is a thousand companions; He alone is a world of friends. That man never knew what it was to be familiar with God, who complains of the want of friends when God is with him." It is this state of constant and unbroken communion with God toward which we should strive.

Let the life of prayer flow into the busiest hours of the busiest days. It will be a defense against temptations. It will give us power in Christian service. It will hallow all our influence. It will make holy and pure every nook and cranny of our lives. It will give us peace in the presence of dangers, help in all darkness, comfort in all sorrows, companionship in all loneliness, friendship in all heart hunger. If we know how to get help in prayer, we need never fail at any point in life, for then God's might is back of us as the ocean is back of the bay.—*J. R. Miller*

May 20

Pray without ceasing.—1 Thessalonians 5:17

It is quite evident that when Paul wrote these words, he had three classes of Christians in mind. They lived in Thessalonica in his day. They exist all over America in this later day, and the Lord would search our hearts with this exhortation. To which class do you belong?

First, there are those who *cease without praying.* These are quite ready to accept Jesus Christ as Savior from the guilt of their sins, but they have been far from ready to accept Him as Lord of their lives. They are struggling through the Christian life on the little strength they can muster themselves. To them it would appear a sign of weakness if they should put their own fancied efforts aside, and turn the whole matter over to the Lord—and that is their main weakness, for the highways and byways of life are strewn with the spiritual wreckage of those who have struggled in and with themselves, only to end up defeated.

Second, there are those who *pray with ceasing.* These are quite willing to accept the truth contained in the hymn, "Take it to the Lord in prayer," but the pressures of an adverse world and a trying life conspire to go back again and "take it from the Lord without prayer." "Ye did run well; who did hinder you?" (Gal. 5:7) may well refer to them, these wonderers, and wanderers, and wishers instead of warm warriors when it comes to the serious business of prevailing prayer. What is begun in prayer cannot be finished with good intentions.

Third, there are those who really *pray without ceasing.* Paul could commend the Thessalonians for their faithfulness in this. And can the Holy Spirit, who inspired this word through His servant, commend us likewise? What, after all, is the heart of our prayer life? We should pray and we should engage in "holy wrestling" (prayer without ceasing) before the throne of grace. There is the crux and the core for much of the Christian life. For unto him who presses through, who carries on, who resists the subtle temptation to cease, to shorten, to taper off, to minimize, to weaken, unto him, who for the glory of God will "pray without ceasing," is there power, promise and provision! —*Edwin Raymond Anderson*

May 21

We do not present our supplications before thee for our righteousness, but for thy great mercies. O Lord, hear: O Lord, forgive; O Lord, hearken and do.—Daniel 9:18, 10

Every true prayer has its background and its foreground. The foreground of prayer is the intense, immediate desire for a certain blessing which seems to be absolutely necessary for the soul to have; the background of prayer is the quiet, earnest desire that the will of God, whatever it may be, should be done.

What a picture is the perfect prayer of Jesus in Gethsemane! In it burns the strong desire to escape death and to live; but, behind, there stands, calm and strong, the craving of the whole life for the doing of the will of God.

Leave out the foreground—let there be no expression of the wish of him who prays—and there is left a pure submission which is almost fatalism. Leave out the background—let there be no acceptance of the will of God—and the prayer is only an expression of self-will, a petulant claiming of the uncorrected choice of him who prays.

Only when the two, foreground and background, are there together, balancing one another—the special desire resting on the universal submission, the universal submission opening into the special desire—only then is the picture perfect and the prayer complete! —*Phillips Brooks*

May 22

In quietness and in confidence shall be your strength.— Isaiah 30:15

Isaiah prophesied during some of the stormiest years of Judah's history. Indeed, tradition tells us that Isaiah ended his ministry of more than fifty years as a martyr, cut in pieces during wicked Manasseh's assumption of the throne. In the Bible's "Faith Hall of Fame," Hebrews 11, the writer says of those heroic martyrs: "They were stoned . . . sawn asunder . . . slain with the sword. . . ."

Isaiah lived an equally tumultuous life, prophesying during the changing reigns of Jotham, Ahaz, and Hezekiah. Facing such a tragic and painful end, he could still write the triumphant words, "In quietness and in confidence shall be your strength." In a later chapter he reveals the secret of his strength and confidence in the midst of death and destruction. In chapter 32 he writes: "And the word [effect] of righteousness shall be peace; and the effect of righteousness, quietness and assurance forever."

Isaiah's secret arsenal of spiritual "spunk" is available to you as well. Remember, it is God who is in control of your affairs. He has a wonderful plan for your life. But you must want that plan with all your heart, you must be yielded to His control, accepting what comes as His will, opening the deepest areas of your life to His command.

As we live quietly and confidently in a disordered and stormy world, we show forth the validity of our faith, the strength of our confidence in God to do with us as He has promised. Everything that happens to the Christian has a purpose—to build him up in the faith, or perhaps to chasten him that he might become even stronger. Accept what comes in that light and experience faith's "growing pains." God is good and "will not suffer you to be tempted above that ye are able, but will with the temptation provide a way of escape"! This is the Christian's quietness... and confidence... and strength!

May 23

Praying in the Holy Spirit. —Jude 20

We all admit the place the Father and the Son have in our prayer. It is to the Father we pray and from whom we expect the answer. It is in the merit, and name, and life of the Son, abiding in Him and He in us, that we trust to be heard. But have we understood that in the Holy Trinity all three persons have an equal place in prayer, and that the faith in the Holy Spirit of intercession as praying in us is as indispensable as the faith in the Father and the Son?

How clearly we have this in the words, "Through Christ we have access by one Spirit to the Father." As much as prayer must be *to* the Father, and *through* the Son, it must be *by* the Spirit. And the Spirit can pray in no other way in us than as He lives in us. It is only as we give ourselves to the Spirit living and praying in us that the glory of the prayer-hearing God, and the ever-blessed and most effectual mediation of the Son, can be known by us in their power.

Without the Holy Spirit no man can call Jesus Lord, or cry, Abba, Father; no man can worship in spirit and truth, or pray without ceasing. The Holy Spirit is given the believer to be and do in him all that God wants him to be or do. He is given him especially as the Spirit of prayer and supplication. Is it not clear that everything in prayer depends upon our trusting the Holy Spirit to do His work in us? Yielding ourselves to His leading, depending only and wholly on Him?

We read that "Stephen was a man full of faith and the Holy Spirit." The two ever go together, in exact proportion to each other. As our faith sees and trusts the Spirit in us to pray, and waits on Him, He will do His work, and it is the longing desire, and the earnest supplication, and the definite faith the Father seeks. —*Andrew Murray*

May 24

Abide in me, and I in you.—John 15:4

We ought to notice the order of this twofold abiding. The condition of having the Lord dwelling in us is that we ourselves should be dwelling in Him. We must abide in Him if we would have Him abiding in us. The whole chapter sets forth the deep and mysterious truth of the soul's union with Christ. There is a union of life and there is a union of will. Fellowship cannot be known unless the latter, as well as the former, is a reality in our experience.

Another point we must remember is declared in this chapter: Christ is not the root or the stem only; He is the whole vine. He says, "I am the vine." So that what Christ is, covers every branch and every leaf and every tendril of the whole plant. Remember, Paul in another place designates the name "Christ" is given to the whole body (see 1 Cor. 12:12).

The believer is to abide in Christ as the branch abides in the vine. The function of the branch is to maintain connection with the stem, to receive the life-sap at one end and to bear the fruit at the other. The branch cannot *produce* the fruit —its responsibility is to *bear it.* —*Evan H. Hopkins*

May 25

And all things, whatsoever ye shall ask in prayer, believing, ye shall receive.—Matthew 21:22

There are other scriptures qualifying this promise. In the first place, not all asking is really praying, and therefore not all asking receives. James says, "Ye ask, and receive not, because ye ask amiss, that ye may spend it in your pleasures" (James 4:3). A man asks for money, not to use it for the glory of God and the good of others, but for his own glory and pleasure. Again the Psalmist says, "If I regard iniquity in my heart, the Lord will not hear me." That is, if one is cherishing a secret sin in his heart while he is trying to serve God, no prayers that he offers will be heard or answered. So here are at least two kinds of asking that will not bring an answer.

Then there are conditions. One is that we must ask in Christ's name. That implies that we believe in Christ as our Saviour, and are His faithful friends, and therefore have a right to use His Name. This condition narrows down the promise to the true followers of Christ. Another condition is that we are abiding in Christ and His words are abiding in us. So there is a double "if." Even a Christian who is following afar off does not come within the circle of this promise.

Then there is another qualification which belongs to all promises to prayer. God himself must be the judge as to the things we ask, whether they would really be blessings to us or not. There may be things we desire greatly that it would be the greatest unkindness to grant us. Is God then bound by this promise to give us what we crave? By no means. "What is *good* the Lord will give." "No *good* thing will be withhold from them that walk uprightly." But He will withhold even from the most upright the things which in His divine wisdom He sees would not be good things. This is implied in every such promise as this. —*J. R. Miller*

May 26

Abraham prayed unto God: and God healed. . . . When Moses prayed unto the Lord, the fire was quenched. —Genesis 20:17, Numbers 11:2

Just think for a moment of the men of prayer in Scripture, and see in them what the life was that could pray with such power. What gave Abraham such boldness in prayer? He knew that God had chosen and called him away from his home and people to walk before Him that all the nations might be blessed in him. He knew that he had obeyed and forsaken all for God. Implicit obedience, even to the sacrifice of his son, was the law of Abraham's life. He did what God asked; he dared to trust God to do what he asked.

Why did Moses have such power in prayer? He too had forsaken all for God, counting the reproach of Christ greater riches than all the treasures of Egypt. He lived at God's disposal: "as a servant he was faithful in all his house." How often it is written of him, "According to all that the Lord commanded Moses, so did he." No wonder he was so bold; his heart was right with God: he knew God would hear him. No less is this true of Elijah, the man who stood up to plead with the God of Israel. *The man who is ready to risk all for God can count upon God to do all for him.*

It is as men live that they pray. It is the life that prays. It is the life that, with wholehearted devotion, gives up all for God and to God that can claim all from God. Our God longs exceedingly to prove himself the faithful God and mighty helper of His people. He only waits for hearts wholly turned from the world to himself, and open to receive His gifts.

It is only as our own wills, and strength, and effort, and pleasure, even where it appears perfectly natural and sinless, is cut down, so that the whole energies of our being are free and open to receive the sap of the heavenly Vine, the Holy Spirit, that we shall bear much fruit. It is in the surrender of what nature holds fast, it is in the full and willing submission to God's holy pruning knife that we shall come to what Christ chose and appointed us for—to bear fruit that whatsoever we ask the Father in Christ's name, He may give it to us.

—*Andrew Murray*

May 27

And Hezekiah . . . spread it before the Lord.—Isaiah 37:14

Those who come to God must "believe that he is, and that he is a rewarder of them that diligently seek him." Hezekiah was one who believed that God *is*. Even his enemies could not help but see that he professed unbounded confidence in God. "Let not your God," said they, "in whom you trust deceive you."

Hezekiah's perfect trust in the Lord led him to place his difficulty in God's hands. He "received the letter from the hand of the messengers and read it, and then went up to the temple and spread it before the Lord."

This, too, must be our strategy: lay all matters before God with implicit faith and confidence that He will undertake for us.

Next comes Hezekiah's prayer. He knew how to pray; he had often prayed before, both in times of gladness and sadness. In his prayer we are able to see how he desired victory only for God's glory: "Save us," said he, "that all the kingdoms of the earth may know that thou art the Lord."

Such a prayer immediately reached the ear and heart of God, and the prophet was commissioned at once to go to him and say: "Thus saith the Lord . . . whereas thou hast prayed to me . . . I will defend this city to save it." Thus God not only heard the king's prayer, but also gave him a glorious and speedy answer.

Let me learn from Hezekiah's conduct:

(1) To live for God and trust Him at all times.

(2) Whenever trials and difficulties are permitted to cross my path, to "spread" them at once before the Lord.

(3) Desire blessing on my life and victory all along the line, entirely and only for God's glory.

Then may I expect at all times both His presence and His blessing.　　　　　　　　　　　　　　　　　　—*John Roberts*

May 28

When thou prayest, enter into thy closet, and when thou hast shut thy door, pray to thy Father which is in secret.
—Matthew 6:6

In our word for today we have one of our Lord's plainest and most significant instructions about the manner and the nature of prayer. He is speaking, not of public prayer, as when the minister leads the congregation, but of personal prayer, when the child of God wants to talk to his Father of his own affairs and lay at His feet his own individual burdens. We should seek to be alone in all such praying. Other presences about us disturb our thoughts and restrict our freedom. So we are to go into our closet and shut the door.

This shutting of the door is significant in several ways. It shuts the world out. It secures us against interruption. It ought to shut out worldly thoughts and cares and distractions as well as worldly presences. Wandering in prayer is usually one of our sorest troubles. Shutting the door also shuts us in, and this also is important and significant. It shuts us in alone with God. No eye but His sees us as we bow in the secrecy. No ear but His hears us as we pour out our heart's feelings and desires. Thus we are helped to realize that with God alone have we to do, that He alone can help us. As we are shut up alone *with* God, so also are we shut up *to* God. There is precious comfort in the assurance that when we thus pray we are not talking into the air. There is an ear to hear, though we can see no presence, and it is the ear of our Father. This assures us of loving regard in heaven, also of prompt and gracious answer. —*J. R. Miller*

May 29

And when he had sent the multitudes away, he went up into a mountain apart to pray: and when the evening was come, he was there alone.—Matthew 14:23

The primary purpose of Christ in seeking a place to pray seems to have been that He might be alone with God. The mountains were His "secret" place. Further than this, the mountains, in their majesty, seem to bring God wonderfully near to us, and us wonderfully near to God. And it may have been that Jesus felt this, too. At any rate, He sought their quietude and their majesty, and there poured out His soul to His Father, and there received sustaining grace.

There is doubtless a sense in which we can find a solitary place in our crowded streets, but it is well to follow Christ's example literally and get alone with God. If you have never known what it is to kneel down in the woods where no human voice could be heard, or beneath a tree in the silent starlight, and look up with open eyes toward the face of God, you have missed a blessing that cannot be described, but that every child of God should know.

If we commune with God more and more, His beauty will illumine and reflect itself in our lives. Moses' very face shone because He had been with God. So will our lives shine with heavenly glow and glory if we habitually walk and talk with God. —R. A. Torrey

May 30

I have heard thy prayer.—2 Kings 20:5

"The power of prayer!" exclaims the unbeliever with a skeptical sneer. But the good soldier of Jesus Christ replies, from a happy heartfelt experience: "Thank God for the privilege of prayer!" Many a time troubled warriors have fallen upon their knees with hearts full of sadness, but risen to their feet strengthened and filled with gladness. Hezekiah was one who knew the value and the power of this divine art. He had learned *how* to pray and to *whom* to pray. But multitudes since his day have learned the same.

Weak in the body and sad in heart, John Roberts was seated on a stool in a prison cell for Christ's sake. These words of Joseph's, when he was in prison, came to him, "Bring me out of this...dungeon" (Gen. 40:14, 15). He had been longing for liberty, and felt somewhat condemned for his impatience when he came across Joseph's words, and saw that, though Joseph was determined at all costs to do right, he had no love for the prison, but prayed to his friend to bring him "out." Roberts then saw clearly that Joseph preferred liberty to imprisonment, but preferred imprisonment to grieving God or ceasing to do his duty both to God and man.

Though the prison gate was closed, the gate of heaven opened wide. At the throne of grace Roberts knelt and prayed in tears for help. He arose from prayer, and, opening a small Bible, read the words: "I have heard thy prayer, I have seen thy tears; behold, I will heal thee."

The words came as a message from the skies. The cell was filled as with the presence of God, and the enemy of souls, for the time being, was gone. Thank God for the privilege of prayer! "Man is born unto trouble," but those who pray will never die of a broken heart. When trouble comes they hear God's voice, "Call upon me," and as they call they obtain deliverance and go on their way glorifying God. The Lord teach us more and more the divine art of prayer!

May 31

Hereby perceive we the love of God, because he laid down his life. . . . —1 John 3:16

We have to turn to the work of Christ, and especially His death, if we would estimate the love of God. The most wonderful revelation of that divine heart lies in the gift of Jesus Christ. The apostle bids me, "Behold what manner of love. . . ." and I turn to the cross and see there a love which shrinks not from sacrifice, but gives "Him up to death for us all." I see there a love not in response to my own lovableness, but a love that comes from the depth of His own infinite being who loves because He must, because He is God. So, streaming through the darkness of that awful day on the cross, and speaking to me even in the awful silence in which the Son of Man died there for sin, I "behold," and I hear the "manner of love that the Father hath bestowed on us." Undeserved and Infinite, boundless and endless, immeasurable and transcendent—the love of God to me in Jesus Christ my Saviour.

Similarly, if we would estimate the "manner of this love," we have to think of the divine life like His own which comes to us as a gift of His sacrifice. Bestowing this love upon us is not altogether the same as simply loving us; there is a greater depth in it than that. Paul speaks of it as "the love of God shed abroad in our hearts" by the Spirit which is given to us. At all events this communication of divine life, which is after all divine love—for God's life is God's love—is His great gift to men.

The gift of Christ and the gift of His Spirit are one gift, embracing all that the world needs. Christ *for* us and *in* us must both be taken into account if you would estimate the manner of the love that God has bestowed upon us.

—Alexander Maclaren

June 1

In Christ shall all be made alive.—1 Corinthians 15:22

If I have Christ I have no other need.

We strive for things. Help us, O Christ, to strive for Thee.

Christ is truth. The knowledge learned at the fountain of man's wisdom is uncertain, variable, and does not satisfy. He who has Christ has truth, the basis of all proper approach to life's perplexities. No falsehood is found in Christ.

Christ is eternal. Changeableness is written on all the universe. Christ is ever changeless. Nowhere but in Christ can the soul bathe in the warm sunlight of eternalness.

Christ is the way—the way out of the confusion of my own self-efforts. The way to God. The way to peace and deliverance for man. The way from sin to holiness, from bondage to freedom, from darkness to light—and there is no other way.

Christ is hope—without His sweeping promises life is desolate, the future filled with dark misgivings. Because He told of the Father's many-mansioned home a rainbow arches the sky. Because He declared, "I will come again and receive you unto myself; that where I am, there ye may be also," I face the uncharted future unafraid.

Our hope is not soldiers but salvation; not a great supply of well-trained scientists but a great number of praying saints; not regimenation but regeneration through Christ. The hope of the world on every level of its existence is Christ Jesus the Lord.

Christ is rest for the weary, strength for the weak, light for the confused, comfort for the bereaved, companionship for the lonely. Christ is all in all. In a world that is seeking gluttonusly for things, seek Christ. You will discover Him to be the foundation of peace, the river of pure pleasure, the joy that abides when all things temporary are swept away.—*O. G. Wilson*

June 2

He shall not be afraid of evil tidings: his heart is fixed, trusting in the Lord.—Psalm 112:7

Here is a man whom we may call the lord of circumstance. He does not feel that the end has come when some threatening rumor reaches his ears. He is not the victim of panic, he is not the bondslave of paralyzing fear. He is calm, self-possessed and quietly confident. What is the secret of his strength and assurance?

"His heart is fixed." This is the first part of his great secret. His heart no longer wanders. It has settled down, and has resolved to put life to the proof in one supreme test. And that must be our secret, too. There are some souls who are always on the road. They are vagrants. They spend a night with Theosophy, then a night with Christian Science, then a night with New Thought, then a night with Spiritualism, then a night with Jesus Christ, then—so on and on! One never knows their spiritual address. But this man of the Psalm had ceased his flirtations with everything and everyone. His heart was fixed. He had settled down.

"Trusting in the Lord." That was the second part of his great secret. God could be trusted, and he would trust Him! That was the home of his soul where his heart was stayed. All his thinkings about everything began with God, who supplied the major premise in all his reasonings. His confidence rested in God; there he made his rest. In the hurricane of circumstances he hears the still, small voice. In the threatening furnace he sees one like unto the Son of Man. And therefore he is not "afraid of evil tidings." —*J. H. Jowett*

June 3

Weeping may endure for a night, but joy cometh in the morning. —Psalm 30:5

David, the sweet Psalmist, seems to be echoing the message of his beloved Psalm 23 in the words of this Psalm. It is a fact of life that the child of God must travel the valley of the shadow of death on his triumphant way to eternal life. But life will inevitably follow hard upon the heels of death, as inevitably as day succeeds night. Later in the Psalm David expresses this truth in a different way: "Thou hast turned . . . my mourning into dancing; thou hast put off my sackcloth, and girded me with gladness" (v. 11).

This truth is taught elsewhere in the Scriptures as well. In 1 Kings 17:14, Elijah tells the widow of Zarephath: "The barrel of meal shall not waste, neither shall the cruse of oil fail. . . ." Outwardly, the situation for this poor widow looked pretty bleak. But the love of God shines through the circumstances, like sunlight filtering through a cloud, and suddenly it breaks forth into glorious beaming light to bathe the believer in its warmth. God's barrel is bottomless, never failing; the supply of His meal is measureless, never ending.

Christian, if you believe this, it will make a difference in your life. It will add a dimension to your joy in spite of circumstances, an aura of serenity in a chaotic and restless world. The Source of that joy is both inside and outside the believer. The Spirit within causes the joy to flow out; the glory of God outside saturates the believer in His peace.

June 4

If any man thirst, let him come unto me and drink. — John 7:37

Every word here is full of meaning. "If" marks the one condition to which the Savior's invitation is addressed. Of course if we do not thirst, we will not care to come to the well and drink. Souls are dying all about us, not because there is no water near, but because they are not thirsty. Intense thirst is a pitiable condition; but the lack of soul-thirst is infinitely more pitiable: it is hopeless. The words "any man" show us how universal is our Lord's invitation. The cry was not to "any Jew," nor to "any man of good character," but to "*any* man." No one is left out.

The word "thirsty" describes the need which Christ is able to supply. It is not bodily thirst, but thirst of the soul, which He offers to quench. For the soul as well as the body has its thirsts, and there is no spring of earth at which they can be satisfied.

The words "let him come" show us the gate to the fountain flung wide open. There is no barrier in the way. "Let him come" reminds us, however, that if we would have our thirst quenched by Christ we must really come to Him. We must leave our dry wastes, where no water is, and come to Christ. We cannot find Christ while we are still in our sins.

The word "drink" tells us that we must receive Christ himself into our hearts if we would have our thirst satisfied in Him. Merely going to a spring and looking at its sparkling waters will never quench anyone's thirst; we must drink of the waters. So, looking at Christ is not enough to bless us; we must take Him into our life and let His Spirit fill our hearts. This new picture of Christ presents Him as a great well in the desert. The water gushes from a cleft in the rock. We understand the meaning of the cleft—Jesus died that there might be water for our soul's thirst.   —*J. R. Miller*

June 5

The living God, who giveth us richly all things to enjoy.
—1 Timothy 6:17

The apostle, we see from the context, charges Timothy to warn those of their peril "who are rich in this world." Charge them, he says, "not to be highminded." Pride may be found without wealth; but it is hard to have wealth without pride. Instead of trusting in wealth, the apostle would say, "Let us trust in the living God, to whom all riches belong, and who is the giver of every good gift.

"It is He who gives us richly all things to enjoy. It is God's will, therefore, that we should accept His gifts—earthly as well as spiritual—and enjoy them as bestowed by His loving hand."

"All things are yours," says the same apostle in another epistle (1 Cor. 3:21).

"Trust in the living God" is the mark of the true disciple (1 Tim. 4:10).

How often we forget that the God who has redeemed our souls and supplies our spiritual needs is the God who bestows all our temporal blessings!

He gives us all things to *enjoy*. God delights in the happiness of His children. It is when they take His gifts and forget the God who gave them that His name is dishonored.

—*Evan H. Hopkins*

June 6

Seek ye me and ye shall live. —Amos 5:4

The dangers of seeking places of blessing is very prevalent. Bethel, for instance, was the place of divine blessing historically; it was there Abraham built an altar to the Lord, there Jacob had visions of God. What place could be more suitable to seek than Bethel, there to have the spirit of communion revived and quickened by sweet and divine meditation? And yet God says in verse 5, "But seek not Bethel, nor enter into Gilgal." Gilgal was the place of the first encampment of the children of Israel after crossing the Jordan; what could be better after sanctification than to return in memory to the place of our first encampment in the promised land? Yet God says to "pass not to Beersheba." Beersheba was the place of wonderful refreshing; Abraham dwelt there; Hagar was relieved there; Jacob was comforted there. What could be better than a pilgrimage back to our "Beershebas"? The place where outcasts have been received, the discouraged encouraged, the failures revived and made successes? Yet God says no.

At first reading of these verses one might wonder what their message is when applied spiritually, and yet very little attention will reveal that it is the old story that it is the Lord himself and not the places of blessing the children of God are to seek. The place of former victories for God, the place that was heaven on earth in days gone by, will be places of defeat and failure if you persist in going there as a means of reviving. The message of God is, "Seek ye me, and ye shall live." It is the message that runs all through God's Book and all through the experiences of the saint's life.

I wonder how many of us are trying to haunt places instead of seeking the Lord? There are places of revival to which the people of God take pilgrimages and spend hours and days and weeks there, trying to get a jaded life back again into communion with God, trying to revive by meditation and the power of association what can never be made alive apart from the living presence of God himself. God is not confined to places, and where He once blessed, He may not bless again; it depends on the motive in seeking it.

"Seek ye me and ye shall live." Oh, the joy of that life with God and in God and for God! It takes a sharp discipline to learn that "my goal is God himself, not joy nor peace, or even blessing, but himself, my God." —*Oswald Chambers*

June 7

But rather seek ye the kingdom of God; and all these things shall be added unto you. —Luke 12:31

"Happiness in this world," wrote Nathaniel Hawthorne, "when it comes, comes incidentally. Make it the object of pursuit and it leads us on a wild goose chase, and is never attained. Follow some other object and very possibly we may find that we have caught happiness without dreaming of it."

Real happiness, enduring happiness, can be found only in the soul's right relationship to God. This is the sole source of true happiness, and it may be discovered by all, for all are welcome to return to the Father's house "where there is bread and to spare."

If you would be happy, "seek ye first the kingdom of God," emphasizes Matthew (6:33) in his parallel text to our verse for today. Happiness is like a bottle of rare perfume. Its aroma permeates the atmosphere until all who come in contact with it enjoy its fragrance. Some seem to think that happiness lies in the bottom of a bottle, that it can be prescribed by doctors and dispensed by druggists. This is the day when we try to fight our way to peace, buy our way to eternity, drink our way to pleasure, and force God to do our bidding by putting Him in some kind of a box. Many feel that just a few more pay increases will put them where they want to be and assure them of lasting happiness.

Pascal said, "Happiness is neither within us nor without us. It is in the union of our selves with God." Lincicome pointed out, "Happiness is the greatest paradox in nature. It can grow in any soil, live under any conditions. It defies environment. The reason for this is that it does not come from without but from within. Whenever you see a person seeking happiness outside himself, you can be sure he has never yet found it."

Yes, happiness is a very elusive thing. Yet it can be found in the simplest places; it knocks at our very door, but we do not recognize it. It is not free, yet we cannot buy it. But true happiness is a by-product of our wholehearted search for "the kingdom of God."

June 8

My soul followeth hard after thee; thy right hand upholdeth me. —Psalm 63:8

The word translated "followeth" here literally means to "cleave," or to "cling." And there is a beautiful double idea of a twofold relationship expressed in that somewhat unusual expression, "cleave after thee," the former word giving the idea of union and possession, the latter suggesting the other idea of search and pursuit: so that the two main currents of thoughts in the psalm are repeated in that little phrase. And verse 1, "My soul thirsts for thee"; here "the soul cleaveth after"—both expressive of pursuit, but the latter speaks of a profounder possession and a less sense of want.

"My soul cleaveth after God." That is to say, inasmuch as He is infinite, this nature of mine is finite. Each new possession of Him will open the elastic walls of my heart so that they will enclose a wider space and be capable of holding more of God, and therefore I shall possess more. Desire expands the heart; possession expands the heart. More of God comes when we can hold more of Him.

The world's gifts never satisfy; God satisfies and never cloys. If we are His children, we have the double delight of a continual fruition and a continued desire. So we shall ascend, if I may so say, in ever higher and higher spirals, which will rise further and draw in more closely toward the unreached and unatainable—Christ himself.

Then there is pictured here very beautifully the cooperation and reciprocal action of the seeking soul and the sustaining God. We hold and we are held. We hold because we are held, and we are held while we hold. We follow, and yet He is with us; we long, and yet we possess; we pursue and yet in the very act of pursuit we are upheld by His hand. We follow only because He holds us up. He will not hold us up unless we follow. Here all controversies of grace and free will are reconciled.

—*Alexander Maclaren*

June 9

He maketh my feet like hinds' feet.—2 Samuel 22:34

It is said that the feet of the hind are so constructed that she is able to run anywhere, stand everywhere, and slip nowhere. When she wishes to scale the mountaintops, she can go dashing along with the greatest ease, and stand upon the highest point without the slightest danger of either falling or slipping.

King David had been brought through so many dangers that when he remembered how "the Lord had delivered him out of the hand of his enemies," his heart overflowed with gratitude, and he "spake unto the Lord the words of this song." Again and again throughout the song he speaks as a soldier:

"By thee," says he, "I have run through a troop."

"By my God have I leaped over a wall."

"He teacheth my hands to war, so that a bow of steel is broken by mine arms."

"Thou hast given me the shield of thy salvation" and "thou

hast girded me with strength to battle."

What a picture of one of God's soldiers clothed with armor provided by Jehovah. It is our privilege also to be good soldiers of Jesus Christ, to "put on the whole armor of God," so that our heads are covered with the "helmet of salvation," our heart preserved with "the breastplate of righteousness," and our "feet shod with the preparation of the gospel of peace." Then indeed will they become like unto "hinds' feet," and we shall be able to run in the way of God's commandments without slipping or falling all the way.   *—John Roberts*

June 10

He uncovers the deeps out of darkness, and brings deep darkness to light.—Job 12:22 (RSV)

But a man may be in darkness, and yet in motion toward the light. I was in the darkness of the subway, and it was close and oppressive, but I was moving toward the light and fragrance of the open country. I entered into a tunnel in the Black Country in England, but the motion was continued, and we emerged amid fields of loveliness. And therefore the great thing to remember is that God's darknesses are not His goals; His tunnels are means to get somewhere else. Yes, His darknesses are appointed ways to His light. In God's keeping we are always moving, and we are moving towards Emmanuel's land, where the sun shines, and the birds sing night and day.

There is no stagnancy for the God-directed soul. He is ever guiding us, sometimes with the delicacy of a glance, sometimes with the firmer ministry of a grip, and He moves with us always, even through "the valley of the shadow of death." Therefore, be patient, my soul! The darkness is not your place, the tunnel is not your abiding home! He will bring you out into a large place where you will know "the liberty of the glory of the children of God."   *—J. H. Jowett*

June 11

Blessed are they that mourn: for they shall be comforted.
—Matthew 5:4

We do not usually regard sorrowing people as blessed. Here, however, is a special beatitude for mourners. Probably Jesus meant particularly penitent mourners. In all this world there is nothing so precious before God as tears of contrition; no diamonds or pearls shine with such brilliance in His sight. It was Jesus himself who said there is joy in the presence of the angels of God over one sinner that repents. Truly blessed, therefore, are those who in true penitence grieve over their sins; a holy light from heaven shines upon all such mourners. They are comforted with God's pardon and peace.

But no doubt the beatitude also refers to those children of God who are in sorrow, from whatever cause. Blessing is never nearer to us than when we are in affliction. If we do not get it, it is because we will not receive it. Some day we shall see that we have gotten our best things from heaven, not in the days of our earthly joy and gladness, but in the times of trial and affliction. Tears are lenses through which our dim eyes see more deeply into heaven and look more fully upon God's face than in any other way. Sorrows cleanse our hearts of earthliness and fertilize our lives.

The days of pain really do far more for us than the days of rejoicing. We grow best when clouds hang over us, because clouds bear rain and rain refreshes. Then God's comfort is such a rich experience that it is well worthwhile to endure trial, just to enjoy the sweet and precious comfort God gives in it. But to receive from our sorrows their possibilities of blessing, we must accept the affliction as a messenger from God, and pray for true comfort—not the mere drying of our tears, but grace to profit by our affliction, and to get from it the peaceable fruit of righteousness.　　　—*J. R. Miller*

June 12

For as the rain cometh down ... from heaven, and ...
watereth the earth ... that it may give seed to the sower
and bread to the eater. ... —Isaiah 55:10

God's Word is a seed. The "seed-thought" idea is one that preachers and evangelists need to remember. We imagine we have to plough the field, sow the seed, reap the grain, bind it into sheaves, put it through the threshing machine, make the bread—all in one discourse. "For herein is the saying true, One soweth, and another reapeth," said our Lord.

Let each one be true to the calling given him by God. The truth is we don't believe God can do His work without us. We are so anxious about the Word, so anxious about the people who have accepted the Word. We need not be; if we have preached what is a word of God, it is not our business to apply it; the Holy Spirit will apply it. Our duty is to sow the Word, see that it is the Word of God we preach and not "huckster" it with other things, and God says it will prosper whereunto He sends it.

In some cases it will be a savor of life unto life; in others, a savor of death unto death. But rest assured that no individual and no community is ever the same after listening to the Word of God. It profoundly alters life.

The force and power of a word of God will work and work and bring forth fruit after many days. Hence the necessity of revising much of what we preach and what we say in meetings. God has not said that the relating of my experiences will not return unto Him void; He says, "My word shall not return unto me void." Every temptation to exalt the human experience ... will fall short. The only thing that prospers in God's hands is His own Word.

"As the rain that cometh down from heaven, so shall my word be." Thank God for the sweet and radiant aspect of the falling of rain from heaven; after a time of drought it is almost impossible to describe its beauty. So when the Word of God comes to a soul after a time of difficulty and perplexity, it is almost impossible to tell the ineffable sweetness of that word as it comes with the unction of the Holy Spirit. —*Oswald Chambers*

June 13

Grow in grace, and in the knowledge of our Lord and Saviour, Jesus Christ.—2 Peter 3:18

The Bible is a garden book. There's one at the beginning, a better one at the end, and the Gethsemane garden in between. Every man should be a gardener, and his life the garden. There's sowing and sunshine, dewfall and rain, and special watering in dry spells. Then there's weeding, watching for hurtful insects, and pruning, a cutting back to get better fruit. Let's be good gardeners, with the Man of Gethsemane to help.

Evil, like weeds, grows rank and fast without cultivation, we *think*. But it isn't so. There's another gardener, a special, unseen gardener for evil. He sows, and waters, and cultivates, and tries to weed out the good. He's an old hand at gardening. He stays up nights, watching for chances. We must fight him. The best way is to get our crop in *first*; weed and work it sleeplessly. The best work in this garden is done down on your knees. —*S. D. Gordon*

June 14

Know ye that the Lord he is God: it is he that hath made us, and not we ourselves; we are his people, and the sheep of his pasture.—Psalm 100:3
But now, O Lord, thou art our father; we are the clay, and thou our potter; and we all are the work of thy hand.—Isaiah 64:8

Have you ever observed an artist at work? I watched a chalk artist one night in church—and learned a striking spiritual lesson that wasn't a part of his excellent presentation.

He began with the background! For the first several minutes he was busily smearing his easel with a veritable rainbow of colors, blending them together until suddenly I saw a beautiful sunset sky emerging from the seeming chaos of color. His next step was to insert several harsh black lines in the foreground. These slowly took shape as mountains. Skillfully blending his colors, he began to add dimension to his landscape, even adding a quiet lake at the bottom of his picture, which reflected all the glorious color he had already laid on his canvas. By the time he completed his picture, I was a part of it, so closely did I watch.

God is the divine Artist of our lives, and they will not be completed until He adds the final touch of color, the last detail, as did my artist friend at his chalkboard. We are God's canvas, and our task is simply to receive the colors He has designed for us—the darks and the lights, the somber and the bright. Some of the details may seem meaningless until the last colors are added, but someday we will see it all—our life painting completed by the Master Artist. Only then will we see the reason for the dark background—perhaps as a contrast to the final brilliant flourish of His brush as He completes His work and our lives culminate in His glorious presence.

June 15

I know whom I have believed. —2 Timothy 1:12

The apostle had become personally acquainted with his Lord, and this acquaintance filled him with perfect joy. He had no desire to boast of his parentage, position, training, or education. He had been brought to know Christ, and in Him he boasted all the day long.

Many persons love to glory in their circumstances, friends, home, family, or situation, but Paul had sufficient to do to glory in Christ Jesus. His heart was full of love to Christ, his mind was constantly occupied with the Lord Jesus, and his whole soul was continually going out after Him. So all his time, talents, influence, and powers were consecrated to Christ, and spent in making known Christ's love and power to save and keep. Paul knew what Christ could *do*, "who both saved us and called us with an holy calling," and therefore "He is able to keep."

Paul also knew the secret of Christ's keeping power: "He is able to keep that which I have committed unto him against that day." He committed himself entirely and eternally to Christ. He knew Christ could keep him, because he knew Christ possessed him. This committal of ourselves to Christ is *re-*

quired (Rom. 12:1). And the death of Christ has made it possible (Titus 2:14). Therefore, may my experience be as full of assurance as was Paul's, for Christ is equally able to keep me—if I am as fully committed unto Him—against that day as He was the apostle Paul.

> I know in whom I have believed,
>   Who, when this precious faith He gave,
> My soul, into His hands received,
>   And bade me trust His power to save.
>
> His Spirit doth my heart assure
>   That what I still to Him commend,
> His constant love shall keep secure
>   Till faith fulfilled in sight shall end.
>   —*John Roberts*

June 16

Search me, O God, and know my heart. —Psalm 139:23

It has been said that all deception begins with self-deception, and this is the very worst form of deception. "The heart is deceitful above all things, and desperately wicked, who can know it?" (Jer. 17:9).

We must beware of tricking ourselves into thinking we are wholly following the Lord when the facts are that there are wide areas of souls unsurrendered to God. We are tuned to detecting falsehood and insincerity in others and are often stone deaf to the discords in our own lives. Self-righteousness is a disabling disease, a vision-destroying malady. Our enemies could point out our failures but we would not listen to them. We would conclude they were prejudiced by their hatred. Our friends may see our inconsistencies, but they gloss over them, excuse them, and explain them as "just our way."

The writer of this beautiful Psalm, David, went to the right source to have the fallacies of his inner life exposed. The soul that God searches stands on the threshhold of new discoveries and adventures with God.

"The God of all grace" will search out ways to bring into the soul new revelations of His grace. He will point out the leaks in the devotion through which worldly self-indulgence seeps into the soul to cool the ardor.

He will expose the tendency to ease and self-indulgence.

He will examine the excuses offered for our smallness of faith.

He will lead the soul to examine itself in the light which shines from Calvary, rather than in the light with which contemporary society examines itself.

Search me, O God!—the inner springs of my emotions, the

compelling impulses of my life. Let everyone who reads these words pray this prayer sincerely, honestly. Eternity will be richer for those who will thus pray. —O. G. Wilson

June 17

I will never leave thee, nor forsake thee.—Hebrews 13:5

This was a promise given by the Lord to more than one Old Testament saint (Gen. 27:15; Deut. 31:6, 8; Josh. 1:5; 1 Chron. 28:20). The inspired writer of the Epistle to the Hebrews has no hesitation, however, in applying the words to the needs of New Testament believers.

"Be content with such things as ye have: *for he hath said.*" It is the word that Jehovah has spoken that is the sure ground of our confidence. Resting on that foundation, we may add, "So that we may boldly say, The Lord is my helper, and I will not fear what man shall do unto me."

All spiritual blessings are comprehended in that one promise. Let our faith grasp that fact. Let us not only pray, "Lord, be Thou with me"; let us rise to the apprehension of the actual present reality, "Lord, Thou *art* with me!"

"Yea, though I walk through the valley of the shadow of of death, I will fear no evil: for thou art with me; thy rod and thy staff they comfort me" (Ps. 23:4). Such assurance equips me for whatever life—or death—can bring. Let me live in that assurance today and every day! —*Evan H. Hopkins*

June 18

For by grace have ye been saved through faith; and that not of yourselves: it is the gift of God.—Ephesians 2:8

No man can be saved by praying, by believing, by obeying, or by consecration; salvation is a free gift of God's almighty grace. We have the sneaking idea that we earn things and get into God's favor by what we do—by our praying, by our repentance. But the only way we get into God's favor is by the sheer gift of His grace. The first thing we consciously experience is a sense of underserving-ness, but it does take some of us a long while to know we don't deserve to be saved. "I really am sorry for what I have done wrong"; "I really am sick of myself"—if only I am sick enough of myself, I will be sick to death; I am driven to despair, I can do nothing; then I am exactly in the place where I can receive the overflowing grace of God. . . .

"God is able to make all grace abound unto you" (2 Cor. 9:8). In talking to people you will be amazed to find that they much more readily listen if you talk on the line of suffering, of the attacks of the devil. But get on the triumphant line of the apostle Paul, talk about the super-conquering life, about God making all His divine grace to abound and they lose interest. "That is all in the clouds," a sheer indication that they have never begun to taste the unfathomable joy awaiting them if they will only take it. All the great prevailing grace of God is ours by drawing on it, and it scarcely needs any drawing on; take out the stopper and it comes out in torrents. Yet we just manage to squeeze out enough grace for the day—"sinning in thought, word and deed every day"!

You don't find that note in the New Testament. We have to keep in the light, and the grace of God will supply supernatural life all the time. Thank God there is no end to His grace if we will keep in the humble place. The overflowing grace of God has no limits, and we have to set no limits to it, but "grow in grace, and in the knowledge of our Lord and Saviour, Jesus Christ." —Oswald Chambers

June 19

The grace of our Lord was exceeding abundant.— 1 Timothy 1:14

By definition, grace is "the unmerited love and favor of God toward man" and "divine influence acting in man to make him pure and morally strong." This grace was obviously operative in the life of the apostle Paul so that when he wrote to Timothy, he was not mouthing empty platitudes, but he was speaking from blessed experience, having walked with God through the ups and downs of life for many years. His first introduction to that grace had come on the Damascus road; his last earthly touch with it would come on the martyr's altar.

Grace is a frequent theme throughout Paul's writings. In the next verse (v. 15) he calls himself the "chief of sinners" and marvels that God would enter his life, causing an abrupt about-face, so that the chief of sinners would become the chief spokesman for the Christian faith in New Testament times (he's still pretty influential today). What an example of grace Paul himself was—and what encouragement he could give young Timothy because of his own remarkable experience of forgiveness on the basis of "unmerited favor." If ever anyone deserved God's judgment, that man was Paul. If ever any man experienced the apex of God's gracious favor, that man was Paul!

There is another side or facet of grace brought out in Webster's definition, however, and that is the active aspect, "divine influence acting in man to make him pure and morally strong."

Notice, however, that it is God's action *in* the believer, not the believer's action toward God. If we struggling Christians could only learn the lesson of surrender to God's activity in our lives, rather than trying to generate our own spirituality like high school students at a pep rally, complete with cheerleaders and pep band, what a difference it would make in our lives! We could experience serenity in the midst of the world's confusion and chaos. This is that ageless and endless "exceeding abundant" grace applied to the tumultuous twentieth century.

June 20

Blessed are they which do hunger and thirst after righteousness: for they shall be filled. —Matthew 5:6

It strikes us somewhat strangely at first that there should be a beatitude for dissatisfaction. We know that peace is promised the Christian, and peace is calm repose and satisfied restfulness. The words "hunger and thirst after righteousness" appear to suggest something incompatible with rest and peace. But when we think a little more deeply, we see that spiritual hunger must form a part of all true Christian experience. Hunger is a mark of health. It is so in physical life; the loss of appetite indicates disease. So a healthy mind is a hungry one; when one becomes satisfied with one's attainments, one ceases to grow. The same is true in spiritual life. If we become satisfied with our faith and love and obedience, and our communion with God, and our consecration to Christ, we have ceased to grow.

Invalids die often amid plenty—die of starvation; not because they can get no food, but because they have no appetite. There are many professing Christians who are starving their souls in the midst of abundance of spiritual provision because they have no hunger. There is nothing for which we should pray more earnestly and more sincerely than for spiritual longing and desire. It is indeed the very soul of all true prayer. It is the empty hand reached out to receive new and richer gifts from heaven. It is the heart's cry which God hears with acceptance and answers with more and more of life. It is the key which unlocks new storehouses of divine goodness and enrichment. Spiritual hunger is indeed nothing less than the life of God in the human soul, struggling to grow up in us into the fullness of the stature of Christ. Such spiritual hunger never fails of blessing. —*J. R. Miller*

June 21

Peace I leave with you, my peace I give unto you: not as the world giveth, give I unto you. —John 14:27

If we are really Christ's, then back into the very bosom of the Father where Christ is hidden, there will He carry us. We too shall look out and be as calm and as independent as He is. The needs of men will touch us just as keenly as they touch Him, but the sneers and gibes of men shall pass us by as they pass by Him and leave no mark on His unruffled life and spirit.

For us, just as for Him, this will not mean a cold and selfish separation from our brothers. We will be infinitely closer to their real life when we separate ourselves from their outside strifes and superficial pride, and know and love them truly by knowing and loving them in the Lord.

This is the power and progress of true Christianity. It leads us into, it abounds in peace. It is a brave, vigorous peace, full of life, full of interest and work. It is a peace that means thoroughness, that refuses to waste its force and time in little superficial tumults which come to nothing, while there is so much real work to be done, so much real help to be given, and such a real life to be lived with God. That peace, His peace, may Jesus give to us all. *—Phillips Brooks*

June 22

Jesus then took the loaves, and when he had given thanks, he distributed them to those who were seated; so also the fish, as much as they wanted. —John 6:11 (RSV)

The Lord who came to save His people was sensitive to His people's hunger. In the presence of the supreme need the smaller need was not forgotten. He knows the body as well as the soul. He ministers to the transient as well as the eternal. That is ever the characteristic of true kingliness; it has a kingly way of doing the smaller things. I can measure my own progress toward spiritual maturity by the importance I place on spiritual principles. "He that is faithful in that which is least, the same also is great."

The Lord is not oppressed by the multitude of His guests. "He himself knew what he would do." We need not jostle one another for His bounty. We shall not crowd one another out. "There is bread enough and to spare."

Even in the material realm this is true, and everybody would have his daily bread if the will of the Lord were done. There is no stinginess in the divine Host! It is the greed of the guests which mars the satisfaction of the feast.

Finally, notice how carefully the Lord of glory gathered up the fragments (v. 12). Our infinitely wealthy Lord does not throw things away. He does not waste bread. Can He afford to lose a soul? "He goes out after that which is lost until he finds it"!
—*J. H. Jowett*

June 23

Then the devil leaveth him, and behold, angels came and ministered unto him.—Matthew 4:11

While it is evident that in those terrible hours (of the Temptation) the whole nature of Jesus was submitted to a fearful struggle, and that, as not the least among the elements that made up the ordeal, His intellectual judgments were shaken, His knowledge of truth was invaded by tumultuous doubt, His sight of the Father was obscured—yet, at the last, and as the sum of all, the question was not one of intelligence but of will. It was a choice of obediences that made the real crisis.

This choice involved the rejection of Satan's "fall down and worship me," and the clear acceptance of "thou shalt serve the Lord thy God," that marked the victory. "Then the devil leaveth him, and behold, angels came and ministered unto him." The moment that the obedience of the life was established, the mental tumult settled into peace within it.
—*Phillips Brooks*

June 24

He came unto his own, and his own received him not.
—John 1:11

The picture here is of Christ coming with infinite grace to those He loved, to His own people, only to be rejected by them and turned away from their doors. This was one of the saddest aspects about the Saviour's mission to the world. He was the God of glory and of life; He came to bring heaven to earth: but when He stood at men's doors and knocked, the doors were kept closed to Him, and He had to turn away, taking with Him the precious gifts and blessings He had brought and wished to leave.

We say the Jews, "His own," were very ungrateful to treat their Messiah in this way; and also that their rejection was a terrible wrong to themselves, for they thrust away in Christ the most glorious things of heaven and eternity. But how is it with ourselves? Christ comes to us; He is continually coming. His hands are full of blessings; He has eternal life to give. Do we receive Him? Is it not true of us that He comes unto His own, and His own receive Him not?

Do we really take from the hand of Christ all that He

offers us? Do we not daily grieve Him and rob ourselves of blessings by refusing what He brings? Especially do we reject Christ often when He comes to us in the garb of pain or sorrow. Many times the blessings He brings to us then are the very richest and the most precious in all His store. But how many of us receive Christ gladly, and take the gifts from His hand as cheerfully and gratefuly when He comes in grief or suffering as when He comes in joy or worldly prosperity? Why not? Can we not trust His love and wisdom? He never sends pain unless pain is best. He never chastens unless there is a blessing in chastening. *—J. R. Miller*

June 25

But he knoweth the way that I take: when he hath tried me, I shall come forth as gold.... Take therefore no thought for the morrow; for the morrow shall take thought for the things of itself. Sufficient unto the day is the evil thereof.—Job 23:10; Matthew 6:34

If he had lived in a later day, Job would have affirmed the truth of Jesus' words in Matthew 6:34. It is vital to our emotional health (and physical as well) that we learn one all-important lesson: approach life "one day at a time." Don't get bogged down in needless worry about tomorrow. Earlier Jesus asked the probing question: "Which of you, by taking thought, can add one cubit to his stature?" (Matt. 6:27). If worry doesn't accomplish anything, why worry? Someone has said that 99 percent of the things we worry about never happen, and the other 1 percent aren't that important anyway!

God provides light enough for a day. If He gave more than that, the resulting heat from "double exposure" to sunlight would be too much for us to handle. Rest assured that God knows your need. He is as completely aware of what is happening to you as He was of every trouble that Job faced so courageously. Did God abandon Job in his trouble just because He allowed calamity to fall upon him? No, for His benign hand of blessing was continually upon Job as that good man underwent every test Satan could devise and took from him every material and familial advantage he had enjoyed.

As a result, Job came out of the testing fire "as gold" with all waste refined away, and only the purest metal remaining. It may be difficult to understand *why* a test comes your way, but never forget *what* the test is accomplishing: refining and purification. Determine to profit from the experience, learning from it rather than fighting it. This is what Job was concluding when he said, "When he hath tried me, I shall come forth as gold." That is reacting positively to testing, building on it rather than blasting it for interfering with life's joys.

The trials that come into the Christian's life are the fulfillment of God's gracious purpose as He seeks to build up His child in the most precious faith, developing in His loved one the Christlike spirit that leads to joy and "gold."

June 26

As thy days, so shall thy strength be. —Deuteronomy 33:25

There are two ways of reading these words. According to the common interpretation, they contain an assurance of strength proportioned to the need. Each day has its trials, difficulties, and demands; so for each day there is God's provision of strength. That strength will come as the day comes. Whatever kind of strength is wanted, that kind of strength shall be given. "As thy days so shall thy strength be."

But we may see another thought in the words. Observe that it is not written, "As thy day is . . . " but, "As thy *days*." That is, as your days increase, according to the number of your days, as you grow older. Now, what is the promise here given? It is an assurance of strength that brings out the contrast between the natural and the supernatural. According to natural experience, age brings with it weakness and infirmity. After a certain point in one's life, the older we are the feebler we become. But in the divine life, God promises that if our days are many, our strength shall be great. In other words, He promises that our spiritual strength shall increase with our days. —*Evan H. Hopkins*

June 27

As thy days, so shall thy strength be. —Deuteronomy 33:25

God does not give His grace as He gives His sunshine—pouring it out on all alike. He discriminates in spiritual blessings. He gives strength according to our need. His eye is ever on us in tender, watchful love, and what we need He supplies. He gives us grace for grace. When one grace is exhausted another is ready. The grace is always timely. It is not given in large store in advance of the need, but it is ready always on time. It may not always be what we wish, but it is always what we really need.

There is in the Bible no promise of grace in advance of the soul's need. God does not say He will put strength into our arm for the battle while we are in quiet peace and the battle is yet far off. When the conflict is at hand the strength will be given. He does not open the gates for us, nor roll away the stones, until we have come up to them. He did not divide the Jordan's waters while the people were yet in their camps, nor even as they began their march toward the river.

The wild stream continued to flow as the host moved down the banks, even until the feet of the priests had been dipped in the water. This is the constant law of divine help. It is not given in advance. As we come up to the need the supply is ready, but not before. Yet many Christians worry because they cannot see the way opened and the needs supplied far in advance of their steps. Shall we not let God provide and have faith in Him?　　　　　　　　　　　　　*—J. R. Miller*

June 28

Consider the lilies of the field, how they grow.—Matthew 6:28

What we all need is to "consider the lilies of the field" and learn their secret. Grow, by all means; but grow in God's ways, which is the only effectual way. See to it that you are planted in grace, and then let the divine Husbandman cultivate you in His own way and by His own means. Put yourself out in the sunshine of His presence, and let the dew of heaven come down upon you, and see what will be the result. Leaves, flowers, and fruit must surely come in their season. Only see to it that you oppose no hindrance to the shining of the Sun of Righteousness, or the falling of the dew from heaven. The thinnest covering may serve to keep off the sunshine and the dew, and the plant may wither, even where these are the most abundant. And so also the slightest barrier between your soul and God may cause you to dwindle and fade, as a plant in a cellar.

Keep the sky clear. Open wide every avenue of your being to receive the blessings your God may bring to bear upon you. Bask in the sunshine of His love. Drink the waters of His goodness. Keep your face upturned to Him, as the flowers do the sun. Look, and your soul shall live and grow.

To grow as do the lilies means an interior abandonment of the rarest kind. We are to be infinitely passive regarding ourselves, but infinitely active with regard to our attention and response to God. Self must step aside to let God do the work. Maybe you feel yourself planted in a desert soil where nothing can grow. Even so, trust fully in God, the divine Husbandman. He will make that very desert blossom as the rose and you "shall be as a tree planted by the waters . . . and shall not see when heat cometh . . . neither shall cease from yielding fruit."　　　　　　　　　*—Hannah Whitall Smith*

June 29

He that hath my commandments, and keepeth them, he it is that loveth me.—John 14:21

Yes, but how can I keep them? Someone sent me a bulb which requires a certain kind of soil, but he also sent me the soil in which to grow it. He sent instructions, but he also sent power. And when I am bidden to keep a commandment I feel as though I have received the bulb but not the soil! But is this God's way of dealing with His people? I will read on if perhaps I may find the gift of the soil.

"He that abideth in me . . . the same bringeth forth much fruit." That is the gift I seek. For the keeping of His commandments the Lord provides himself. I am not called upon to raise fruits out of the soil of my own will, out of my own infirmity of aspiration or desire. I can rest everything in God! I can "abide in Him," and I may have the holy energies of the Godhead to produce in me the fruits of a holy and obedient life. The good Lord provides both the bulb and the soil.

It is the tragedy of life that we forget this, and seek to make a soil-bed of our own. And thus do we experience the discouragement of fruitless labor, the heavy drudgery of tasks beyond our strength. "Come unto me, all ye that labour and are heavy laden, and I will give you rest."   —*J. H. Jowett*

June 30

As newborn babes, desire the sincere [pure, spiritual] milk of the word, that ye may grow thereby.—1 Peter 2:2

Peter is not trying here to spread some new doctrine in urging the Christians of his day to adopt a diet of spiritual milk. Jesus had said, probably in his hearing, "Whosoever shall not receive the kingdom of God as a little child, he shall not enter therein." However, there is a sense in which milk is for babies and not for mature Christians. As Paul points out, "I have fed you with milk and not with meat: for hitherto ye were not able to bear it, neither yet are ye able" (1 Cor. 3:2). And the writer to the Hebrews, in his early and able defense of the Christian faith, came down pretty hard on those early Christians when he wrote: "Of whom we have many things to say, and hard to be uttered, seeing ye are dull of hearing. For when for the time ye ought to be teachers, ye have need that one teach you again which be the first principles of the oracles of God; and are become such as have need of milk, and not of strong meat. For every one that useth milk is unskilful in the word of righteousness: for he is a babe. But strong meat belongeth to them that are of full age, even those who by reason of use have their senses exercised to discern both good and evil" (5:11-14).

A growing tree reaches up into the sky, and at the same time reaches out to the world around it. In a sense, this is what should happen to the growing Christian. In 2 Peter 3:18, Peter says: "But grow in grace, and in the knowledge of our Lord and Saviour Jesus Christ," and this speaks of our *upward* maturity. We are also admonished by Paul to "grow up into him in all things, which is the head, even Christ: from whom the whole body fitly joined together and compacted by that which every joint supplieth ... maketh increase of the body unto the edifying of itself in love" (Eph. 4:15, 16).

The agent of this growth is the Bible, the Word of God. Desire it!

July 1

But as for you, ye thought evil against me; but God meant it [for] good. —Genesis 50:20

I can empathize with Joseph in this statement to his brethren. Not long ago, my world seemed about to cave in around me. Men upon whom I had counted as "brethren in the Lord" seemed determined to ruin my life, to rob me of what had come to be a false sense of earthly security and spiritual blessing. My spiritual underpinnings were threatened and my first reaction was to complain to God about my lot, the poor deal I was getting. Hadn't I been faithful, doing my job as unto the Lord, carrying out my daily responsibilities with a certain degree of dedication? True, some of the enthusiasm and creativeness of my younger days had disappeared along with some of the energy of youth, but wasn't that to be expected? After all, along with "maturity" had come a certain feeling of accomplishment. But some of the magic was gone. I had lost it somewhere along the path to "security."

Do you know what happened when my spirits hit the bottom in the wake of real persecution? I turned to God with a greater sense of urgency and desperation than I had evidenced in many a year. And He answered. Out of the depths I cried unto Him, and He heard me! Among the exciting things that began to happen—this book came into being. Thrilling new insights into His Word and will became my almost daily companions. I, who had thought that life could no longer challenge and stir me, found my spiritual "batteries" being recharged, a youthful feeling of adventure and wonder being reborn within me. My creative spirit was revived and I wanted to make a contribution to those around me once again. I thank God that "He meant it for good." My valley experience led me back to the mountaintop again. What could have made me *bitter* has made me *better!* As John Greenleaf Whittier wrote:

So darkness in the pathway of Man's life
Is but the shadow of God's providence,
By the great Sun of Wisdom cast thereon;
And what is dark below is light in Heaven.

July 2

Ye are not as yet come to the rest and to the inheritance, which the Lord your God giveth you. —Deuteronomy 12:9

We miss the chief lesson of the passage if we take the inheritance to be mainly typical of heaven. It would be equivalent to saying to the child of God, "You have not as yet entered into heaven." But this would carry with it no particular lesson.

Rather, regard these privileges as representing the blessings that belong to the believer *now*; they are intended for his *present* realization. Then we see at once that the passage opens up to us a subject of great practical importance. God has not only called us out of bondage, but into liberty; not only out of poverty, but into wealth. He has redeemed us to enter into the land of plenty by faith now. It is emphatically the land of rest.

Though we have come out of bondage, there is a danger that we should come short of entering into His rest. Many things belong to the soul redeemed and delivered, of which he has not yet taken possession, though God has already given them. What he has to do is go up and by faith enter into them (2 Pet. 1:3; Deut. 1:21).

Hebrews 4:3 points out, "We which have believed do enter into rest." The RSV translated it *"that* rest." It is not heaven, let us bear in mind; it is not by *faith* that we enter into heaven. But there is a rest that remains to us who have come out of Egypt, which we may now enter into by faith. It lies between us and glory.

Not all those Israelites who came out of Egypt entered into the promised land. Not all who have been delivered from the authority of darkness have entered into the rest spoken of here. It is to Christians this privilege belongs; it is in this that Christians are in danger of falling short. God has provided it for them. He has already bestowed it; but because of unbelief they are kept out of it.

What is this rest? Not something negative, merely deliverance—but something positive, satisfaction in God. It is God's own rest. Not a mere spiritual luxury, but the essential condition of all consistent walking, all sound judgment, and all effective service. God's rest is the center of all true action and the spring of all victorious power. —*Evan H. Hopkins*

July 3

The ark of the covenant of the Lord went before them . . . to search out a resting place for them. —Numbers 10:33

After we are brought to know the blessings of deliverance, we are then ready to learn the secret of guidance. How wonderful is the sight here presented to us! Instead of Israel seeking to find a resting place for God, it is God who would find a resting place for them. Shelter and guidance were here provided for His redeemed people.

"The cloud of the Lord was upon them by day, when they went out of the camp." They were thus protected from the scorching rays of the midday sun. And "the ark of the covenant of the Lord went before them" in order to show them the path of His will. They were not left to choose their own way, or to use their own wisdom in discovering God's way. The symbol of the divine presence preceded them. They had but to follow.

So it is with God's children today. He who died to redeem, now lives to lead and direct. He seeks for us continually not merely places of safety, but of "rest." He is concerned in the welfare of His people and delights in their comfort and joy. —*Evan H. Hopkins*

July 4

I will instruct thee and teach thee in the way which thou shalt go: I will guide thee with mine eye. —Psalm 32:8

Reading this passage in the King James Version, one is impressed with the majestic cadence of these sentences, but puzzled by the real meaning of "I will guide thee with mine eye." Here is the way the RSV renders it: "I will counsel you with my eye upon you." Sounds a little more contemporary, doesn't it? Looking at some of David's other references to God's guiding activity in the Christian's life opens up other facets of this exciting truth:

"Good and upright is the Lord; therefore he instructs sinners in the way" (Ps. 25:8).

"Behold, the eye of the Lord is on those who fear him, on those who hope in his steadfast love" (Ps. 33:18).

In this complex and troubled world, we desperately need guidance—guidance that includes "counsel." In fact, human counselors have never been busier than they are today—and more subject to error when they ignore the spiritual dimension. What greater Guide and Counselor could we ask for than God himself, who over and over in His Word expresses His willingness to guide and care for His children? Guidance includes the concept of trust, for a guide will do us no good if we do not take him at his word and follow him unquestioningly. St. Augustine said: "Beware of despairing about yourself; you are commanded to trust in God, and not in yourself." Thomas Benton Brooks adds a contemporary dimension when he points out: "We trust as we love, and where we love. If we love Christ much, surely we will trust Him much."

Where is your trust today? If it is in the divine Guide, you will enjoy divine guidance!

July 5

Then said she, Sit still, my daughter. . . . —Ruth 3:18

The habit of reckoning on Christ is the key to a restful life. Not only to depend on His promises, but also to count on himself. A good man, one of those for whom some would even dare to die, is more than his words or assurances, because a case may arise not covered by either of them, and then we can fall back on what we know him to be. Christ is more than His spoken and recorded words. Boaz, in the story of Ruth, is a picture of our Kinsman-Redeemer, Jesus Christ. Just as Boaz turned Ruth's bitterness into blessing, so Christ does for His redeemed children.

Is there some great perplexity in your life? Is there a lurking evil in your life, which you have tried in vain to defeat? Is there some anxiety about one dearer to you than life, who is drifting beyond your reach? Is there a yearning for all that can be realized of deliverance from sin, the filling of the Spirit, the life and love of God? Go to the great Kinsman, find Him when you can speak to Him without interruption, tell Him everything. Hand it all over to Him, then go home and sit still.

If there is anything for you to do, He will tell you what it is, and give you the grace to do it. But if not, sit still, wait patiently, quiet yourself. He cannot forget, He will not procrastinate, He cannot fail. He is allowing no grass to grow under His feet. He is making haste, though He appears to tarry. And presently at the door there will be a shout of joy. Then the bridal bells shall ring out over an accomplished purpose, and your life shall be no more Marah, but Naomi, and bitterness shall be swallowed up in blessing. —*F. B. Meyer*

July 6

God hath not given us the spirit of fear; but of power
... love, and a sound mind. —2 Timothy 1:7

"The only thing we have to fear is fear itself." So said the late President Franklin D. Roosevelt in his first inaugural address. Consciously or not, he was echoing Paul's words of warning to his spiritual son, Timothy. Fear causes most of the emotional (and many of the physical) problems so prevalent in our world today—not the least of which is that sickness, that instability of mind so characteristic of modern life.

The stresses of modern life are a shocking seedbed for sick minds. However, those minds which are "stayed" or solidly based on the Lord Jesus Christ are sound and healthy because of their relatedness to Him. Isaiah says, "Thou wilt keep him in perfect peace, whose mind is *stayed* on thee; because he trusteth in thee" (26:3). The healthy mind described here to Timothy by Paul was also "stayed" on the Lord.

Elsewhere in the New Testament James says of the mind of man, "A double-minded man is unstable in all his ways" (James 1:8). He contrasts the "sound mind" with the "double mind," and labels the individual so afflicted as "unstable," the very opposite of "sound."

There is a unity about the descriptions of sound minds in the New Testament. Jesus Christ promises us that if we love the Lord our God with all our minds, healthiness (singleness) of mind will be the result (Matt. 22:37; Mark 12:30; Luke 10:27). In the face of this overwhelming evidence on the side of the Christian's secret of a sound mind, we as children of our heavenly Father should enjoy real mental health; ours should be a life of spiritual power exercised in a spirit of love, that spirit which characterized our Savior. If we are plagued with some of the sickness saturating our world, we need to get back to the heaven-sent message of freedom from fear that Paul proclaimed to Timothy. All Christians are called upon to live for Christ in a world which so desperately needs Him! Put that power to work in your life.

July 7

For whatsoever is born of God overcometh the world: and this is the victory that overcometh the world, even our faith.—1 John 5:4

You can be victorious. Does that seem impossible? It is not. You can be. This life of victory is not realized in your own strength but in the name and power of the living Christ.

His expressed statement is, "I am with you alway." He is by your side, a strong friend who cares for your well-being, and who is concerned with the things that concern you. He has declared: "Call... and I will answer thee." If you are in trouble, depressed, discouraged or blue, call upon Him and He will come to your help.

Many who had the same faults to contend with as you have are now saints in heaven. They made it through to the celestial city despite their sinful dispositions and the fierce onslaughts of Satan. You, too, can one day enter the city where "they need no sun."

Victory is assured every believer. Not by dogged determination on his part but by divine mercy on God's part. "Casting all your care upon him, for he careth for you."

Only have patience, perseverance. "More haste, less speed" is an old saying that has its parallel in the Scriptures: "They that wait upon the Lord shall renew their strength"; "Stand still and see the salvation of the Lord."

The sweet peace of God comes wrapped in personal resignation. Soul rest is sure when you cease struggling. It is then that you will hear God whisper: "Yield cheerfully thy will. Be submissive and I will come to thine aid."

"And the peace of God that passeth all understanding shall keep your hearts and minds through Jesus Christ our Lord." Do not settle for less than a life of victory, a life filled with peace and joy in the Holy Ghost. This is not an ideal for a day only, but a day-by-day possibility when the life is hid with Christ in God. —*O. G. Wilson*

July 8

Let the people renew their strength. —Isaiah 41:1

All things on earth need to be renewed. No created thing continues by itself. "Thou renewest the face of the year," was the Psalmist's utterance. Even the trees, which wear not themselves with care, nor shorten their lives with labor, must drink of the rain of heaven and suck from the hidden treasures of the soil. The cedars of Lebanon, which God has planted, only live because day by day they are full of sap freshly drawn from the earth. Neither can man's life be sustained without renewal from God. As it is necessary to repair the waste of the body by the frequent meal, so we must repair the waste of the soul by feeding upon the Book of God, or by listening to the preached Word....

Without constant restoration we are not ready for the perpetual assaults of hell, or the stern afflictions of heaven, or even for the strifes within. When the whirlwind shall be loosed, woe to the tree that has not sucked up fresh sap, and grasped the rock with many intertwisted roots. When tempests arise, woe to the mariners that have not strengthened their mast, nor cast their anchor, nor sought the haven. If we suffer the good to grow weaker, the evil will surely gather strength and struggle desperately for the mastery over us; and so, perhaps, a painful desolation, and a lamentable disgrace may follow. Let us draw near to the footstool of divine mercy in humble entreaty, and we shall realize the fulfillment of the promise, "They that wait on the Lord shall renew their strength."

—*C. H. Spurgeon*

July 9

I will seek that which was lost.—Ezekiel 34:16

Our passage today sounds like a New Testament gospel statement. In Matthew 18:11 the good and great shepherd has said: "The Son of Man is come to save that which was lost." And here in this Old Testament record we have the same glorious fact stated: "I will seek that which was lost." The shepherds of Israel had forsaken their sacred trust and neglected to seek "that which was lost." But "thus saith the Lord God, Behold I, even I, will both search my sheep, and seek them out."

The Good Shepherd also promises to "feed" them, and to "cause them to lie down," denoting perfect peace, safety, and rest. As I read over these gracious promises and statements, am I able to exclaim, "The Great Shepherd of the sheep has not only sought me, but in His mercy He has found me and brought me safely to His fold"? If so, then I am able to add with my whole heart, "The Lord is my Shepherd," and therefore wherever I may be and whatever my surroundings, of one thing I may be perfectly certain: "I shall not want."

—*John Roberts*

July 10

The Lord shall be thy confidence, and shall keep thy foot from being taken.—Proverbs 3:26

Confidence means complete reliance. To rely on anything, or anyone, is to depend or lean upon that person or thing, with the assurance that we have something there that is trustworthy. Confidence in something is natural to any man.

Now when that confidence is *in the Lord*, the man passes from the natural to the spiritual. Confidence in the Lord means *repose* or rest in Him. This is the secret of composure, and composure is the secret of power. "The Lord shall keep thy foot from being taken" (or *caught* as the RSV has it). This implies that we walk in the midst of danger. The enemy of souls sets many a trap to catch the feet of God's children. But the Lord "will keep the feet of his saints" (1 Sam. 2:9).

"The steps of a good man are ordered by the Lord; and

he delighteth in his way" (Ps. 37:23). But how does the Lord keep the feet of His people? Not by dealing with them as if they were machines. He keeps us by giving us the grace of holy vigilance; by teaching us ever to be looking unto Him, not to watch the enemy so much as the Lord, who is our Confidence. —*Evan H. Hopkins*

July 11

Let not your heart be troubled.—John 14:1

The Lord of all harvests said, "Let not your heart be troubled." Surely, then, my daily bread will be given to me—and on time.

The world's Sin-bearer said, "Let not your heart be troubled." That means there is a sovereign remedy for sin, a Balm in Gilead to make the wounded whole, power in Jesus' blood to heal the sin-sick soul.

The God of all comfort said, "Let not your heart be troubled." Then I am to find a place of comfort and soul rest when all earthly comfort has failed, and the source of all human comfort is swept away.

The God of all grace said, "Let not your heart be troubled." Then I am to find grace sufficient amid slander, opposition, and vicious satanic attacks.

The coming world Sovereign, whose right it is to rule, said, "Let not your heart be troubled." Then let military braggarts march, let blatant atheists make their threats, let arrogant unbelievers scorn and deride, let vicious criminals frighten the land with their evil. The dawn of a day of righteousness is certain. He said, "I will come again." The angels said, "This same Jesus . . . shall so come again in like manner."

Be not troubled about tomorrow—"sufficient unto the day is the evil thereof." Tomorrow is in His hands. He that hath not failed thee in six troubles will not fail thee in the seventh!

Let every troubled soul repeat five times aloud the first phrase of Psalm 23, "The Lord is my shepherd," each time emphasizing a different word. As one meditates on each word each succeeding time there will come to the soul a song borne on angel wings, a song of blessed assurance. Be not troubled—believe. God has His way in the storm and He rides on the wings of the wind! —*O. G. Wilson*

July 12

Jesus therefore, being wearied with his journey, sat thus on the well.—John 4:6

In all the gospel story there are few more tenderly suggestive pictures of Jesus than that which we have in these words.

He has been travelling all day in the hot sun, and coming to this resting place He sits down on a well curb. He is weary and wayworn with His long journey. He is both hungry and thirsty. This is the picture of Jesus for tired people. As we look at it we see the human side of Christ's life. Here is one of His experiences which we can understand. As we see Him healing, teaching, raising the dead, transfigured, He is far above us, and we cannot enter into His feelings. But in His bodily weariness, after His long journey in the heat and dust, He is down among us, and we can tell just how He felt. The chief comfort comes to us from the fact that He is able now to sympathize with us when we are tired, because that day, so long since, He was tired.

Do we get all the blessing we might get from the truth of our Lord's actual human experiences? When we have been working hard all day, and are weary and faint, let us remember this picture—Jesus, footsore and dust-covered, sinking down in sheer exhaustion on the stone curb. He has not forgotten even in His glory how He felt that day, and as He sees us in our weariness, His heart feels tenderly for us. He looks down upon us in compassion, and sends to us a benediction of strength and cheer. Let all the people whose work is hard, and who ofttimes are very tired, frame this picture in their memory and keep it always hanging up on the wall of their heart. —*J. R. Miller*

July 13

I am the good shepherd, and know my sheep, and am known of mine.—John 10:14

The Good Shepherd knows His sheep, and knows them by name. And that is what I am tempted to forget. I think of myself as one of an innumerable multitude, no one of whom receives personal attention. "My way is overlooked by my God." But here is the good news—the Savior would miss me, even me!

At a great orchestral rehearsal, which Sir Michael Costa was conducting, the man who played the piccolo rested his fingers for a moment, thinking that his trifling contribution would never be missed. At once Sir Michael raised his hand, and said: "Stop! Where's the piccolo?" He missed the individual note. And my Lord needs the note of my life to make the music of His kingdom, and if the note be absent He will miss it, and the glorious music will be broken and incomplete.

There is a common vice of self-conceit, but there is also a common vice of excessive self-depreciation. "My Lord can do nothing with me!" Yes, my Lord knows you and needs you! And by the power of His grace you can accomplish wonders! —*J. H. Jowett*

July 14

Thou hast enlarged my steps under me, that my feet did not slip.—Psalm 18:36

When first we experience the grace of God, we have the feeling that if ever we should become what Jesus Christ wants us to be, He would have to take us straight to heaven! But when by God's grace we get there, we find we are not on a perilous mountain peak, but on a broad plateau, with any amount of room to walk—as safe and eternal as the hills. "Thou hast enlarged my steps under me." The great note of strength is to "walk and not faint"; to "mount up with wings" is exceptional. Everywhere your foot treads, at home or abroad, should bring a preparation of the gospel of peace. Sometimes when you put down a prepared foot for God it is anything but peace! It is disturbance and upset, but that is the way God prepares for the coming of His peace. Jesus is the Prince of Peace, yet He said, "I came not to bring peace, but a sword."

Are you strengthened from above—mentally, physically, morally, spiritually, and circumstantially? Do you know how to draw on the resurrection life of Jesus? The guidance in work for God is to notice where you are exhausted without recuperation. We take on a tremendous amount of stuff which we call work for God, and God puts a sentence of death on it, for we are exhausted by it without being recuperated, because our strength is drawn from somewhere other than the Highest.

The sign that what we are doing is God's work is that we know the supernatural recuperation. Are we strong enough to be abject failures in the eyes of the world, or are we set upon success? Our work for God is not of any value saving as it develops us; the one thing of value in God's sight is our relationship to Jesus Christ. The branch knows nothing about its fruit; it only knows the pruning knife (see John 15:2). "Am I a blessing?" No, certainly not, if you are looking at the outflow. Keep rightly related to the Highest and out of you will flow "rivers of living water."   —*Oswald Chambers*

July 15

Walk in newness of life.—Romans 6:4

Both life and liberty are needed before we are ready to "walk." The life is secured to us in Christ. He is our life. So, too, is liberty. Deliverance from sin's power, as well as from sin's penalty, is the fruit of Christ's death. "Stand fast in the liberty wherewith *Christ hath made us free*" (Gal. 5:1). We are set free, not for idle contemplation or personal enjoyment, but for practical service.

Walking in newness of life embraces the whole of that life

that glorifies God. It is the apostle's favorite term for moral conduct. He says *"newness* of life" instead of *"new* life," because he would make prominent the idea of the new nature of this second life. The old life terminates at the cross. If we died with Christ, then the life that belongs to the "man of old" has been brought to an end; and if we are risen with Christ, we have entered into the life of the "new man." That is a life of freedom and power.

Walking in this life is not a hard, irksome struggle, but free and joyous action. What physical exercise is to the man who is in robust health, "walking in newness of life" is to the soul who is in the power of Christ's resurrection.

—Evan H. Hopkins

July 16

Are they not all ministering spirits, sent forth to minister for them who shall be heirs of salvation?—Hebrews 1:14

To him to whom life is but an episode, a short stage in the existence of eternity, who is always aware of the great surrounding world of mystery, grief comes as angels came to the tent of Abraham. Laughter is hushed before them. The mere frolic of life stands still, but the soul takes the grief in as its guest, meets it at the door, kisses its hand, washes its travel-stained feet, spreads its table with the best food, gives it the seat by the fireside, and listens reverently for what it has to say about the God from whom it came (see Genesis 18).

I beg you, if God sends you grief, take it largely by letting it show you first of all how short life is, and then prophesy eternity. Such is the grief of which the poet sings so nobly:

> Grief should be
> Like joy, majestic, equable, sedate;
> Confirming, cleansing, raising, making free;
> Strong to consume small troubles; to commend
> Great thoughts, grave thoughts, thoughts lasting
>   to the end.

But grief, to be all that, must see the end; must bring and forever keep with its pain such a sense of the shortness of life that the pain will seem but a temporary accident, and that all that is to stay forever after the pain has ceased, the exaltation, the unselfishness, the mystery, the nearness to God, shall seem to be the substance of the sorrow.   *—Phillips Brooks*

July 17

Wait on the Lord: be of good courage, and he shall strengthen your heart. . . .—Psalm 27:14

Some people find their courage in a bottle, a pill, or even in an artificially induced emotional "high" of some kind, but the child of God finds his courage to meet life's rigors in God himself. His confidence comes from within himself, from his heart which derives its strength from the divine Source.

Moses told the spies who went into the Promised Land, Canaan, to "be of good courage, and bring some of the fruit of the land" (Num. 13:20). They were facing the unknown enemy, but they were obeying the direct command of God "to spy out the land . . . which I [God] give to the people of Israel" (Num. 13:1). With a commission like that, their courage should have been equal to the task, but ten of the spies lost their courage, while only two, Joshua and Caleb, allowed God to strengthen their heart. We as Christians can stifle the Spirit's activity within us by our unbelief, and unfortunately that is the path the majority (the ten) too often follow—the "path of least resistance."

Daniel in his vision recognized the truth of this strengthening process in spite of (or because of) opposition, for he points out, "The people who do know their God shall stand firm and take action" (Dan. 11:32, RSV). Just as our physical muscles grow strong when they are exercised, just so our "spiritual" muscles take on new strength when they are put to the test. So don't feel that just because you are encountering difficulties, God has deserted you. *No!* He is with you in the midst of your difficulties, He is teaching you through the obstacles He allows in your path. "Be of good courage," for with the testing He also supplies the strength to overcome.

July 18

Thou wilt keep him in perfect peace, whose mind is stayed on thee.—Isaiah 26:3

These words bring before us the Keeper, the Keeping, and the Kept. The *Keeper* is none other than Jehovah himself. Nothing less than God himself was needed for man's salvation. And this not merely to deliver him from condemnation, but to keep him from falling. We are kept by the power of God.

The *Keeping* is described in the words, "in perfect peace." This is the nature of it: it is peace in its fullest measure and in its truest sense. Inward and outward peace. Peace of conscience and of soul. Peace with God and the peace of God.

The *Kept.*—What is it that characterizes them? Their minds

are stayed on God. Dr. Kay tells us that the word here rendered "mind" means properly the imagination—the same word as in Gen. 6:5; 8:21; Deut. 31:21; 1 Chron. 28:9 and 39:18. It is in the imagination that we begin to go astray. Let that be stayed on God, and we need not be cast down because of conscious weakness. The word "stayed" occurs only here and implies the entire repose of faith. The reason the believer's mind can rest or repose on "Thee," is "because he *trusts* in thee." It is not a mere clinging or holding on, but *resting* (Phil. 4:6, 7). With the resting comes "the peace of God, which passeth all understanding." —*Evan H. Hopkins*

July 19

This day is this scripture fulfilled in your ears.—Luke 4:21

The words had been written seven hundred years before. Now Jesus reads them and says, "I am the One to whom these golden sentences refer. This scripture is fulfilled before your eyes. I am the Anointed One, and this the mission on which I came to this world." The whole Old Testament was full of Christ. There were a thousand fingers along its pages, every one pointing to Him. All its types and prophecies were fulfilled when He came, and lived, and died, and rose up glorified.

It is extremely interesting to take up Christ's whole public life and ministry, and see how perfectly He lived out the wonderful mission which the prophet here outlined for Him centuries before He came. He preached the gospel to the poor; He was a friend of the poor. He healed the brokenhearted. Wherever He went the sorrowing and the troubled came flocking around Him. As a magnet draws steel filings to itself from a heap of rubbish, so there was something in Him that drew the sad to Him.

There are always two classes of the brokenhearted. There are those whose hearts are broken because of sin. There are those who are crushed by affliction. Both these classes came to Christ. Sinners came and found in Him not a stern, censorious Judge, but a tender, compassionate Saviour. The afflicted came and found true comfort. He loved all men, sympathized with them, and was able to help them. Then He also brought deliverance to sin's captives, setting them free, breaking their chains. He opened blind eyes; not only the natural eyes to see the beautiful things of this world, but the spiritual eyes as well, to behold the things of heaven and everlasting life. Then He lifted the yoke of the crushed and oppressed, inviting all the weary to himself to find rest for their souls. Thus His whole life was simply filling up this outline sketch left by the prophet and "fulfilled in your ears" and eyes.

—*J. R. Miller*

July 20

He maketh my feet like hinds' feet.—Psalm 18:33

> She shall be sportive as the fawn
> That wild with glee across the lawn
> Or up the mountain springs.
> —*Wordsworth*

And it is this buoyancy, this elasticity, this springiness that the Lord is waiting to impart to the souls of His children, so that they may move along the ways of life with the light steps of the fawn.

Some of us move with very heavy feet. There is little of the fawn about us as we go along the road. There is reluctance in our obedience. There is a frown in our homage. Our benevolence is graceless, and there is no charm in our piety, and no rapture in our praise. We are the victims of "the spirit of heaviness." And yet here is the word which tells us that God will make our feet "like hinds' feet." He will give us exhilaration and spring, enabling us to leap over difficulties, and to have strength and buoyancy for the steepest hills. Let us seek the inspiration of the Lord. "It is God that girdeth me with strength, and maketh my way perfect."   —*J. H. Jowett*

July 21

For ye are not under law, but under grace.—Romans 6:14

Here we have suggested the possibility of two types of Christian life. There may be a life partly under the law and partly under grace; or, a life entirely under grace, in the full liberty from self-effort, and the full experience of the divine strength which it can give. A true believer may still be living partly under the law, in the power of self-effort, striving to do what he cannot accomplish. The continued failure in his Christian life to which he confesses is owed to this one thing: he trusts in himself and tries to do his best. He does indeed pray and look to God for help, but still it is he in his strength, helped by God, who is to do the work.

In the epistles to the Romans, Corinthians, and Galatians, Paul tells his fellow Christians that they have not received the spirit of bondage again, that they are free from the law, that they are no more servants but sons; that they must be aware of nothing so much as to be entangled again with the yoke of bondage. Everywhere it is contrast between law and grace, between the flesh, which is under the law, and the Spirit, who is the gift of grace, and through whom grace does all its work. In our modern day, just as in Paul's day, the great danger is living under the law and trying to serve God in the strength of the flesh. With the great majority of Christians it appears to be the state in which they remain all their lives. Hence the lack to a large extent of true holy living and power in prayer. They do not know that all failure can have but one cause: *Men seek to do in themselves what grace alone can do in them*, what grace most certainly will do.

The law of God could only deliver us into the power of the law of sin and death. The grace of God can bring us into, and keep us in, the liberty of the Spirit. We can be made free from the sad life under the power that led us captive, so that we did not what we wanted to do. The Spirit of life in Christ can free us from our continual failure in prayer, and enable us in this, too, to walk worthy of the Lord.

—*Andrew Murray*

July 22

The Lord was my stay.—Psalm 18:18

It is impossible to overestimate the blessing of a restful heart. To be calm and peaceful "with sorrows surging round"; to be still, yet active, even when "by thronging duties pressed," are privileges that belong only to those who have found rest, the soul's only true resting place.

"The Lord is my rock, and my fortress, and my deliverer; my God, my strength, in whom I will trust." We cannot say "My heart is fixed" until we have found the Rock that cannot be moved. It is not the strength of our efforts to cling that is our stay, but the firmness of the Rock on which we rest. The Lord is our stay.

"Thou wilt keep him in perfect peace whose mind is stayed on thee" (Isa. 26:3). The Scriptures teach us that God is immovable, unchanging, unfailing. The Lord is *immovable*. Of nothing here on earth can this be said. Until we have made Him our Rock we can know nothing of true abiding rest.

The Lord is *unchanging*. What we find Him to be to us today He will be to us tomorrow. He is "the same yesterday, today, and forever" (Heb. 13:8). In Him is "no variation, neither shadow that is cast by turning" (James 1:17, RV).

The Lord is *unfailing*. Men and institutions all around us fail every day—but Jesus Christ, by His very nature and His own declaration, cannot fail.   —*Evan H. Hopkins*

July 23

As for us, the Lord is our God, and we have not forsaken him. . . . Behold, God himself is with us for our captain.
—2 Chronicles 13:10, 12

Israel and Judah had come to the parting of the ways. Israel, God's chosen people, had chosen to serve idols of gold rather than the God who had led her out of Egypt and into the Promised Land. As is so often the case, the majority had taken the wrong path, the wrong fork in the road, whereas the faithful minority, Judah, had chosen the right path, "The Lord is our God, and we have not forsaken him. . . . Behold, God himself is with us for our captain."

Israel had indeed forsaken her God, which was typical of her checkered history. Probably her most obvious and blatant rejection of God came when she chose to follow an earthly king rather than a heavenly Guide. But God, in His grace, went along with Israel's desires. At first, all went well and the fledgling king, Saul, was a spiritual as well as a physical leader. But then Saul began to depend more upon himself than he did on God, and his downward path was set. Ultimately his people followed his example.

When David succeeded Saul, his direction was Godward again, and the people followed his leadership back to God. Eventually David succeeded in uniting Israel and Judah under a common banner and a common allegiance to God. By the time of our text, however, Israel had once again forsaken God and followed foreign, false gods. Judah, that faithful segment that never quite lost its identity, chose to remain faithful —and recognized God's presence as her captain.

The writer to the Hebrews calls Jesus the "captain of their salvation" (Heb. 2:10) and He is that. Not only does He lead His chosen people, the Jews, but He leads His spiritual progeny, the Christians of every age. This is our heritage. All He asks is our allegiance; all we have to offer Him is ourselves. He will do the rest. He will be our Captain!

July 24

And the Lord was with Joseph, and he was a prosperous man; and he was in the house of his master the Egyptian. And his master saw that the Lord was with him.
—Genesis 39:2, 3

We find Joseph filling two roles in the house of Potiphar: first, as a servant and a slave, one who is trusted and loved, but still entirely a servant; second, as master. Potiphar made him overseer over his house and his lands and all that he had, so that we read of him later on that he left everything to Joseph, and he knew of nothing except the bread that came upon his table.

I want to call to your attention Joseph as a type of Christ here. We sometimes speak of entire surrender in the Christian life, and rightly; and here we have a beautiful illustration of what it is. First, Joseph was in Potiphar's house to serve him and help him, and he did that, and Potiphar learned to trust him, so that he said, "All that I have I will give into his hand." Now, that is exactly what is to take place with a great many Christians. They know Christ, they trust Him, they love Him, but He is not Master; He is just a sort of helper. When there is trouble they come to Him; when they sin they ask Him for pardon in His precious blood; when they are in darkness they cry to Him; but more often they live in their own will and seek help in themselves. But how blessed is the man who comes, and like Potiphar says, "I will give everything to Jesus!"

There are many who have accepted Jesus Christ as Lord, but have never yet come to the final, absolute surrender of everything. Christians, if you want perfect rest, abiding joy, strength to work for God, come and learn from that wealthy Egyptian what you ought to do. He saw that God was with Joseph, and he said, "I will give up my house to him." Oh, learn to do that. There are some who have never accepted Christ: some who are seeking after Him, thirsting and hungering, but they do not know how to find Him; let all come and learn the true secret of the victorious Christian life—surrender!

—Andrew Murray

July 25

Thou art my hope in the day of evil.—Jeremiah 17:17

A day of evil need not be a day of departure from the Lord. In the path of the believer, evil may meet him in the form of fierce temptation, of sore affliction. There may be times when his faith is severely tested, and when the enemy makes a special assault upon his soul. Then it is that he feels his need of a refuge. He finds it in God: "Thou art my refuge in the day of evil" (RV).

Many have rejoiced in the Lord at the beginning and then have lost all their peace the moment that the testing has come because they did not at once hide in their Refuge.

David said, "Thou art my hiding place; thou shalt preserve me from trouble; thou shalt compass me about with songs of deliverance" (Ps. 32:7). It was there he made his refuge until his calamities were past.

It is not the outward trial, after all, that we need to fear. The real evil is the evil of sinning against the Lord and losing His smile. To be kept from that evil is to be kept in peace. "Thou shalt hide them in the secret of thy presence" (Ps. 31:20). *—Evan H. Hopkins*

July 26

My presence shall go with thee, and I will give thee rest.—Exodus 33:14

We can dare anything and go any place if God's presence goes with us. That presence doesn't just go *with* us; it *surrounds* and *overshadows* us, before, behind, above and below. In light of this truth, why are we afraid? Why do we hesitate to follow God completely? Why don't we obey all His commands and fulfill His will as He reveals it to us?

We need to recognize that this promise of God to His people, Israel, applies to the Christian today as well. Our God is alive, present in the world with us. How do I know? He has heard and answered my prayers. He has given me guidance when I asked for it. Therefore will I follow Him without fear, for I will not be walking alone—my Companion is the Lord himself!

Living this kind of a guided, God-directed life implies submission on my part—a willingness to subject myself and my will to Him, a willingness to walk according to His plan and purpose for my life rather than inserting my will ahead of His, substituting my way for His way. How do I know when I am in His will? Our text supplies one aspect of the answer: a restful spirit. If I am doing His will, I have a positive feeling of peace and purpose about the way I am taking. There is a solid sense of "rightness" about my path that is inescapable.

Another unerring source of spiritual direction is available to His child through His Word. Isaiah says, "He shall enter into peace: they shall rest . . ." (57:2). This promise is specifically to the righteous, the godly person, the one who puts God first in his life, who seeks His way. God has promised to walk that way with you, child of His. Walk it with confidence and a restful spirit!

July 27

He is their strength in time of trouble. . . . There remained no strength in me . . . Then there came again and touched me one like the appearance of a man, and he strengthened me.—Psalm 37:39; Daniel 10:17, 18

Daniel knew what it was to walk with God. Yet if any one of God's children was "in trouble," that one was Daniel! But Daniel also had learned the lesson of leaning on the Lord in his "time of trouble." In fact, Daniel made it a practice to turn each day over to the Lord in prayer. Habitually, he knelt and communicated with his heavenly Father.

In spite of his close walk with God, however, Daniel experienced spiritual exhaustion. "There remained no strength in me," he exclaimed, but then he went on to testify that "There . . . touched me one like . . . a man, and he strengthened me."

This "one" was God himself, and as He touched Daniel, the supernaturally given strength renewed Daniel and the exhaustion was replaced with divine exhilaration.

But did Daniel wait until he was in trouble to talk to God? No, prayer was as habitual with him as breathing, and he wasn't afraid to let the unbelieving nation around him know where his trust rested. From his youth, his teen years, Daniel let his light shine, he made his allegiance clear.

Here is a lesson for us today. We cannot expect strength from God if we do not keep the channels of communication open, if we do not uncompromisingly identify ourselves with God—by our very life-style and by our verbal testimony, just as Daniel did. There was no question in the minds of the Babylonians with whom he lived as to his allegiance and relationship to the God of Israel. And we today must not let anything in our lives make our relationship to God fuzzy or ephemeral. Our stand must be firm and solidly committed to the God we serve.

July 28

The Lord bless thee, and keep thee. The Lord make his face shine upon thee, and be gracious unto thee. The Lord lift up his countenance upon thee, and give thee peace.
—Numbers 6:24

This is a part of the Aaronic benediction. It has been observed there is nothing expressed in the apostolic benediction which was not implied in the Aaronic. In blessing Israel, Aaron was to "put the name of the Lord upon the children of Israel." It is into that Name we have been baptized. It is in that Name we enter when we meet together for worship. He blesses us by enclosing us in His presence and encircling us in His power. "Kept by the power of God" is the place of the believer's safety (1 Pet. 1:5).

He blesses us by causing His face to shine upon us and by manifesting to us the riches of His grace. He blesses us by lifting up the light of His countenance upon us and filling our hearts with His peace.

All good is summed up in God's favor. David declares: "There are many that say, Who will show us any good?" He gives us the answer: "Lord, lift thou up the light of thy countenance upon us" (Ps. 4:6). It is "the light of the knowledge of the glory of God in the face of Jesus Christ."

Our need of God's blessing is continual. That need arises not only and merely from the circumstance of the trial, temptation, and difficulty in which we are placed, but also from our condition of personal weakness and sin. Our unworthiness places us in a position of entire dependence upon His sovereign grace.

But God has been pleased to "lift up the light of his countenance upon" us. These words which Aaron had to pronounce on the children of Israel were not the mere utterance of a pious wish, nor were they only a prayer. They were more. They were the divine declaration that God would give effect to all that is here expressed. God's benedictions are not human supplication. A desire expressed in prayer is one thing. A blessing bestowed by a divine declaration is another.

Here then is the believer's privilege—to walk each day beneath the Lord's benediction, within His keeping power, in the light of His favor, in the riches of His grace, and in the enjoyment of His peace. —*Evan H. Hopkins*

July 29

Because thy lovingkindness is better than life, my lips shall praise thee.—Psalm 63:3

A railway passenger once said in my hearing: "There are things in my business I am compelled to do which some people think are not right, but if I did not do them, I could not live as things are now. I have my family to provide for, taxes to pay, and we must live."

I listened to his speech, and then replied: "You are quite right, my friend, because from your point of view life is the supreme good. But I can tell you of men who are acting upon another principle. They look at life as a great blessing, but not *the* blessing. They have learned to say with David, the Psalmist in the wilderness of Judah, 'God's lovingkindness is better than life.' They love to pray as he did: 'Cause me to hear thy lovingkindness in the morning, for in thee do I trust. Cause me to know the way wherein I should walk, for I lift up my soul to thee.' If they could not live without losing His favor, the friendship of the Lord Jesus, and the comfort of the Holy Spirit, they would be quite willing to die, because God's favor to them is better than life."

But my friend was in error in supposing that in order to live he was compelled to do wrong. It is God who gives us life, and He alone can sustain it, and if we resolve by His help to seek first His kingdom and His righteousness, He will see that we shall not suffer by so doing, but will, according to His promise, supply all our needs, not only for soul and spirit, but also for the body. Therefore, let the doing of God's will be our supreme good, be to us "better than life," and we will prove godliness to be profitable unto all things.

David found it so. God stood by him and eventually delivered him from the hand of Saul and raised him to the throne, after which he assures that "in His favor is life." That is it: living in God's favor will assure real life while here on earth, and eternal life hereafter in His presence forevermore.

—John Roberts

July 30

Jesus saith unto him, I am the way.—John 14:6

The mother of a child mentally retarded because of brain injury wrote: "We might call it the great tragedy of our lives were it not for the fact that because of this we have come to know God better. Our keen disappointment when the expected development did not occur cannot be fully expressed. However, it gave us to understand how God feels when His children fail to develop spiritually."

Most of God's assigned lessons are difficult to master. They often take years of self-discipline, yet always they take the learner to the heart of God. James Russell Lowell wrote: "After all, the kind of world one carries about within oneself is the important thing, and the world outside takes all its grace, color, and value from that within."

The mother of the above letter has found life's true meaning —to fit oneself graciously into the place Almighty God has selected.

Dr. Erich Fromm once said: "If the average group of citizens were confined to their rooms alone without any of the standard doodling devices or avenues of escape—radio, television, card playing, aimless conversation, detective stories— there would be an almost one hundred percent of incidences of 'nervous breakdowns' at the end of three days." People everywhere are turning to religions, seeking in desperation for life's answers to the enigma with which man is surrounded. This can end only in frustration and deeper despondency unless they turn to God through Jesus Christ. "I am the way," was spoken long ago by Jesus Christ the Lord. He is still The Way:

To soul rest, though gripped by tragedy.

To enlightenment and peace when surrounded by darkness and confusion.

To security for time and eternity. He is the answer to the soul's cry: "Who am I and where am I going? Where are the fixed poles in a world of chaos?" Those of you reading these lines who have faced a great tragedy, do as did this mother: convert your tragedy into triumph. You too can find in Christ a faith that will help you not only survive sickness, affliction, loss, but transform them into jewels for the eternal crown.

—O. G. Wilson

July 31

He that saith he abideth in him ought himself also so to walk, even as he walked. —1 John 2:6

Abiding in Christ and *walking like Christ:* these are the two blessings of the new life which are here set before us in their essential unity. The fruit of a life *in Christ* is a life *like Christ.* As the fruit of our surrender to live wholly in Him, His life works so mightily in us that our walk, the outward expression of the inner life, becomes like His. The two are inseparably connected. The abiding in always precedes the walking like Him. And yet the aim to walk like Him must equally precede any large measure of abiding.

Every believer is in Christ; but not everyone abides in Him, in the consciously joyful and trustful surrender of the whole being to His influence. You know what abiding in Him is. It is to consent with our whole soul to His being our life, to reckon upon Him to inspire us in all that goes to make up life, and then to give up everything most absolutely for Him to rule and work in us. It is the rest of the full assurance that He does, each moment, work in us what we are to be, and so himself enables us to maintain that perfect surrender in which He is free to do all His will.

Let all who do indeed long to walk like Christ take courage at the thought of what He is and will prove himself to be if they trust Him. He is the *True Vine*; no vine ever did so fully for its branches what He will do for us. We have only to consent to be branches. Honor Him by a joyful trust that He is, beyond all conception, the True Vine, holding you by His almighty strength, supplying you from His infinite fullness. Thanks be to God, in the blessed life of God's redeemed these two are inseparably one: abiding in Christ and walking like Christ! —*Andrew Murray*

August 1

Serve the Lord with gladness. —Psalm 100:2

Delight in divine service is a sure sign of genuine gladness. Those who serve Christ with a long face and a sad countenance, as if what they are doing is unpleasant to them, are not serving Him at all; they bring the form of homage, but the life is absent. They have a form of godliness, but deny the power thereof.

Our God requires no slaves to grace His throne; He is the Lord of the empire of love and would have His servants dressed in uniforms of joy. The angels of God serve Him with joy and songs, not with groans and grumblings; a murmur or a sigh would be a mutiny in their ranks. That obedience which is grudging and not voluntary is disobedience, for the Lord looks on the heart, and if He sees we serve Him from force, and not because we love Him, He will reject our offering.

Service coupled with cheerfulness is heart-service, and therefore true. Take away joyful willingness from the Christian, and you have removed the test of his sincerity. If a man must be driven into battle, he is no patriot; but he who marches into the fight singing, with flashing eye and beaming face, proves himself to be sincere in his patriotism.

Cheerfulness is the support of our strength; in the joy of the Lord are we strong. It acts as the remover of difficulties. It is to our service what oil is to the wheels of industry. Without oil the axle soon grows hot, and accidents occur; and if there be not holy cheerfulness to oil our wheels, our spirits will be clogged with weariness. The man who is cheerful in his service of God, proves that obedience is his element; that true joy is his portion.

Reader, let me ask you this question—do *you* serve the Lord with *gladness*? Let us show the people of the world, who think our religion to be slavery, that it is to us a delight and a joy! Let our gladness proclaim that we serve a good Master.   —*C. H. Spurgeon*

August 2

Martha was cumbered about much serving.—Luke 10:40

Her fault was not that she *served:* the condition of a servant well becomes every Christian. "I serve" should be the motto of all those who are in God's family. Nor was it her fault that she had *"much serving."* We cannot do too much. Let us do all we possibly can; let head, and heart, and hands be engaged in the Master's service. It was no fault of hers that she was busy preparing a feast for the Master. Happy Martha to have an opportunity to entertain so blessed a guest; and happy, too, to have the spirit to throw her whole soul so heartily into the engagement.

Her fault was that she grew *"cumbered* with much serving,"* so that she forgot *Him* and only remembered the service. She allowed service to override communion, and so presented one duty stained with the blood of another.

We ought to be Martha and Mary in one: we should do much service and have much communion at the same time. For this we need great grace. It is easier to serve than to commune. Joshua never grew weary fighting with the Amalekites; but Moses, on the top of the mountain in prayer, needed two helpers to sustain his hands.

The more spiritual the exercise, the sooner we seem to tire in it. The choicest fruits are the hardest to rear; the most heavenly graces are the most difficult to cultivate. Beloved, while we do not neglect external things, which are good enough in themselves, we ought also to see to it that we enjoy living, personal fellowship with Jesus. See to it that sitting at the Savior's feet is not neglected, even though it be under the specious pretext of doing Him service. The first thing for our soul's health, the first thing for His glory, and the first thing for our own usefulness is to keep ourselves in perpetual communion with the Lord Jesus, and to see that the vital spirituality of our Christian faith is maintained over and above everything else in the world. —*C. H. Spurgeon*

August 3

Have this mind in you, which was also in Christ Jesus, who, being in the form of God, emptied himself, taking the form of a servant, being made in the likeness of men; and being found in fashion as a man, he humbled himself, becoming obedient unto death, yea, the death of the cross.
—Philippians 2:5-8 (RV)

Christ's example teaches us that it is not sin that must humble us. This is what many Christians think. They consider daily falls are necessary to keep us humble. This is not so. There is indeed a humility that is very necessary, consisting in the acknowledgment of transgression and shortcomings. But there is a humility even more meaningful which is like Christ's. This consists in the self-abasement that can wonder that God should bless us, and delights to be as nothing before Him to whom we owe all, even when grace keeps us from sinning. It is grace we need, and not sin, to make and keep us humble.

The heaviest laden branches always bow the lowest. The greatest flow of water makes the deepest riverbed. The nearer the soul comes to God, the more His majestic presence makes it feel its littleness. It is this alone that makes it possible for each to count others better than himself. Jesus Christ, the holy One of God, is our example of humility: it was knowing that the Father had given all things into His hands, and that He was come from God and went to God, that He washed the disciples' feet. It is the divine presence, the consciousness of the divine life and divine love in us, that will make us humble.

The blessedness of a Christlike humility is unspeakable. It is of great worth in the sight of God: "He giveth grace to the humble." In the spiritual life it is the source of rest and joy. To the humble all God does is right and good. Humility is always ready to praise God for the least of His mercies. Humility does not find it difficult to trust. It submits unconditionally to all that God says. The two whom Jesus praised for their great faith are just those who thought least of themselves: the centurion and the Syrophenician woman. The humble man is ever willing to serve his neighbor, because he has learned from Jesus the divine beauty of being a servant.

—*Andrew Murray*

August 4

Bear ye one another's burdens, and so fulfil the law of Christ.—Galatians 6:2

"If you must needs impose *burdens* on yourselves, let them be burdens of mutual sympathy. If you must needs observe a *law*, let it be the law of Christ" (Lightfoot). "These are the burdens I would have you bear—not the vexatious ritual of the law, but your neighbour's errors and weaknesses, his sorrows and sufferings."

Cultivate a tender sense of brotherhood. We who are joined to the Lord are members one of another. We cannot have the mind of Christ and be indifferent to the sufferings and difficulties of others. "Look not every man on his own things, but every man also on the things of others. Let this mind be in you, which was also in Christ Jesus" (Phil. 2:4, 5).

The Lord Jesus came to be God's faithful servant. He "came not to be ministered unto, but to minister, and to give his life a ransom for many" (Mark 10:45). This is to be manifested in our prayers and in our efforts. In intercessory prayer, we should seek to identify ourselves with others in their distress, or sorrow, or difficulty.　　　　　　—*Evan H. Hopkins*

August 5

Blessed be the Lord . . . : there hath not failed one word of all his good promise.—1 Kings 8:56

"There hath not failed one word of all his good promise." Supposing one word had failed, how then? If one golden promise had turned out to be counterfeit, how then? If the ground had yielded anywhere, we should have been fearful and suspicious at every part of the road. If the bell of God's fidelity had been broken anywhere, the music would have been destroyed. But not one word has failed. The road has never given way in time of flood. Every bell of heaven is perfectly sound, and the music is full and glorious. "God is faithful, who also will do it."

"God is love," and "love never faileth." The lamp will not die out at the midnight. The fountain will not fail us in the wilderness. The consolations will not be wanting in the hour of our distresses. Love will have "all things ready."

"He has promised, and shall he not do it?" All the powers of heaven are pledged to the fulfillment of the smallest word of grace. We can never be deserted! "God cannot deny himself." Every word of His will unburden its treasure at the appointed hour, and I will be rich with the strength of my God. —*J. H. Jowett*

August 6

Behold the fowls of the air . . . your heavenly Father feedeth them. Are ye not much better than they?—Matthew 6:26

Are we to draw the inference that since the birds neither sow nor reap, we are not to exert ourselves to provide for our own needs? No: if we did nothing to earn our own bread, we should soon starve. God would not feed us as He feeds the birds. He has bestowed on us powers by which we can make provision for our own wants. He feeds us, not by bringing the bread to us, but by making us able to sow and reap and gather into barns. God nowhere encourages that "trust" which sits idly down and waits to be cared for. Little babies, people who are too ill to care for themselves, may live as the birds do, and may expect to be cared for. But healthy people, with active brains and strong hands, will fare very poorly if they try to live the birds' way.

The point of this illustration lies in another direction. God's care extends even to the birds. There are two reasons, then, why it will more certainly extend to His people. First, they are better than birds. Birds have no souls, do not bear the divine image, have no spiritual nature. They cannot worship nor voluntarily serve God; they have no future and immortal life. The God who cares for a little soulless bird will surely care much more thoughtfully for a thinking, immortal, godlike man.

Then the other reason is that God is our Father. He is the creator and provider for the birds, but He is not their Father. Surely a father will do more for his children than for his chickens! A mother will give more thought to her baby than to her canary! Will not our heavenly Father provide more certainly and more tenderly for His children than for His birds? So from the birds we get a lesson of trust. Every time we see a bird sitting on its branch, or hear it singing its sweet song, it ought to lead us to renewed confidence in the care of our Father. —*J. R. Miller*

August 7

The children of Reuben . . . and Gad, and the half tribe of Manasseh have built an altar over against . . . Canaan.
—Joshua 22:11

Two and one-half tribes of the children of Israel were content to settle for an inheritance near Canaan. They left Egypt, endured the hardships of the wilderness, but settled for an inheritance short of what God had promised.

There are those in the Christian experience who are willing to settle for an experience short of full deliverance from the power of indwelling sin. They have made many necessary separations. They have denied themselves many things for which the flesh craved. But they stop short of full and complete deliverance.

There is always some one thing on which the final battle for the Canaan land experience turns. With the two and one-half tribes the inducement was grass—fine pastures for fine cattle. In the lives of men today it may be financial advantage, it may be social prestige, it may be personal honor. Whatever it is that causes the soul to settle short of an experience of full deliverance is a trick of Satan.

The two and one-half tribes were soon lost to Israel and nothing is ever heard of them again—they took their possession outside of Canaan. Nail down this fact: he who stops short of the Promised Land, on the wilderness side of Canaan, dwarfs his own soul immeasurably. Canaan only is the land of beauty, abundance, gladness—"a land of corn and wine." Only in Canaan can you get "honey from the rock" and find every man living "under his own vine and fig tree." Keep moving, keep believing until you enter your possessions in Canaan. —*O. G. Wilson*

August 8

He first findeth his own brother Simon.—John 1:41

This case is an excellent pattern of all cases where spiritual life is vigorous. As soon as a man finds Christ, *he begins to find others.* I will not believe that you have tasted of the honey of the gospel if you keep it all to yourself. True grace puts an end to all spiritual monopoly. Andrew *first* found his own brother Simon, and then others.

Relationship has a very strong demand upon our first individual efforts. Andrew did well to begin with Simon. I doubt whether there are not some Christians giving away tracts at other people's houses who would do well to give away a tract (or genuine love) at their own; whether there are not so ᴜ engaged in works of usefulness abroad who are neglecting their special sphere of usefulness at home. You may or may may not be called to evangelize the people in any particular locality, but certainly you are called to minister to your own household, your own kinfolk and acquaintances.

Let your religion begin at home. Many merchants export their best commodities; the Christian should not. He should have a good witness wherever he goes, but let him be careful to put forth the sweetest fruit of spiritual life and testimony in his own family.

When Andrew went to find his brother, he little imagined how eminent Simon would become. Simon Peter was worth ten Andrews so far as we can gather from what is recorded of their exploits in sacred history; yet Andrew was the instrument God used to bring Simon to Himself. You may not have much talent yourself, and yet you may be the means God uses to draw one to himself who will become eminent in grace and service.

Ah! dear friend, you little know the possibilities which are in you. You may but speak a word to a child, and in that child there may be slumbering a noble heart which will stir the Christian church in years to come. Andrew had only one talent, but he found Peter. "Go thou and do likewise."

—*C. H. Spurgeon*

August 9

Beginning to sink, he cried, saying, Lord, save me.— Matthew 14:30

Sinking times are praying times with the Lord's servants. At the beginning of his watery adventure, Peter neglected prayer. But when he began to sink, his danger made him a beggar, and his cry though late was not too late. In our hours of bodily pain and mental anguish, we find ourselves as naturally driven to prayer as the wreck is driven upon the shore by the waves. The fox goes to its hole for protection; the bird flies to the wood for shelter; even so the tried believer runs to the mercy seat for safety. Heaven's great harbor of refuge is all-prayer; thousands of weather-beaten vessels have found a haven there, and the moment a storm comes on, it is wise for us to make for it under full sail.

Short prayers are long enough. There are but three words in Peter's petition, but they were sufficient for his purpose. Not length but strength is desirable. A sense of need is a mighty teacher of brevity. If our prayers had less of the tail feathers of pride and more wing, they would be all the better. Verbiage is to devotion as chaff is to the wheat. Precious things lie in small scope, and all that is real prayer in many a long address might have been uttered in a petition as short as Peter's.

Our extremities are the Lord's opportunity. The moment a keen sense of danger forces an anxious cry from us, the ear of Jesus hears, and with Him ear and heart go together, and the hand does not long linger. At the last moment we appeal to the Master, but His swift hand makes up for our delays by instant and effectual action. Are we nearly engulfed by the boisterous waters of affliction? Let us then lift up our souls unto our Savior, and we may rest assured that He will not suffer us to perish. When we can do nothing, Jesus can do all things; let us enlist His powerful aid upon our side, and all will be well. —*C. H. Spurgeon*

August 10

The Lord appeared to Abram, and said unto him, I am the Almighty God; walk before me, and be thou perfect.
—Genesis 17:1

Walk before me, and be thou perfect. It is in the life fellowship with God, in His realized presence and favor, that it becomes possible to be perfect with Him. Walk before me: Abraham had been doing this. God's Word calls him to a clearer and more conscious understanding of this as his life calling. It is easy for us to study what Scripture says of perfection, to form our ideas of it, and argue for them. But let us remember that it is only as we are walking closely with God, seeking and in some measure attaining, uninterrupted communion with Him, that the divine command will come to us in its divine power, and unfold to us its divine meaning. Walk before Me, *and* be thou perfect. God's realized presence is the school, is the secret, of perfection. It is only he who studies what perfection is in the full light of God's presence to whom its hidden glory will be opened up.

That realized presence is the great blessing of the redemption in Jesus Christ. The veil has been rent, the way into the true sanctuary, the presence of God, has been opened; we have access with boldness into the Holiest of all. God who has proved himself God Almighty in raising Jesus from the dead and setting Him, and us in Him, at His right hand, speaks now to us: "I am the God Almighty; *walk before me, and be thou perfect.*"

That command came not only to Abraham. Moses gave it to the whole people of Israel: "Thou shalt be perfect with the Lord thy God" (Deut. 10:13). It is for all Abraham's children; for all the Israel of God; *for every believer.* O think not that before you can obey you must first understand and define what perfection means. No, God's way is the very opposite of this.

Abraham went out, *not knowing whither he went.* You are called to go on to perfection: go out, not knowing whither. It is the land God will show you. —*Andrew Murray*

August 11

For whosoever will save his life shall lose it; but whosoever shall lose his life for my sake and the gospel's, the same shall save it. —Mark 8:35

At first glance, this teaching of Jesus seems to contradict the facts of life; it is one of those paradoxes that the human mind cannot accept. Our natural conclusion would be that the best way to live, at least the most profitable, is to run as fast as possible so as to miss as little as possible of what life has to offer. Above all, to the modern mind at least, it seems important to put oneself first and gain as much in the way of material possessions as possible. This style of life is exactly the opposite of what Jesus was advocating here as He prepared His followers for His coming death, resurrection, and second coming as the true facts of life.

This is not the only time Jesus taught this truth of selflessness: In Matthew 10:39 He said, "He that findeth his life shall lose it: and he that loseth his life for my sake shall find it." In talking about His coming kingdom in Luke 17:33 He reminded His disciples: "Whosoever shall seek to save his life shall lose it; and whosoever shall lose his life shall preserve it." John 12:25 tells us: "He that loveth his life shall lose it; and he that hateth his life in this world shall keep it unto life eternal." All of Jesus' teachings are contrary to life as the natural man lives it.

What is Jesus saying to you and me as His disciples? After all, we aren't that different from His first followers, and the temptation to put self and substance first existed then, too. This selfless attitude was perfectly exemplified in the Lord Jesus. He came to give himself that others might live, the ultimate sacrifice. Most of us are like the rich young man who sought pleasure in the frantic pursuit of fun, only to find himself strangely empty. Then he found Christ and began to live for others as a lowly Christian servant on the mission field. There he felt finally fulfilled and truly happy. Selfserving had been a breathless kind of bondage for him, but serving others brought a glorious freedom. With Martin Luther he could say: "A Christian man is the most free lord of all, and subject to none; a Christian man is the most dutiful servant of all, and subject to everyone."

August 12

Thou art a God ready to pardon, gracious and merciful.
—Nehemiah 9:17

God does not need our entreaties to move Him to be gracious unto us. He is not a hard, relentless being, needing our supplications before He will be gracious unto us. He does not say, "Repent, and then I will have mercy on you." The revelation of His love toward us comes before our faith. Remember, "it is the goodness of God" (Rom. 2:4) that "leadeth thee to repentance." It is not the fear of hell or of future punishment that brings the soul to contrition.

The change of mind, of which true repentance consists, comes from having our false impressions of God removed. It is when we see that, even while we were yet sinners and rebels, God gave His only begotten Son, that melts our hearts. It is a view of His wondrous grace toward us—His attitude of love—that brings us in repentance to His feet.

This is the great message of the gospel which we may proclaim to all men: He is "a God ready to pardon, gracious and merciful." We are called to repentance on the ground of God's gracious and tender mercies toward us (Joel 2:13).

—Evan H. Hopkins

August 13

The bread of God is he which cometh down from heaven.—John 6:33

No bread that is grown on earth will furnish food for a human soul. In all our earthly striving and ambitions we are thinking only of our perishing part; we are looking only after the poor, frail outer tent, while we are allowing the dweller within to die of hunger. Recently, in a well-furnished home in a city, a family was found starving for bread. There are many souls starving in bodies that are luxuriously cared for. A soul cannot feed on grains and fruits. The finest luxuries of earth will never quench a soul's hunger.

Manna is once called in the Bible "angels' food" (Ps. 78: 24, 25), but this was only a poetical designation, referring to its falling from the sky. Manna did not really come down from heaven. It was not angels' food. It was food for bodies, not for spirits. Angels could not have lived on it. Imagine an angel taking up his abode in some millionaire's mansion on earth. Would he care for the magnificent things filling every room? Would he sit down and feed at the rich man's luxurious table? And souls and angels are much alike in their needs; both are spirits, unable to subsist on material food. Yet many people live as if their souls could be clothed in earth's finery and fed and satisfied with earth's dainties.

Bread for souls must literally come down from heaven. It is the nature of the soul to feed upon immortal things. Its hungers and cravings are for pardon of sin, for peace, for communion with God, for holiness of character, for Christlikeness, for restoration to divine favor. The bread for these spiritual hungers must come down from heaven. It must come in the form of mercy, of grace, of love, of divine friendship, of gifts of life. Such food is found on no table on earth; it grows in no earthly garden; it can come only from God. It is for God, the living God, that our souls hunger and thirst—the bread that "cometh down from heaven." —*J. R. Miller*

August 14

A faithful man will abound with blessings, but he who hastens to be rich will not go unpunished.—Proverbs 28:20 (RSV)

Do not be in too great a hurry. "To everything there is a season, and a time to every purpose under the heaven" (Eccles. 3:1). There is a time for everything that has to be done. He who gave you your life work has given you just enough time to do it in. The length of life's candle is measured out according to the length of the required task. You must take necessary time for meditation, for sleep, for food, for the enjoyment of human love and friendship; and even then there will be time enough left for your necessary duties. More haste, less speed! The feverish hand often gives itself additional toil. "He that believeth shall not make haste."

Where does making a living come in? Is it to be the first consideration or the last? According to Satan's way of looking at life, the bread question is paramount; according to Christ, secondary. Have you ever seriously considered which policy is yours and what you would do if you had to choose in any supreme crisis? This temptation which came to our Lord occurs to us all; sooner or later the devil comes to us with the suggestion that we must *live*, and in the last resort we must make or get our bread, leaving consideration of purity, truth, honor, God, and eternity to come in second best. Jesus answered Satan, "Man shall not live by bread alone, but by every word . . . out of the mouth of God" (Matt. 4:4). Our hunger may be for food, for love, for knowledge; we are tempted to gratify it apart from God. But He who gave us these strong appetites and desires knows that we need food. The body is more than meat, and He that gave the one is responsible for meeting the other. Throw all the responsibility upon Him; they cannot be ashamed who wait for Him.

—*F. B. Meyer*

August 15

I have commanded a widow woman there to sustain thee.—1 Kings 17:9

God uses weak instruments to accomplish His purposes. Elijah needed help, but I wonder if he would have chosen a penniless, starving widow as the source of his sustenance. The widow was God's choice, however, and through her He intended to bless Elijah.

Too often we tend to limit God and insist that He work by our human standards and carry out His will using our methods. But God sometimes uses the small things to accomplish the big tasks. A truly biblical principle is finding expression here. In the New Testament Paul put it this way, "... not many wise men after the flesh, not many mighty, not many noble, are called: but God hath chosen the weak things of the world to confound the things which are mighty" (1 Cor. 1:26, 27).

Take heart, wounded Christian. God can use the smallest vessel to hold the greatest blessing. He can use even you to accomplish His great purpose. All He asks is your willingness to be used. The widow of Zarephath was not even aware of the role she was destined to play in Elijah's life, but she recognized his God (see v. 12) and His inner promptings and she did as that God told her to do for His spokesman, Elijah.

Interestingly enough, Jesus in the New Testament used a widow woman to illustrate the concept of true and sacrificial giving (Mark 12:42, 43). The lesson for us is twofold: God can use the frailest vessel to help us in time of need, or He can use even *us*, a weak vessel, to work out His program. All He asks is our availability!

August 16

The barrel of meal wasted not, neither did the cruse of oil fail, according to the word of the Lord, which he spake by Elijah.—1 Kings 17:16

See here the faithfulness of divine love. You observe that this woman had *daily necessities.* She had herself and her son to feed in a time of famine; and now, in addition, the prophet Elijah had to be fed, too. But though the need was now threefold, yet the supply of meal wasted not, for she had a *constant supply.* Each day she made calls upon the barrel, yet each day it remained the same.

You, dear reader, have daily necessities, and because they come so frequently, you are apt to fear that the barrel of meal will one day be empty and the cruse of oil will fail you. Rest assured that, according to the Word of God, this will not be the case.

Though each day brings its trouble, it also brings its help; and though you should outlive Methuselah, and though your needs should be as many as the sands of the seashore, yet always shall God's grace and mercy last through all your necessities, and you will never know real lack.

For three long years, in this widow's days, the heavens never saw a cloud and the stars never wept a holy tear of dew upon the wicked earth. Famine, desolation, and death made the land a howling wilderness, but this woman never was hungry, but always joyful in abundance.

So shall it be with you. You will see the sinner's hope perish, for he trusts in his native strength; you will see the proud Pharisee's confidence totter, for he builds his hope upon the sand; you will see even some of your own plans blasted and withered, but you yourself will find that your place of defense shall be a fortress of rocks: "Your bread shall be given you, and your water shall be sure." Better have God for your guardian than the Bank of England for your possession. You might spend the wealth of the Indies, but the infinite riches of God you can never exhaust.　　　　—C. H. Spurgeon

August 17

If I then, your Lord and Master, have washed your feet;
ye also ought to wash one another's feet.—John 13:14

All was ready for the last supper, to the very water to wash the feet of the guests, according to custom. But there was no servant to do the work. Each one waited for the other: none of the twelve thought of humbling himself to do the work. Even at the table they were full of the thought as to who would be the greatest in the kingdom they were expecting (Luke 22:26, 27). All at once Jesus rises (they were all still reclining at the table), lays aside His garments, girds himself with a towel, and begins to wash their feet. What an example of service He was! Thus I must live, moving about among God's children as the servant of all. If we first learned from our Lord to associate with others in the blessed spirit of a servant, what a blessing we would become!

The foot washing speaks of a double work: (1) the cleansing and refreshing of the body; (2) the cleansing and refreshing —the saving of the soul. During our Lord's earthly life these two things were ever united: "The sick were healed, to the poor the gospel was preached."

The disciple must not lose sight of this when he receives the command, "Ye ought to wash one another's feet." Remembering that the external and bodily is the gate of the inner life, the spiritual, He makes the salvation of the soul the first object in His holy ministry of love, at the same time, however, seeking the way to the hearts by the path of service, not censure.

The spirit which will enable one to live such a life of service can be learned from Jesus alone. John writes, "Having loved his own which were in the world, he loved them to the end" (John 13:1). For love nothing is too hard. Love never speaks of sacrifice. It was love made Jesus a servant. It is love alone will make the servant's place and work so blessed that we will persevere in it at all costs. Like Jesus, we may have to wash the feet of some Judas who will reward us with ingratitude and betrayal. We may meet many a Peter, impetuous and changeable. Only love, a heavenly unquenchable love, gives us the patience, the courage, and the wisdom for this great work the Lord has set before us in His holy example: "Wash ye one another's feet." —Andrew Murray

August 18

In quietness and in confidence shall be your strength.
—Isaiah 30:15
Be still, and know that I am God. —Psalm 46:10

Tension is the worst of all depressants of the spirit. It draws off energy needed for daily tasks. It places all social contacts in a distorted light and causes the soul to see slights where none are intended.

"Be still," that is, reduce your activity, stop your rushing about, be quiet, quit your talking. Agitation wears us out. Anger burns us up. Disturbed people burn out their life forces. Fussiness does not get us anywhere.

When you have slowed down your tempo of life and quit your efforts at self-vindication, then you are ready to hear the voice for which the soul is listening: "I am God."

Above the human scene hovers the divine order. We cannot derive satisfaction from our feelings, but we can gain deep springs of contentment from our faith in God. Realize that you cannot run the universe. You are not arbiter of other men's lives. Leave those things to God.

When your tensions mount because of "the prosperity of the wicked," sit down and wait in patience upon God. Life is full of examples which show that implicit reliance on God is a sure way to victory. There grows within the soul the exultant feeling that here is reality—certainty. Here is a balm for our aching hearts and troubled spirits.

"The Lord is my light and my salvation: whom shall I fear? The Lord is the strength of my life, of whom shall

I be afraid?" Get out into God's light, and the darkness that has frightened you will be dispelled. Lean upon Him, He knows the end, and He knows how to take you through to complete deliverance. —*O. G. Wilson*

August 19

He also did predestinate to be conformed to the image of his Son, that he might be the firstborn among many brethren.—Romans 8:29

One of the most blessed expressions of God's purpose concerning us in Christ is this word: "Predestinate to be conformed to the image of his Son." The man Christ Jesus is the elect of God; in Him election has its beginning and ending. "In him we are chosen"; for the sake of our union with Him and to His glory our election took place. The believer who seeks in election merely the certainty of his own salvation, or relief from fear and doubt, knows very little of its real glory.

The purposes of election embrace all the riches that are prepared for us in Christ, and reach to every moment and every need of our lives. "Chosen in him that we should be holy and blameless before him in love." It is only when the connection between election and sanctification is rightly understood in the church that the doctrine of election will bring its full blessing (2 Thess. 2:13; 1 Pet. 1:2). It teaches the believer how it is God who must work all in him, and how he may rely even in the smallest matters upon the unchangeable purpose of God to work out itself in the accomplishment of everything He expects of His people. In this light the word "Predestinate to be conformed to the image of his Son" gives new strength to everyone who has begun to take *what Christ is* as the rule of what *he himself is to be.*

And where does this likeness to Christ consist? In sonship It is to the image of His Son we are to be conformed. All the different traits of a Christlike life resolve themselves into this one as their spring and end. We are "predestinated unto the adoption of children by Jesus Christ." It was as the Son that Christ lived and served and pleased the Father. It is only as a son with the spirit of His own Son in my heart that I can live and serve and please the Father. As a son the Father has promised to provide my every need. As a son I live in dependence and trust, in love and obedience, in joy and hope. —*Andrew Murray*

August 20

Thou wast a servant in the land of Egypt, and . . . the Lord thy God brought thee out . . . through a mighty hand and by a stretched out arm. —Deuteronomy 5:15

It is important that we cry for grace from God to see His hand in every trial, and then for grace, seeing His hand, to submit at once to it—not only to submit, but to rejoice in it. "It is the Lord, let him do what seemeth him good." I think there is generally an end to troubles when we get to that, for when the Lord sees we are willing that He should do what He wills, then He takes back His hand and says: "I need not chasten My child; he submits himself to Me. What would have been worked out by My chastisement is worked out already, and therefore I will not chasten him."

There are two ways of getting help. One is to go around to all your friends, be disappointed, and then go to God at last. The other is to go to God first. That is the shortest way. God can make your friends help you afterwards. Seek first God and His righteousness. Out of all troubles the surest deliverance is from God's right hand. Don't go to friends, but pour out your story to God:

> Were half the breath that's vainly spent,
> To heaven in supplication sent;
> Our cheerful song would oftener be,
> Hear what the Lord hath done for me.

Human friends fail us. The strongest arm can be broken, and the most faithful heart will sometimes waver. But our God is eternal and omnipotent; who ever trusted Him in vain?

David learned this lesson well and shared it many times in his songs of love for His Savior God. Here are some of them: "God hath given his angels charge over thee"; "he that dwelleth in the secret place of the Most High, shall abide under the shadow of the Almighty." The Lord said of him: "Because he hath set his love upon me, therefore will I deliver him: I will set him on high, because he hath known my name." He has proved it by trusting in Me alone; therefore will I never fail him. Lean wholly upon God, and since He is everywhere you will stand upright leaning upon Him.

—*C. H. Spurgeon*

August 21

While he yet spake, there came . . . certain which said, Thy daughter is dead. —Mark 5:35

At first glance it seems that Jesus had tarried too long on the road. To us it seems that He should not have stopped to talk to the woman who touched His garment (v. 30) or heal her. The child of Jairus was dying and there was not a moment to lose! Why did the Master not hurry on to get to her bedside before she died?

One thing we learn from this incident is that Jesus is never in a rush. He is never so engrossed in one case of need that He cannot stop to give attention to another. He is never so pressed for time that we have to "wait our turn." No matter what He is doing, He will always hear instantly our cry for help.

A little child's idea of God's listening to her was that when she began to pray God told all the angels to be quiet, saying, "I hear a noise—a little girl's noise"; and then all the angels kept perfectly still until she said amen. The angels did not need to hush for God to hear the humblest little one pray; yet the little girl was not far wrong.

Another thing we learn from this delay is that Jesus never comes too late or waits too long. It certainly seemed that He had tarried too long this time; but when we see how it all came out, we are sure that He made no mistake. True, the child died while He lingered; but this only gave Him an opportunity for a greater miracle. He waited that He might do a more glorious work. There is always a good reason when Christ delays to answer our prayers or come to our help. He waits that He may do far more for us in the end. So we have one more lesson on letting our Lord have His own way with us, even in answering our prayers. He knows best when to answer and what answer to give.　　　　　*—J. R. Miller*

August 22

And Peter said unto him, Aeneas, Jesus Christ maketh thee whole: arise, and make thy bed. And he arose immediately.—Acts 9:34

When a physician heals a patient, he acts on him from the outside, and does something which, if possible and ideally, will ever after render the patient independent of his aid. He restores him to perfect health and leaves him.

With the work of our Lord Jesus it is in both respects the opposite. Jesus works not from the outside, but from the inside, by entering himself in the power of His Spirit into our very life. Bodily healing has as its purpose independency from the physician. Spiritual healing that Jesus works has one condition of success: to bring us into *such dependence upon Jesus himself that we shall not be able for one single moment to do without Him!*

Christ Jesus himself is our life, in a sense about which many Christians have no understanding. The prevailing feeble and sickly life is entirely owed to the lack of understanding of this divine truth: that as long as we expect Christ continually to do something for us from heaven, in single acts of grace from time to time, and each time trust Him to give us what will last only a little while, we cannot be restored to perfect health. But once we see that there is to be nothing of our own for a single moment, that it is to be all Christ moment by moment, and learn to accept it from Him and trust Him for it, the life of Christ becomes the health of our soul.

Health is nothing but life in its normal, undisturbed action. Christ gives us health by giving us himself as our life; so He becomes our strength for our walk. Isaiah's words find their New Testament fulfillment: They that wait upon the Lord shall walk and not faint, because Christ is now the strength of their life.

It is strange how believers sometimes think this life of dependence is too great a strain and a loss of personal liberty. They admit a need for dependence but with room left for their own will and energy. They do not see that even a partial dependence makes us debtors, and leaves us nothing of which to boast. They forget that our relationship to God, and cooperation with Him, is not that He does the larger part and we the lesser, but that God does all and we do all—God all in us, we all through God. He who accepts the life of unceasing dependence on Christ as life, and health, and strength is made whole.

—*Andrew Murray*

August 23

As thou hast sent me into the world, even so have I also sent them into the world. . . . As my Father hath sent me, even so send I you. —John 17:18; 20:21

Our heavenly mission is one of the most glorious aspects of our conformity to our Lord. He says it plainly in the most solemn moments of His life: "that *even* as the Father hath sent" Him, so sends He His disciples. He says it to the Father in His high-priestly prayer, as the ground upon which He asks for their keeping and sanctification. He says it to the disciples after His resurrection, as the ground on which they are to receive the Holy Spirit. Nothing will help us more to know and fulfill our mission than to realize how perfectly it corresponds to the mission of Christ, how they are, in fact, identical.

Our mission is like His *in its object*. Why did the Father send His Son? To make known His love and His will in the salvation of sinners. After the Lord had fulfilled His mission, He ascended into heaven and became to the world like the Father, the unseen One. And now He gave over His mission to His disciples, after having shown them how to fulfill it. They must so represent Him, the invisible One, that from seeing them men can judge what He is. Every Christian must be the image of Jesus—must so exhibit in his person and conduct the same love to sinners and desire for their salvation as animated Christ.

Our mission is like Christ's *in its origin* too. It was the Father's love that chose Christ for this work, and counted Him worthy of such honor and trust. We also are chosen by Christ for this work. Every redeemed one knows that it was not he who sought the Lord, but the Lord who sought and chose him. Whoever you are, and wherever you dwell, believer, the Lord knows you and your surroundings and has need of you. He has chosen you to be His representative in the circle where you are moving. Fix your heart on this truth. He has fixed His heart on you and saved you that you should exhibit His image to others. Your mission is in very truth just like His!

—Andrew Murray

August 24

*For the eyes of the Lord run to and fro throughout the whole earth, to show himself strong in the behalf of them whose heart is perfect toward him.—*2 Chronicles 16:9

What precious lessons these words teach us for the Christian's life. To have God reveal His strength in us, to have Him make us strong for life or work, for doing or for suffering, *our heart must be perfect with Him.* Let us not shrink from accepting the truth. Let no preconceived opinion as to the impossibility of perfection keep us from allowing the Word of God to have its full effect upon us. He shows himself strong to those whose heart is perfect toward Him.

God looks for men who trust Him fully; in them He will show His power. Our minds can form no right conception of what He can do for us. Even when we have His Word and promises, our human thoughts of what He means are always defective. By nothing do we so dishonor God more than limiting Him. By nothing do we limit Him more than by allowing our human ideas of what He purposes, to be the measure of our expectations. The reliance of a heart perfect toward Him is simply this: it yields to Him, as God; it rests upon Him, it allows Him, as God, to do in His own way what He has promised. The heart is perfect toward Him in meeting Him with a perfect faith for all that He is and does as God. Faith expects from God what is beyond all expectation.

The one great need of the spiritual life is to know how entirely it is dependent upon God working in us and what the exceeding greatness of His power is in us who believe. As the soul knows this, and with a perfect heart yields to this Almighty

God to let Him do His work within, oh! how strong He will show himself to usward! —*Andrew Murray*

August 25

The whole family in heaven and earth.—Ephesians 3:15

The Revised Version gives it as "From whom every family in heaven and earth is named." "Every fatherhood," as it is in the margin. The sentence occurs in one of Paul's prayers— one of the most wonderful of the inspired prayers recorded in the Scriptures. In the same epistle the apostle writes: There is "one God and Father of all, who is above all, and through all, and in you all" (Eph. 4:6).

There is a sense in which it may be said that God is the Father of all men. But when the apostle speaks of the relation which we are privileged to occupy toward God as Christians, he says of believers only, "Ye are all the children of God by faith in Christ Jesus" (Gal. 3:26). And when he speaks of the Spirit in the same connection, he writes, "For ye have received not the spirit of bondage again to fear; but ye have received the Spirit of adoption, whereby we cry, Abba, Father. The Spirit . . . beareth witness with our spirit, that we are the children of God" (Rom. 8:15, 16).

Here is the secret of all true and acceptable service. We become God's children before we are called to be His servants. —*Evan H. Hopkins*

August 26

For the arrows of the Almighty are within me, the poison whereof drinketh up my spirit: the terrors of God do set themselves in array against me.—Job 6:4

The path of the Christian is not always bright with sunshine; he has his seasons of darkness and storm. True, it is written in God's Word, "Her ways are ways of pleasantness, and all her paths are peace." It is a great truth that the Christian faith is calculated to give a man happiness below as well as bliss above; but experience tells us that if the course of the just be "as the shining light that shineth more and more unto the perfect day," yet sometimes *that* light is eclipsed. At certain periods clouds cover the believer's sun, and he walks in darkness and sees no light.

There are many who have enjoyed the presence of God for a season; they have basked in the sunshine of the earliest stages of their Christian experience; they have walked among the "green pastures" by the side of the "still waters," but suddenly they find their glorious sky is clouded; instead of the land of Goshen they have to tread the sandy desert; in the place of sweet waters, they find troubled streams, bitter to their taste, and they say, "Surely, if I were a child of God, this would not happen."

Don't say that, you who are walking in present darkness. The best of God's children must drink from the bitter well; the dearest of His people must bear the cross. No Christian has enjoyed perpetual prosperity; no believer can always keep his harp from the willows. Perhaps the Lord allotted you at first a smooth and unclouded path because you were weak and timid. He tempered the wind for the shorn lamb, but now that you are stronger in the spiritual life, you must enter upon the riper and rougher experience of God's full-grown children.

We need winds and tempests to exercise our faith, to tear off the rotten bough of self-dependence, and to root us more firmly in Christ. The day of evil reveals to us the value of our glorious hope. —C. H. Spurgeon

August 27

And I . . . saw the holy city, new Jerusalem, coming down from God out of heaven, prepared as a bride adorned for her husband. . . . He that overcometh shall inherit all things; and I will be his God, and he shall be my son.
—Revelation 21:2, 7

What a stirring vision John must have had as he penned these words under the inspiration of the Holy Spirit. His "pad on Patmos" must have literally vibrated as he gazed upon the streets and houses of gold. After such a vision, Patmos must have looked pretty dim and dingy to his dazzled eyes.

That says something to me about my attitude toward the things of this world. Should I be concentrating my attention earthward when heaven has so much to offer the Christian? Earthly or material things come only to eventually pass away— as does this physical life on which we place so much value.

A better motto for life would be the words of Jesus in Revelation 21:7, "He that overcometh shall inherit all things; and I will be his God, and he shall be my son." This verse tells me that I am a rich man, and I have a legacy so vast that heaven alone could hold it! Why then should I concentrate all my efforts toward earthly gain and what ultimately cannot satisfy the deepest longings of my heart? When death strikes down the unbeliever, he leaves everything he worked so hard to gain. When death comes gently for the believer, on the other hand, he moves on into the timeless storehouse of heaven, the place where he has been "laying up treasures" that will never pass away.

I'm glad for the legacy that is mine as a follower of Christ, and I pray that others may become heirs of that same promise because I show Christ's joy and let it flow through me to others. What a treasure to know that I "shall inherit all things" if I overcome through Him who redeems and keeps me!

August 28

I have chosen thee in the furnace of affliction.—Isaiah 48:10

It has been suggested that this scripture could be translated: "I have chosen thee *for* the furnace of affliction." Those choice saints who spend long days and torturing nights in the refining crucible are chosen by Infinite Wisdom to show what grace does for a man. If life has brought loss and pain, do not take long views but live one moment at a time—this present moment.

"Whom the Lord loveth he chasteneth" (Heb. 12:6).

"As many as I love, I rebuke and chasten" (Rev. 3:19).

The more severe the chastening the more intense the love. This sounds like a paradox, yet it is true. Life's grindings polish us, and life's pressures toughen the moral fiber of the soul.

Calamities enable the soul to give sympathetic help of the highest quality to the distressed. When one sits down beside a tortured soul and says, "I know how you feel, I have been through it," strength is imparted and hope is revived. Those who have suffered much are like those who know many languages: they understand and are understood by all. David, the writer of the Psalms, said, "Before I was afflicted I went astray: but now have I kept thy word" (119:67). He allowed his load to lift him and made capital of his calamities.

"Why should I start at the plow of my Lord that makes the deep furrows on my soul?" asked Samuel Rutherford. "I know He is no idle husbandman. He purposeth a harvest." How are you meeting your afflictions? There are those who give up at the first sign of pain. Those who permit their troubles to make them cynical. But there are those who make capital out of their calamities, and become rich in grace because of the roughness of the way. Bitterness is everywhere if you have it within you; calamities are capital if you shut the door to bitterness. —O. G. Wilson

August 29

A bruised reed shall he not break, and the smoking flax shall he not quench: he shall bring forth judgment unto truth.—Isaiah 42:3

What a beautiful revelation of the delicate gentleness of the Lord! "The bruised reed"—is it the impaired musical reed that cannot now give forth a musical sound and can only be thrown away? He will not snap it and throw it into the fire. The discordant life can be made tuneful again; He will put "a new song in my mouth."

"And the smoking flax"—the life has lost its fire, and therefore its light; its enthusiasm, and therefore its ideals; the life that is smouldering into the cold ashes of moral and spiritual death! He will not stamp it out with His foot. The smouldering fire can be rekindled, a spent enthusiasm can be revived. "He shall baptize you . . . with fire!"

So He comes to minister to those who are ill. He comes to restore the injured member: "to open blind eyes." He comes to give vision to restored sight: "to be a light to the Gentiles." And He comes to endow the restored life with a rich and gracious freedom: "to bring out the prisoners from the prison." Sight, and light, and freedom! My Lord is at the door, and these gifts are in His hand. —*J. H. Jowett*

August 30

Sit still, my daughter.—Ruth 3:18

Stillness of soul is what the great majority of God's children need. Restlessness in Christian service is often mistaken for activity and zeal. The reason of the exhaustion so many experience in working for the Lord is to be found in the lack of inward rest.

Perhaps it is one of the last things we think we ought to do when we first enter upon His service, namely, to let ourselves down, with all our cares, and rest in His almighty arms. And yet it is one of the first lessons the Good Shepherd constrains His following sheep to learn.

"The Lord is my shepherd; I shall not want. He *maketh me to lie down* in green pastures: he leadeth me beside waters of *quietness.*" Before we can work without friction, without exhaustion, and without waste of strength, He teaches us to be *still.* He sets us free from the energy of the flesh and from the fret and disquiet of the natural man.

Here, again, is the secret of all progress in our knowledge of God: "Be still, and know that I am God" (Ps. 46:10). "Mary . . . sat at Jesus' feet, and heard his word" (Luke 10:39). —*Evan H. Hopkins*

August 31

Blessed are they that are [perfect] in the way, who walk in the law of the Lord . . . that seek him with the whole heart. —Psalm 119:1, 2

What is meant by this being "perfect in the way" becomes plain as we study the Psalm. Perfection includes two elements. The one is the perfection of heart, the earnestness of purpose with which a man gives himself to seek God and His will. The other, the perfection of obedience, in which a man seeks, not only to obey some, but all the commandments of his God, and rests content with nothing less than the New Testament privilege of "standing perfect in all the will of God." Of both, the Psalmist speaks: "Blessed are they that seek him with the whole heart"; "With my whole heart have I sought thee"; "O how I love thy law!"

This is indeed the perfect heart, this wholeheartedness. In it, we have the root of all perfection—but it is only the root and the beginning. There is another element lacking. God is found in His will; he who would truly find and fully enjoy God must meet Him in all His will. This is not always understood. A man may have his heart intent on serving God perfectly, and yet may be unconscious how very imperfect his knowledge of God's will is. As far as he knows, he does God's will. But he forgets how much there is of that will that he does not yet know. He can learn a very blessed lesson from the writer of our Psalm.

Hear how he speaks: "I have refrained my feet from *every* evil way"; "I hate *every* false way"; "I esteem *all* thy precepts concerning all things to be right." It is this surrender to a life of entire and perfect obedience that explains at once the need he felt for divine teaching, and the confidence with which he pleaded for it and expected it: "Let my heart be perfect in thy testimonies." The soul that longs for nothing less than to be perfect in the way, and in deep consciousness of its need of a divine teaching pleads for it, will not be disappointed. —*Andrew Murray*

September 1

Jesus, looking upon them, saith, With men it is impossible, but not with God: for with God all things are possible. —Mark 10:27

Doing the impossible! The songwriter put it this way: "God specializes in things thought impossible." He made it rhyme with rivers that were "uncrossable," but God's power extends far beyond crossing rivers without bridges or boats. And He has always been in the business of doing the impossible. Jeremiah said of Him: "Ah Lord God! behold, thou hast made the heaven and the earth by thy great power and stretched out arm, and there is nothing too hard for thee" (32:17).

God's power over the impossible was expressed by Jesus in other contexts as well. In the Mark passage He was referring to the impossibility of the rich man being saved. In Matthew 17:20, He is talking about the all-conquering strength of faith when He says: "If you have faith as a grain of mustard seed, you will say to this mountain, 'Move hence to yonder place, and it will move; and nothing will be impossible to you'" (RSV). In reference to His own blasting of the barren fig tree, Jesus said: "Truly, I say to you, if you have faith and never doubt, you will not only do what has been done to the fig tree, but even if you say to this mountain, 'Be taken up and cast into the sea,' it will be done. And whatever you ask in prayer, you will receive, if you have faith" (Matt. 21:21, RSV).

These verses reveal that the tremendous power resident in God is available to the one who believes in Him. His Spirit takes up residence in the believer, and through that all-powerful Spirit the believer himself can accomplish the impossible. Back in the eighteenth century, the poet Wm. Cowper wrote:

> God moves in a mysterious way
> His wonders to perform;
> He plants His footsteps in the sea
> And rides upon the storm.

That power can work in your life if you are empty of self! What was God's greatest accomplishment in the "impossible" category? He reconciled me, sinner that I was, with my all-powerful and holy God!

September 2

For ye shall not go out with haste, nor go by flight: for the Lord will go before you; and the God of Israel will be your rearward. —Isaiah 52:12

When allied troops were moving toward the Normandy coast on D-Day, mine-sweepers went before the ships filled with soldiers and their equipment. Without this precaution it would have been certain disaster for the whole undertaking.

God is our divine minesweeper. He goes before the trusting soul to prepare a safe way. Our responsibility is to follow carefully the path He marks out. One man on a ship making the first landing on the Normandy coast said, "We were following the minesweeper closely, but at one point we discovered we were out of the cleared channel. We stopped everything until we had corrected our position."

It is of great importance that the child of God follow closely. When he discovers he has missed the path marked out by the Lord, every activity should be stopped until the soul is once again in the protection that comes with close fellowship with God.

Are there towering mountains of difficulty in the path ahead? His obligation is to go before; our obligation is to follow closely; and where He goes He will supply strength and power for us to follow. I know not what tomorrow may bring, but I am secure, for the promise is: "The Lord will go before you." He is never surprised, discomfited, or thrown off balance. He is equal to every emergency and He will not fail. His wisdom prepares the road over which I must travel, and His love allows no thorns or deep valleys but that are good for me. He determines the character of the road I am to travel, and He chooses the weather I am to encounter. "I will trust and not be afraid, for the Lord Jehovah is my strength."
—O. G. Wilson

September 3

He turneth . . . the dry ground into watersprings. —Psalm 107:35

This is one of the miracles of grace. The good Lord makes a dry experience the fountain of blessing. I pass into an apparently waste place and I find riches of consolation. Even in "the valley of the shadow" I come upon "green pastures" and "still waters." I find flowers in the ruts of the hardest roads if I am in "the way of God's commandments." God's providence is the pioneer of every faithful pilgrim. "His blessed feet have gone before." What I shall need is already foreseen, and foresight with the Lord means forethought and provision. Every hour gives the loyal disciples surprises of grace. Let me therefore not fear when the path of duty turns into the wilderness. The wilderness is as habitable with God as the crowded city, and in His fellowship my bread and water are sure. The Lord has strange manna for the children of disappointment, and He makes water to "gush forth from the rock." Duty can lead me nowhere without Him, and His provision is abundant both in "the thirsty desert and the dewy meadow." There will be a spring at the foot of every hill, and I shall find "lilies of peace" even in the lonely valleys.
—J. H. Jowett

September 4

Make me to know thy ways, O Lord; teach me thy paths.—Psalm 25:4 (RSV)

Sometimes we don't know what God's will is, and so we have to pray that God will show us what His will is. We want to know what God's plan is in a particular matter; oftentimes we have to pray a prayer for guidance before we can pray a prayer of faith. "Make me to know thy ways, O Lord; teach me thy paths. Lead me in thy truth, and teach me, for thou art the God of my salvation; for thee I wait all the day long... The friendship of the Lord is for them who fear him, and he makes known to them his covenant" (Ps. 25:4, 5, 14, RSV). This is the concern of the Psalmist; he wants to know what God's will is. He wants to move in the stream of God's commandment. So he prays a prayer for guidance.

The prayer for guidance begins with a period of waiting. You come before the Lord, and you just get quiet. There is no activity, but rather a passivity. You are trying to hear.

Have you ever been in a situation where there is just a faint sound? You say, "Is that a mouse scratching over there in the corner?" You even quit breathing so you can hear better.

We need to get quiet before God. We need to get quiet inside and out. In our day and age that takes some doing. You will be astonished to discover how much noise there is in your mind; in your whole being, how full of noise you are. If you want to hear God's voice, you have to get quiet. Elijah heard a great and strong wind, an earthquake, a raging fire. But God wasn't in any of these things. Then, after all the noise, God began to speak to him in a still, small voice.

—*Larry Christenson*

September 5

They that know thy name will put their trust in thee: for thou, Lord, hast not forsaken them that seek thee.
—Psalm 9:10

To know God's name is to know His character—to know *Him.* Had God not revealed himself, man could never have attained this knowledge. To know Him is to see His trustworthiness; and when we are convinced of that, it is not difficult to put our trust in Him.

Ignorance of God is the secret of all our waywardness. We begin to pray when the first glimmer of the light of the knowledge of God breaks into our souls. "If you only knew what a wonderful gift God has for you," Jesus said to the

Samaritan woman at Jacob's well. What then? "And who I am, you would ask me for some *living* water!" (John 4:10, Living Bible). "I know whom I have believed" (not "in whom," as many inaccurately quote the text).

I know Him whom I have trusted. The whole gospel is comprehended in the divine Names. Let this be our prayer: "Lord, show me thyself. Let me know Thee. Unveil to the eye of my soul Thy glorious attributes. Let me forget my own faith and my own efforts to trust Thee. Let me see Thy glorious trustworthiness, and rest." —*Evan H. Hopkins*

September 6

And therefore will the Lord wait, that he may be gracious unto you.... Blessed are all they that wait for [upon] him.—Isaiah 30:18

The idea of "waiting upon the Lord" is a theme that recurs over and over in the Scriptures. Elsewhere Isaiah says, "But they that wait upon the Lord shall renew their strength ... mount up with wings ... run, and not be weary ... walk, and not faint." In Lamentations 3:25 Jeremiah affirms, "The Lord is good unto them that wait for him, to the soul that seeketh him." The Psalms, too, are replete with admonitions to wait upon the Lord and promises to those who do so.

This posture of patience is particularly difficult for modern man who is accustomed to rapid movement and instant solutions. But here is a lesson we must learn if we are to really discover what it means to depend upon God. We want to move ahead of God even when He "waits for us," but our proper place is on our knees before Him. And this is where the rub comes in. How difficult it is to remain on our knees when we want to be moving! We want immediate action rather than patient waiting. But God in His wisdom knows what is best for us. Today and tomorrow are the same to Him. The past, present, and future are all "now" to Him, so we can confidently rest in His timing and His answers to our prayers.

After all, as Isaiah points out, He wants to "be gracious" unto us. The Living Bible says He wants to "show (us) his love," but in our impatience, we don't give Him the opportunity to do what is best for us. Instead, too often we settle for second best because we can get that sooner. If we want His best, we must wait for His best timing as well. Our seeking must be patient rather than pushy. Then our waiting will be rewarded.

September 7

Simon he surnamed Peter.—Mark 3:16

In a gallery in Europe are shown, side by side, the first and last works of a great artist. The first is very rude and faulty; the last is a masterpiece. The contrast shows the results of long culture and practice. These two names, Simon and Peter, are like those two pictures. "Simon" shows us the rude fisherman of Galilee, with all his rashness, his ignorance, his imperfectness. "Peter" shows us the apostle of the Acts and the Epistles, the rock firm and secure, the man of great power, before whose Spirit-filled eloquence thousands of proud hearts bowed, swayed like the trees of the forest before the tempest; the gentle, tender soul whose words fell like a benediction; the noble martyr witnessing to the death of his Lord. Study the two pictures together to see what grace can do for a man.

It is not hard to take roses, lilies, and all the rarest flowers, and with them make forms of exquisite beauty; but to take weeds, dead grasses, dried leaves trampled and torn, and faded flowers, and make lovely things out of such materials is the severest test of skill. It would not be hard to take an angel and train him into a glorious messenger; but to take such a man as Simon, or Saul, or a John Bunyan, and make out of him a holy saint or mighty apostle—that is the test of power. Yet that is what Christ did and is doing and has been doing ever since Peter's transformation. He takes the poorest stuff—despised and worthless, outcast of men in many cases—and when He has finished His gracious work we behold a saint whiter than snow. The sculptor beheld an angel in the rough, blackened stone, rejected and thrown away; and when men saw the stone again, lo! there was the angel cut from the block. Christ can take us, rough and unpolished as we are, and in His hands our lives shall grow into purity and loveliness until He presents them at last before the throne, faultless and perfect.   *—J. R. Miller*

September 8

Whoso trusteth in the Lord, happy is he.—Proverbs 16:20

We never know the meaning of trust until we learn the nature of trial. It is in the trial that we have to put into practice the theory of believing in God. Trust is to become the habit of the soul.

Often, however, the young disciple is greatly perplexed about faith, because, instead of being occupied with the object of faith, he is thinking of the act of believing. But faith never comes this way. It has no existence apart from Him who is the object of it.

"Whoso trusteth *in the Lord.*" Let our thoughts be occupied with God's revealed character, with what He is to us and what He has done for us, and we shall, without *trying* to believe, begin to put our trust in Him. It is with what God is that we have to be occupied. The mind then finds its resting place. It stays itself on God. A peace is then known that could never be found in the world. We see then how true are the words, "Happy is he."

Trial therefore is the school of trust. It is there we learn the lesson of implicitly confiding in God and of waiting patiently on Him. —*Evan H. Hopkins*

September 9

The Lord knoweth the days of the upright: and their inheritance shall be forever.—Psalm 37:18

As we live our lives, we are painting a picture. We are given a palette on which are placed certain colors by the wise hand of our heavenly Father. These colors we do not choose, but use them we must.

The picture we paint will be determined by our mixing of the colors given us. The dark colors of sorrow, disappointment, and grief are as necessary as the brilliant hues. Not every calamity is a curse. Often adversity is the schoolmaster of life's most valuable lessons.

I looked upon the canvas of a great artist. It was nothing but great blotches of dark paint which was most unattractive. Seeing my apparent dislike, he patiently explained, "This is only the background." Later he showed me the completed picture. It was breathtaking in its beauty, harmony, and splendor.

I asked, "What became of the dark ugly background?" He replied, "It was used to enhance the bright colors of the picture."

Paint on! Do not fear the dark, somber colors. They are as necessary as the sparkling bright ones. A wise providence will help you mix them in the correct proportions for a beautiful life.

Pray about your painting. Your "unseen Partner" will make suggestions, and bring ease of mind as to the outcome. He knows more about mixing colors than you do, and He has a clear idea of what the finished product is to be.

Hold on! Keep on! It has been said that genius is nothing

but continued attention. Skillful sailors gained their reputation as seamen from battling the storms and tempests.

You are painting life's picture. The final showing will be in the eternities of God. So paint that you will not be disappointed or embarrassed at the unveiling in God's great art gallery. —*O. G. Wilson*

September 10

I will give thee the treasures of darkness, and hidden riches of secret places.—Isaiah 45:3

Beloved, take care lest in the very line where your prejudices are setting you off from God's people and God's truth, you are missing the treasures of your life. Take the treasures of heaven no matter how they come to you, even if it be as earthly treasures generally are, like the kernel inside the rough shell, or the gem in the bosom of the hard rock.—*A. B. Simpson*

In Proverbs 25:2 we read, "It is the glory of God to conceal a thing." The Lord conceals that He may the more abundantly reveal. He hides a thing so that we may have the refining discipline of seeking for it, and enjoy the keen delights of discovery. Things obtained easily are esteemed lightly. The pebble that lies in the path is beneath regard. The pearl that lies buried in ocean depths is a treasure of rare price. The pain of getting intensifies the joy of possessing. If everything could be easily picked up from the surface, life would become shallow and superficial.

"The kingdom of heaven is like unto a treasure hid in a field." We have to dig for our wealth. We are called to a life of toil and discipline and research. Things are concealed so that life may be a perpetual inquest. The only healthy life is the life of ardent inquisitiveness: "ask," "seek," "knock." But where shall one search?

One never knows where the wealth may be concealed. The most unpromising piece of ground may be the hiding place of the finest gold. Therefore "I will search in the common places, into the humdrum ways of life; I will pierce into the heart of tame and sober duties; I will look for treasure even in the dark cloud, and I will assume that there is a dowry of grace even in the ministry of pain. I will search for the wealth of poverty, the advantage of apparent disadvantage, the jewels that may be in the heaviest grief. I will look for hidden treasure, for 'it is the glory of God to conceal a thing.'" —*J. H. Jowett*

September 11

Seeing we also are compassed about with so great a cloud of witnesses, let us lay aside every weight, and the sin which doth so easily beset us, and let us run with patience the race that is set before us. —Hebrews 12:1

We are not running a solitary race. Countless eyes are watching us from the heights of heavenly attainment, and glorious lives are calling to us from the records of the past and reminding us that as they have overcome, so may we. Our text is just summing up the sublime chapter which has preceded and of that long catalog of illustrious names which adorned and illustrated the records of faith from the beginning. The writer calls them "witnesses." A witness is not just a spectator, but is also someone who is brought forward to prove something. These witnesses have something to prove, and their testimony from first to last might be summed up in one word, "Cast not away your confidence which has great recompence of reward." Those "who through faith and patience inherit the promises" are calling to us from the heights that they have won, and are telling us that what man once did man can do again.

Not only do they remind us of the necessity of faith, but also of that patience by which faith has its perfect work. Let us fear to take ourselves out of the hands of our heavenly Guide, or to miss a single lesson of His loving discipline by discouragement and doubt. An old blacksmith said the one thing he feared was to be cast on the scrap heap; he said when he tempered a piece of steel he heated and hammered it, and then suddenly plunged it into cold water. If it did not stand the tests, he threw it on the scrap heap and sold it for junk. So the Lord tests us, and if we are not willing to stand the test, or are not fit for the tempering process, He may throw us on the scrap heap. "Reprobate silver." But Jesus is calling us to run the race with Him, the Source of all we need, whispering, *"Thou shalt overcome through Me."* —A. B. Simpson

September 12

I remember thee upon my bed, and meditate on thee in the night watches. —Psalm 63:6

What is the most important treasure, the greatest and most glorious that man can see or find upon earth? *Nothing less than God himself!*

And what is the chief and the best and most glorious activity that a man needs every day and can do every day? Nothing less than to seek and to know, and to love and to praise this glorious God. As glorious as God is, so is the glory which begins to work in the heart and life of the man who gives himself to live for God.

Have you learned what is the first and the greatest duty you have to do each day? Nothing less and nothing greater than to seek this God, to meet Him, to worship Him, to live for Him and for His glory. It is a great step forward in the life of the Christian when he truly sees this and yields himself to consider fellowship with God every day as the most important activity of his life.

Take time and ask whether this be not the truth, the highest wisdom and the one thing for which a Christian is above all to live—*to know his God aright* and to love Him with his whole heart. Believe that it is not only blessedly true, but that God himself desires greatly that you should thus live for and with Him. He will, in answer to prayer, equip you to do so.

"O God, thou art my God; early will I seek thee: my soul thirsteth for thee, my flesh longeth for thee in a dry and thirsty land, where no water is" (Ps. 63:1). "Blessed are they that seek him with the whole heart" (Ps. 119:2).

Repeat these words in deep reverence and childlike longing till their spirit and power enter your heart; and wait upon God till you begin to realize what the blessedness is of thus meeting with Him. As you persevere you will learn to expect that the fear and the presence of God can abide with you through all the day. "I waited patiently for the Lord; and he . . . heard my cry" (Ps. 40:1). —*Andrew Murray*

September 13

The disciple is not above his master.—Matthew 10:24

A disciple is a learner—a learner not only of the Lord's truth, but of the Lord's humility. He has to follow His Master both in doctrine and in suffering. He must always be at his Master's feet. He must never be or strive to be above Him.

And so the true disciple finds that in following he has perpetually to descend. For his Master is the very embodiment of humility. He "made himself of no reputation"—emptied himself. And the disciple must not seek for himself anything above that which his Master sought for himself. "It is enough for the disciple that he be as his master, and the servant as his lord."

The Master was among us as one who served. Though Lord of all, He took the place of a servant. It was as such He glorified His Father. It is as such that we shall glorify *our* Lord.

Oh, for this spirit of self-abnegation—this mind which was in Christ Jesus! There is no real following until we know what it is to ignore self. "If any man will come after me, let him deny himself, and take up his cross, and follow me" (Matt. 16:24). This denial of self is not the end but the condition of following the Master. —*Evan H. Hopkins*

September 14

Looking up to heaven, he sighed, and saith unto him, Ephphata....—Mark 7:34

How it must have saddened the heart of Jesus to walk through this world and see so much human misery! There is a story of a sculptor who wept as at his feet he saw the shattered fragments of his breathing marble, on which he had spent years of patient, loving toil. Jesus walked through this world amid the ruin of the noblest work of His hands, man. Everywhere He saw the destruction wrought by sin. So His grief was twofold: tender sympathy with human suffering, and sorrow over the ruinous work of sin.

It is a precious thought to us that we are so dear to Jesus that the beholding of our grief touches and stirs His heart. What a wonderful revelation it is to us that we are thought of by Him, and that He cares enough for us to be moved to sorrow by our woes and sufferings!

Then Christ's help does not end in the thrill of sympathy. That is about as far as human help usually goes. People stand over us when we are in misfortune or trouble, and heave a sigh, and then pass on. Sometimes this is all they can do. Human sympathy in suffering is a wonderful help; but the assurance of divine help is infinitely more uplifting. Then Christ gives real help. He was moved with compassion when He saw the widow of Nain in her lonely sorrow, and He restored her dead son to her. He wept with Mary and Martha, and then raised their brother. He sighed as He looked on the misfortune of this deaf man in our text, and then He opened his ears.

He is "touched with the feeling of our infirmities," and then gives "grace to help in time of need." Not only does He pity us when He finds us deaf to all the sweet voices of love and grace, but He is ready to open our ears. We have only to bring to Christ our infirmities, and He will take them and give us back in their places souls with all their lost powers restored.
—*J. R. Miller*

September 15

He leadeth me beside the still waters... in the paths of righteousness....—Psalm 23:2, 3

Despite the devious road over which David had traveled, he could trustingly say: "God leadeth me." God's leadership had led through the cave of Adullam and into the land of the Philistines. There were by the way many injustices, much grief and slander, but David still affirmed, "God leadeth me."

"He leadeth me beside the still waters." The greatest hindrance to a life of deep devotion is our feverish rushing about.

We talk about "God's minutes," about "a word of prayer," as though that were all we could possibly spare to God in whose hands is our very breath. His admonition is, "Be still and know that I am God." Quiet down! Do not be in such a hurry—as though you were greedy for the graveyard. Listen to God.

"By the still waters." Often this means to stand and wait. Others may rush past us to intense activity, but we are in the calm of "still waters." But God may lead from the still waters to the raging tempest. But He leads!

He was as truly leading the apostle Paul when in the storm at sea as when Paul gave the unsurpassed oration on Mars' Hill. We want God to lead us, to be sure, but we want to have something to say as to the direction and the nature of the road we take. However, when He leads He is in full command. He chooses the road, the weather, and the loads.

"He leadeth me." This means guidance but it also means discipline. He takes me over the road which His love and wisdom know is best for me. Make sure of this one thing—His leading will take us through the valley of humiliation and suffering. He allows testings to come, not that He may know what is in us, but that He might *develop* what He knows is in us. He is concerned for us . . . and He "leadeth me."—*O. G. Wilson*

September 16

For we are not contending against flesh and blood, but against the principalities, against the powers, against the world rulers of this present darkness.—Ephesians 6:12 (RSV)

When God takes charge of our warfare, He opens our eyes to see who the real enemy is. You can test this in your own experience. When you find yourself getting unaccountably irritated with a person or impatient with a situation, "step back." Let the Lord give you an awareness of the agitating activity of Satan. He may be beaming a thought or an attitude or a feeling into your mind (see John 13:2, 27). It's necessary to recognize this.

You must stop aside and disassociate yourself from that which you have been accepting as your own thought or feeling. You say: "Now that—that's the enemy! Get thee behind me, Satan!" It's amazing to see the complexion of the situation change. That person isn't so irritating after all. That impossible situation isn't as impossible as you thought it was. Then you realize that you have been under attack by an exceedingly clever enemy.

Surely this does not mean that a person begins to attribute all difficulties to the activity of Satan. Human failure and plain old cussedness still account for their share. What we do mean is that we should not fall into the opposite error, of attributing *nothing* to satanic activity.

Secondly, when Jesus takes charge of our warfare, we learn what is expected of us. "Resist Satan, firm in your faith, knowing that the same experience of suffering is required of your brotherhood throughout the whole world." This is the great theme of embattled Christians: Endure—*endure*—ENDURE. Stick it out. Don't panic. Don't stop until you've reached the end of the race. "I have fought the good fight, I have *finished* the race," Paul could say as he was ready to be martyred (2 Tim. 4:7).

Have you finished the battle God has put you in right now? Or is your call yet to endure for a little while?

—*Larry Christenson*

September 17

Take no thought, saying, What shall we eat? or, What shall we drink? or, Wherewithal shall we be clothed? ... For your heavenly Father knoweth that ye have need of all these things.—Matthew 6:31, 32

Our Lord here warns His hearers against the sin of anxious thought. There is nothing in these words to encourage the careless neglect of means. It is concerning unbelieving anxiety that He speaks. No doubt the besetting sin in those days, as it is now, was anxiety: worrying and fretting about things that perish. The same questions people asked then are absorbing the minds of multitudes today, as if a man's life consisted in the abundance of the *things* that he possessed.

One secret of freedom from these anxious doubts and thoughts lies in the fact that our heavenly Father knows all about us—knows exactly what we need, not just on the surface of our lives, but deep down where men cannot see or understand.

The other secret of freedom is found in following the divine direction: "Seek ye *first* the kingdom of God, and his righteousness; and all these things shall be added unto you" (Matt. 6:33).

—*Evan H. Hopkins*

September 18

The Lord had said unto Abram, Get thee out of thy country ... unto a land that I will shew thee. ... So Abram departed, as the Lord had spoken unto him.—Genesis 12:1, 4

Abraham, as this passage shows, first met the call of God with a mingled and partial obedience; and then for long years neglected it entirely. But the door still stood open for him to enter, and that gracious hand still beckoned him, until he struck his tents and started to cross the mighty desert with all that he owned. Sarah may have been broken down with bitter regrets, but Abraham did not falter. He staggered not through unbelief. "He was fully persuaded that what God had promised, he was able also to perform."

Moreover, already some glimpses of the "city which hath foundations" and of the "better country, the heavenly," had loomed upon his vision; and that fair sight had loosened his hold upon much which otherwise would have fascinated and fastened him.

Ah, glorious faith! This is your work, these are your possibilities!—contentment to sail with sealed orders, because of unwavering confidence in the love and wisdom of the Lord High Admiral; willingness to arise up, leave all, and follow Christ because of the glad assurance that *earth's best cannot bear comparison with heaven's least.* —*F. B. Meyer*

> He fought his doubts and gathered strength,
> He would not make his judgment blind,
> He faced the specters of the mind
> And laid them; thus he came at length
> To find a stronger faith his own,
> And Power was with him in the night,
> Which makes the darkness and the light,
> And dwells not in the light alone.
> —*Alfred Tennyson*

"For he looked for a city which hath foundations, whose builder and maker is God" (Heb. 11:10).

September 19

And as Jesus passed by, he saw a man which was blind from his birth.—John 9:1

An infirmity becomes doubly burdensome when we give it a false interpretation. The weight of a thing is determined by our conception of it. If I look on my ailment as the stroke of an offended God, I wear it like the chains of a slave. If I look upon it as the fire of the gracious Refiner, I can calmly and confidently await its effect in my life. It is my Lord, involved in chastening His jewels!

So our Master first of all relieves the blind man of the false interpretation of his infirmity. "Neither did this man sin, nor his parents"—that is our Lord's judgment. That lifts the sorrow out of the winter into the spring. It sets it in the warm, sweet light of grace. It becomes transfigured and wears a new face, placed there in "the light of His countenance."

Then our Lord relieves the blind man of the infirmity itself. The ministry of blindness was accomplished and sight was given. No man is kept in the darkness a moment longer than infinite love deems good. Our Lord does not overlook the prison house and leave us there forgotten. "He that keepeth Israel shall neither slumber nor sleep" (Ps. 121:4).

So, cheer up, my soul! The Lord is on your side. The miracle-worker knows His time and "the dreariest path, the darkest way, shall issue out in heavenly day." —*J. H. Jowett*

September 20

He [God] is their strength in time of trouble. And the Lord shall help them.—Psalm 37:39, 40

The gospel song asks the question: "Where can I go but to the Lord?" When trouble comes, where *can* the unbeliever go? He is overcome and overawed by it, but the righteous man has God to go to. Trouble either drives a man *to* God or *away* from Him. David, the writer of these words, knew trouble. It seemed to be his daily companion through most of his early life. And it was *in* these troubles that David drew close to the Lord. In fact, I believe one of the reasons David was "a man after God's own heart" was his attitude in and reaction to trouble in his life. The way he handled his troubles reflected his relationship to his God.

David wasn't like the little old lady carrying her bundle on her back along the road one day. A farmer picked her up and gave her a ride in the back of his truck. He noticed that she did not put her heavy burden down, but sat with it strapped to her back. When he asked her why she didn't put it down, she replied that she didn't want to be any extra trouble to him. Instead of letting the truck carry her load, she went right on carrying it herself. Isn't that the way we treat God sometimes? We have a chance to turn our burdens over to Him, but we go right on carrying them ourselves. Look to God for His help— and rest in His competence to carry your load, to more than meet your needs. "Take your burden to the Lord and leave it there!"

September 21

And he went a little farther, and fell on his face, and prayed, saying, O my Father, if it be possible, let this cup pass from me: nevertheless not as I will, but as thou wilt.—Matthew 26:39

Jesus did not spend His life in trying not to do wrong. He was too full of earnest love and longing to do right—to do His Father's will.

And so we see, by contrast, why so many of our attempts at purity fail by their very negativeness. It seems that we break almost all our resolutions *not* to do wrong, while we keep a large proportion of our resolutions that we *will* do what is right. Habit, which is the power by which evil rules us, is only strong in a vacant life. It is the empty, swept, and garnished house to which the devils come back to revel still more.

—Phillips Brooks

September 22

The Lord hath been mindful of us: he will bless us. . . .
—Psalm 115:12

"The Lord hath been mindful of us: he will bless us." In that joyful assurance there is both retrospect and prospect. There is the tried path of Providence, and there is the star of hope! The eyes are refreshed and renewed in sacred memories, and then they gaze into the future with serene and happy confidence. And so the Ebenezer of the soul becomes both a thanksgiving and a reconsecration (see 1 Samuel 7:12).

Now perhaps our hopes are thin because our praises are scanty. Perhaps our expectations are clouded because our memories are dim. There is nothing which awakens hope like a journey among the mercies of our yesterdays. The heart lays aside its fears among the accumulated blessings of our God. Worries pass away like mists in the warmth of a summer morning. And the recollections of God's goodness always make summer even in the wintriest day.

Now I see why the New Testament is so urgent in this matter of praise. Without praise many other virtues and graces cannot be born. Without praise they have no breath of life. Praise arouses and enlivens a radiant company of heavenly presences, and among them is the shining spirit of hope.   *—J. H. Jowett*

September 23

Be of good courage, and he shall strengthen your heart, all ye that hope in the Lord. —Psalm 31:24

All of us face difficulties and dangers that frighten and discourage us. It's "par for the course" so far as this life is concerned. Some of us have more difficulties than others, so we need to pay particular attention to our word for the day: "Be of good courage." Does the Psalmist ask us to whip up our own courage, to "think positively" as it were, and lift ourselves by our own bootstraps? No, as he so often does, the sacred writer not only tells us *what* to do, but *how* to do it as well. Our strength to face life with courage "cometh from the Lord," for our "hope [is] in the Lord"!

There's a childish prayer that begins, "God is great, God is good. . . ." Nothing that faces you is too great for Him to control, and since His greatness is matched by His goodness, you can trustfully leave your life in His hand. Your problems do not perplex Him as they do you—for He is the God who controls the universe, and nothing is too small to escape His notice. You can count on it! He doesn't miss a thing!

What should this infinite truth mean to you? This great God has committed himself to be with you in this life and the next. He has promised that nothing coming into your life is beneath His notice, for you are His child, His beloved one. That is the Christian's "hope in the Lord." The Living Bible gives it an even stronger thrust, for it tells us: "Cheer up! take courage if you are depending on the Lord." What better promise do you want than that? We should put into practice the advice of Jesus given in Mark 5:36, "Be not afraid, only believe." Once again, the promise stated in the Old Testament is proved out in the New!

September 24

I know their sorrows.—Exodus 3:7

God was not dependent upon the complaints of the people for His knowledge of their troubles. When He came down to meet Moses at Horeb, He said, "I know their sorrows." There is unspeakable comfort in the thought in time of unusual trial, "Well, He *knows* all about it." Even before the deliverance comes, a sense of relief is found in knowing that He knows.

Sorrow is not sin, though it has come into the world in consequence of sin. With sin Christ can have no sympathy, but He was the "Man of sorrows, and acquainted with grief" (Isa. 53:3). He is therefore "touched with the feeling of our infirmities" (Heb. 4:15).

Every varying circumstance in life is a fresh occasion for a deeper knowledge of the Lord Jesus Christ. We cannot learn the precious truths of the tenderness of His humanity without passing through times of deep suffering in which His divine sympathy is needed and realized. Such occasions are the peculiar opportunities which God gives us to know Him in a still fuller and deeper sense. The Lord is never nearer His children than when they are suffering for His sake. —*Evan H. Hopkins*

September 25

I looked on my right hand, and beheld, but there was no man that would know me: refuge failed me; no man cared for my soul. I cried unto thee, O Lord: I said, Thou art my refuge and my portion in the land of the living.
—Psalm 142:4, 5

Have you ever trusted in men, only to have your trust betrayed, your confidence turned to ashes? On the surface of it, this may seem a hard lesson—an almost impossible instruction to receive. But be assured that God is in it when men fail us. For it is at this point that we *must* turn to Him. When men fail us, and all seems dark around us, then God can and will work if we turn to Him. A light is not visible in the bright sunlight; but even a dim light shows clearly in the darkness of midnight.

Someone has said, "Man's extremity is God's opportunity," and that is blessedly true when we face disillusionment and discouragment in our relationships with others. Man is finite and prone to imperfection, disappointing himself and others because of his weaknesses and inconsistencies. But God is infinite and changeless, perfect in all His attributes and just in all His actions.

Why do we wait until we are driven to some extremity before we turn to God? What is it in our mental make-up that deceives us into thinking we can go it on our own? Only as we are compelled by circumstances to go to God do we discover that He alone is equal (and abundantly able) to solve our problems, to take us through (or over) that obstacle or discouragement.

If only we would turn to Him at the outset, if only we could live in daily submission to His control, how different our lives would be—for then *He* would be our refuge, the shadow of His wings, our covering, the comfort of His arms, our protection. Inner peace is not the result of outward tranquillity; it is the reflection of an attitude of complete dependence upon the God of all peace who keeps His child no matter what the outward circumstances. If *He* is our "portion in the land of the living," what more do we need?

September 26

Let the beauty of the Lord our God be upon us.—Psalm 90:17

Too few Christians live radiantly, beautifully, abundantly. We do not rise to the joys of God's heirs. We do not know the love of Christ in the sense that we are conscious ourselves of being loved by Christ with all infinite tenderness. There are far deeper joys within our reach than we have experienced. The beauty of the Lord does not shine always in our faces and glow in our characters and appear in our dispositions and tempers. We are like the Galilean fishermen, toiling and taking nothing. Is it any wonder some of us are discouraged and almost ready at times to give up?

But listen to the Master's voice as it breaks on our ears: "Launch out into the deep and let down your nets for a draught." The trouble with us is, we have been trying only in shallows of God's love. Half consecration knows nothing of the best things of divine grace. We must cut the last chain that binds us back to the shore of this world, and like Columbus, put out to sea to discover new worlds of blessing. We can best hasten the coming of the Kingdom of Christ in its full glory by letting love have its victories in us—the love that bears all things and endures all things and does ever the gentle deeds that comfort lonely hearts and relieve suffering and distress.

—*J. R. Miller*

September 27

My meditation of him shall be sweet: I will be glad in the Lord.—Psalm 104:34

Perhaps, in these busy days, what Christians need most is the habit of devout meditation. There may be stated times for prayer and Bible reading, and yet little or no meditation. It is in those quiet seasons of prayerful meditation, over some fact or declaration of God's Word, that our faith strikes its root down deep into the truth. Time is needed to appropriate, personally, what is already ours in Christ. It is in this way that our knowledge, which at the first is elementary, though true and saving, becomes deepened and developed.

References to this fuller knowledge are frequent in Paul's epistles. For the lack of it many of God's children are weak and superficial. Our meditation, if it is to be profitable, will be "of Him." He is the Center, and Sum, of all revealed truth.

By meditation, too, we sow the seeds for future action. As out of the heart are the issues of life, so by meditation we lay up in our heart that word of life which will occupy our thoughts, purify our desires, and direct our wills (Jer. 15:16). We feed on the Word, and then we assimilate it into our being. It is sweet to our taste, and it makes us "glad in the Lord."

—*Evan H. Hopkins*

September 28

Obey his voice.—Exodus 23:22

The word "obey" in the Revised Version is "hearken." We first listen, then hear, and then obey: "If thou shalt indeed hearken unto his voice and do all that I speak." Then God says: "I will be an enemy unto thine enemies, and an adversary unto thine adversaries."

The children of Israel had nothing to fear while they listened, hearkened, and obeyed His voice. God speaks now through His Word, by His Spirit, and by His providence, and obedience to His voice will insure His favor, and this is better than life itself. By obeying His will as expressed by His voice,

I will have perfect peace in my heart and perpetual victory in my life.

The prophet Samuel said to King Saul when he disobeyed the Lord's command: "Obedience is better than sacrifice." Oh, that I may have grace to prove my love to the Lord Jesus by being always upon the altar as "a living sacrifice" and by remembering His injunction to His disciples, "If ye love me, keep my commandments."

> Lord, let me hear Thy voice today,
> And by Thy grace I will obey;
> To love Thee is my heart's delight,
> To serve Thee keeps my armor bright.
> —*John Roberts*

September 29

I am crucified with Christ: nevertheless I live; yet not I, but Christ liveth in me.—Galatians 2:20

What a noticeable change had come between the time when Paul cried submissively, "Lord, what wilt thou have me to do?" looking to an outside Christ for commandment, and the same Paul crying, "Not I who live, but Christ liveth in me!" rejoicing in the inspiration of an inward Savior. This is a dramatic illustration of what it means to "grow in grace." This was the perfect victory after which Paul was always striving so intensely.

The victory did not come perfectly to him in this world. It cannot to any of us. Dependent as victory is upon the knowledge of Christ by the soul, it cannot be perfect until the soul's knowledge of Christ shall be perfect in heaven.

The great privilege of the Christian is deepening personal intimacy with Him who is the Christian's life, the Lord Jesus Christ. All comes down to that at last. Christianity begins with many motives. It all fastens itself at last upon one motive, which does not exclude, but is large enough to comprehend, all that is good in all the rest.

"That I may know him." Those are Paul's words. How constantly we come back to his large, rounded life, as the picture of what the Christian is and should become. —*Phillips Brooks*

September 30

When he hath found it, he layeth it on his shoulders.— Luke 15:5

He does not drive the poor, weary sheep home. This is not the way of the gentle Eastern shepherd. He stoops down, and lifts it up, and lays it on his own shoulder, and carries it back. There is a wonderful picture of Christ as the Good Shepherd here.

We all know that Christ carried our sin when He went to the cross. We know, too, that we may cast our burdens upon Him. But here we learn that Christ wants to carry, not our sins only, not our burdens and cares only, but *ourselves.* The Shepherd took up the sheep itself and laid it upon His shoulder.

> I am the Burden-bearer; I
> Will never pass the o'erladen by.
> My feet are on the mountain steep;
> They wind through valleys dark and deep;
> They print the hot dust of the plain,
> And walk the billows of the main;
> Wherever is a load to bear
> My willing shoulder still is there.

He does this with "rejoicing." Can this be true? Has Christ really interest enough in any human being on this earth to be made sad by his wandering, and glad by his recovery? The thought overwhelms me. We can understand a shepherd's rejoicing when he bears home a sheep that has been lost. We can understand a mother's joy when her lost child is brought to her door. But that the heart of Jesus rejoiced when He found us, and bore us back toward home, seems too amazing to be true. Yet here the word stands. Listen to Zephaniah: "The Lord thy God in the midst of thee is mighty; he will save, *he will rejoice over thee* with joy; he will rest in his love; *he will joy over thee* with singing." How dear we are to Christ! —*J. R. Miller*

October 1

Be ye holy; for I am holy.—1 Peter 1:16
To those who are made holy in Christ Jesus, called to be holy.—1 Corinthians 1:2

Holy! In Christ! In these two expressions we have perhaps the most wonderful words of all the Bible. *Holy!* The word with unfathomable meaning, the word in which all God's perfections center, and of which His glory is but the reflection. *In Christ!* The word in which all the wisdom and love of God are unveiled. The Father giving His Son to be one of us. The Son dying on the cross to make us one with himself. The Holy Spirit dwelling in us to establish and maintain that union! *In Christ!* What a summary of what redemption has done, and of the inconceivably blessed life in which the child of God is permitted to dwell.

What wealth of meaning and blessing in the two words

combined: *Holy in Christ!* Here is God's provision for our holiness, God's response to our question, How to be holy. Often as we hear the command, "Be ye holy as I am holy," it is as if there were a great gulf fixed between the holiness of God and man. *In Christ* is the bridge that crosses that gulf; no, rather, His fullness has filled it up. *In Christ* God and man meet. *In Christ* the holiness of God has found us and made us its own; has become human, and can indeed become our very own.

All God's teaching on the subject can be summed up in three broad statements: the first a revelation, "I am holy"; the second a command, "Be ye holy"; the third a gift, the link between the two, "Ye are holy in Christ." —*Andrew Murray*

October 2

That I may win Christ, and be found in him.—Philippians 3:8, 9

It is not enough to cut loose from the old life: the Christian must enter the new life. Leaving the service of one master, he must enlist in that of another. Ceasing to do evil, he must also learn to do well. No longer a servant of sin, he must become a servant of righteousness. Mere repentance is not enough; there must also be a devoting of the life to Christ. The heart cannot be left empty. The whole allegiance of the life should be instantly transferred to Him. This is conversion; it is going over to Christ fully, wholly, freely and forever. It is coming to Him, believing on Him, following Him, loving Him, obeying Him.

We are always to do God's will, and it is as much His will that we should be diligent in business as that we should be fervent in spirit. But, "Whatsoever ye do, do all to the glory of God." We must live carefully that in the smallest things we may honor Him. The world is reading our lives, and it reads no other Bible; we must make sure therefore that our daily actions spell out a true gospel, so that no one who sees us may ever get from us a wrong thought of Christ or a wrong sense of His religion.

Holy living is itself highest service. Someone has given this test: "Whatever weakens your convictions, impairs the tenderness of your conscience, obscures your view of God or takes off the relish of spiritual things is *sin to you,* however innocent it may be in itself." A life so ruled by conscience and by the Word and Spirit of God will grow into a living power of incalculable value. —*J. R. Miller*

October 3

Walk after his commandments. —2 John 6

If we do this we may be quite sure that "the love of God is shed abroad in our hearts by the Holy Ghost," for this "is love, that we walk after his commandments." Our Lord has said, "If ye love me, keep my commandments," and "He that hath my commandments, and keepeth them, he it is that loveth me: and he that loveth me shall be loved of my Father, and I will love him, and will manifest myself to him" (John 14:15, 21). And again our Lord says, "If ye keep my commandments, ye shall abide in my love," and, "Ye are my friends if ye do whatsoever I command you" (John 15:10, 14).

In 1 John 5:3 we learn that "His commandments are not grievous." The prophet Micah inquired, "What doth the Lord require of thee?" and the reply came: "To do justly, to love mercy, and to walk humbly with thy God" (Micah 6:8). Can such requirements be "grievous"? Not when our hearts are filled with the love of God. Then we delight to do God's will and to "walk after his commandments," and in so doing we experience the truth of our Lord's words in Matthew 11:30, "My yoke is easy and my burden is light."

> In full and glad surrender,
> I give myself to Thee—
> Thine utterly and only
> And evermore to be.
>
> O Son of God, who lovest me,
> I will be Thine alone:
> And all I have, and all I am,
> Shall henceforth be Thine own.
>
> Reign over me, Lord Jesus!
> Oh, make my heart Thy throne!
> It shall be Thine, dear Savior,
> It shall be Thine alone.
> —*John Roberts*

October 4

I will walk among you, and will be your God, and ye shall be my people. —Leviticus 26:12

The Bible says that Enoch walked with God and then "was not," for God took him to be with himself. What a benediction on a life well lived! But what does our daily fellowship with God really involve—what does He do for us because we are His "people"? Unfortunately, we humans tend to become so wrapped up in the pursuit of the material and the mundane that we neglect this greatest of all rights—the right to walk with God daily.

To begin with, every new day is a gift from Him. If we really believed this, I wonder if our attitude toward our "daily grind" wouldn't be different. Wouldn't we feel that there was something special about each new day and treat it as the fragile and priceless gift it really is? Out of such an attitude would come days that are truly special as they are spent in His presence.

Remember, too, that every new experience is a gift from God. And every new experience, whether it be difficult or easy, is for our benefit that we might grow spiritually as a result of it. This outlook upon our difficulties will have a telling effect on our attitude and reaction to them.

Walking with God has another aspect as well—if He is granting us daily blessings and benefits, we should in turn be giving each day back to Him. Just as His gifts come to us without limit or "strings attached," we should be giving back to Him our entire selves, without reservation. There have been people who lived this way, and their lives are a monument of faithfulness. Some of them are recorded for us in the annals of church history and the Bible, but others have gone to their eternal reward without fanfare or recognition. But what does it matter if we receive recognition from men? The important thing is that we be "His people" and that He is "our God," walking with us through whatever comes our way.

October 5

He preserveth the way of his saints.—Proverbs 2:8

Both the ways and the feet of His saints God promises to keep (1 Sam. 2:9). How little we realize our need of His preserving grace continually! It is not the deliverance of our souls from death only that we need God himself to accomplish. Even after we have realized that blessing, it is His power again we need perpetually to keep our feet from falling.

We may think of the way as the path along which we have to travel. God prepares and preserves it. It is the way of holy obedience. Along that path we shall find the "good works, which God hath before ordained that we should walk in them" (Eph. 2:10). One great business of life is to be kept constantly "prepared unto every good work" (2 Tim. 2:21). This also God undertakes to do if we are willing to give ourselves into His hand for this purpose.

We need not be anxious as to our future, as to marking out our path and planning our ways. We have but to seek His guidance and daily to be taught His way concerning us. He will say unto us, "This is the way; walk ye in it."

—Evan H. Hopkins

October 6

Forasmuch then as Christ hath suffered for us in the flesh, arm yourselves likewise with the same mind: for he that hath suffered in the flesh hath ceased from sin.
—1 Peter 4:1

There is suffering that is preventable, but there is an inevitable suffering that is essentially God's will for us. We do not know the preface of our own story any more than Job did; we suffer, and God alone knows why. It is beside the mark to say that it is because we deserve to suffer; Job did not deserve to suffer, for he was a man "perfect and upright, and one that feared God and eschewed [turned away from] evil." Neither is it at all satisfying to say that suffering develops character. There is more in Job's suffering than was required to develop his character, and so it is with the sanctified soul. The preface to Job's story lets in the light from the revelation point of view, viz., that God's honor was at stake, and the issue fought out in this man's soul vindicated God's honor.

This point of view does not deny that we receive whippings from our Father for being willful and stupid, or that we are chastened to purity; or that any of the obvious or beautiful and sentimental things that are said and known about suffering are not true. They are true, but there is a deeper suffering in connection with sanctification that cannot be exhausted by any or all of these views.

The sufferings of the sanctified are caused by growing into the idea of the will of God. God did not spare His own Son, and He does not spare His sanctified ones from the requirements of saintship. A child is a perfect specimen of the genus homo; so is a man. The child as it develops, suffers; it is a false mercy that spares a child any requirements of its nature to complete the full stature of manhood, and it is a false mercy that spares the sanctified child of God any of the requirements of its nature to complete "the measure of the stature of the fulness of Christ." We do not evolve into holiness, it is a gift. We evolve *in* it, attainment after attainment, becoming sons and daughters of God, brothers and sisters of the Lord Jesus. —*Oswald Chambers*

October 7

Why art thou cast down, O my soul? And why art thou disquieted within me? hope in God. . . . Christ in you the hope of glory.—Psalm 43:5; Colossians 1:27

Problems along life's way come to everyone, to a greater or lesser degree. But come they do. Trials make some people bitter—and some people better. Why the difference? One's reaction to the trial. The Psalmist provides the key in our verse for today—faith in God. If we take the "hope" road, we will be blessed in the midst of persecution, uplifted despite difficulties.

The apostle Paul was a great exponent of hope. In Colossians he pins our hope on Christ. And what better hope is there than Christ "in you"? If He is in your heart, He brings with Him all the blessings of His Spirit: love, joy, peace, all those positive gifts that are to be apparent in the believer's life. Blending the messages of these two verses, one from the Old and one from the New Testament, the Christian gets a glimpse of what his life *can* be if it is truly yielded to Christ's control.

Think of some of the implications of having Christ in you:

You will never be alone again.

You can "cast all your care on him, for he careth for you."

You can count on the gifts of His Spirit bearing fruit in your life.

You will not only have "hope for heaven," but you will also have hope for each day of this earthly life, despite outward circumstances and the difficulties created by your situation.

This is just a part of the spiritual legacy that is ours as we "hope in God" and claim the promise of "Christ in you the hope of glory." The broad vistas of victorious living into which this door of "hope" leads us are too vast to contemplate, too deep to comprehend. But they await the believer who obeys the command to "hope"!

October 8

They have no wine.—John 2:3

Another version has it: "The wine failed." This incident is a very fitting illustration of the failure of all this world's joy. The wine gave out before the end of the wedding feast. This is the way it is with all earthly pleasure. It comes in cups, not in fountains, and the supply is limited and soon exhausted. This is particularly true of sin's pleasures. The prodigal son soon runs through his abundance and begins to be in want. A poet compared the pleasures of sin to a snowflake on a river—"a moment white, then gone forever." But it is true in a sense also of pure pleasures. Even the sweetness of human love is but a cupful which will not last forever. The joy which so fills us today, tomorrow is turned to sorrow. Even amid the gladness of the marriage altar there is the echo of the end in the words, "till death do us part." One of every two friends must bid the other farewell at the edge of the valley—must stand alone by the other's grave and walk alone part of the way.

The best wine of life and love will fail inevitably. If there were nothing better in this world, how sad it would be! But it is right here that we see the glory of Christ's gospel. Jesus comes when earth's wine fails, and gives heaven's wine to supply the lack. How beautiful and how true is the picture here—the failing wine, and then Jesus coming with power and supplying the want! That is what He is doing continually.

He takes lives which have drained their last drop of earthly gladness and satisfies them with spiritual good and blessing, so that they want nothing more. When human joy fails, if we have Jesus with us, He gives new joy, better than the world's, and in unfailing supply. How sad it is for those who have not taken Christ into their lives, and who have nothing but the empty cup when earth's wine gives out!   —*J. R. Miller*

October 9

The fire came down.—2 Chronicles 7:1

No sooner did the fire descend than "the glory of the Lord filled the house." The temple which Solomon had erected became fully sanctified when "the glory of the Lord filled it." This is clear from verse 16 where God says: "Now I have chosen and sanctified this house . . . and mine eyes and mine heart will be there perpetually."

We are also reminded of the same thing happening before in the wilderness. When Moses had completed the tabernacle "the glory of the Lord filled it," previous to which God had said: "The tabernacle shall be sanctified by my glory" (Ex. 29:43).

Here, then, we learn, both from Exodus and the Chronicles, the secret of entire sanctification. "The fire" must come "down from heaven," and "the glory of the Lord" must fill us. We thus become filled with God. His presence, power, fire, and glory cleanses, removes, fills, and sanctifies. And then His "eyes" and "heart" are upon and with us "perpetually." This relationship gives us power to resist temptation, to overcome Satan, and to live both a holy and useful life. May the prayer of our heart today therefore be—

> Oh, that in me the sacred fire
> Might now begin to glow;
> Burn up the dross of base desire,
> And make the mountains flow!
>
> Oh, that it now from heaven might fall,
> And all my sins consume!
> Come, Holy Ghost; for Thee I call;
> Spirit of burning, come.

Refining fire go through my heart,
Illuminate my soul;
Scatter thy life through every part,
And sanctify the whole.

—*John Roberts*

October 10

Ye are Christ's; and Christ is God's.—1 Corinthians 3:23

Think of yourself as living in an apartment building. You live there under a landlord who has made your life miserable. He charges you exorbitant rent. When you can't pay, he loans you money at a fearful rate of interest, to get you even farther into his debt. He barges into your apartment at all hours of the day or night, wrecks and dirties the place, then charges you extra for not maintaining the premises. Your life is miserable.

Then comes Someone who says, "I've taken over this apartment building. I've purchased it. You can live here as long as you like, free. The rent is paid up. I'm going to be living here with you, in the manager's apartment." What a joy! You are saved! You are delivered out of the clutches of the old landlord!

But what happens? You hardly have time to rejoice in your new-found freedom when a knock comes at the door. And there he is—the old landlord! Mean, glowering, and demanding as ever. He has come for the rent, he says.

Do you pay him? Of course you don't! Do you go out and pop him on the nose? No—he's bigger than you are! You confidently tell him, "You'll have to take this up with the new Landlord." He may bellow, threaten, wheedle, and cajole. Just quietly tell him, "Take it up with the new Landlord." He'll come back a dozen times, waving legal documents, shouting threats and arguments, but tell him once again, "Take it up with the new Landlord." In the end he has to, and he knows it. He just hopes he can bluff and threaten and deceive you into doubting that the new Landlord will really take care of things.

Now this is the situation of a Christian. Once Christ has delivered you from the power of sin and the devil, you can depend on it: that old landlord will soon come back knocking at your door. And what is your defense? How do you keep him from getting the whip hand over you again? You send him to the new Landlord. *You send him to Jesus!*

—*Larry Christenson*

October 11

Seek ye first the kingdom of God.—Matthew 6:33

Who is God? The great being through whom alone the universe exists; in whom alone it can have its happiness. It cannot find any joy or rest but in Him. Oh, that Christians really understood and believed that God is the fountain of happiness, perfect, everlasting blessedness! What would be the result? Every Christian would say, "The more I can have of God, the happier I'd be. The more of God's will, and the more of God's love, and the more of God's fellowship, the happier it would make me."

How Christians, if they believed with their whole heart, would give up everything that could possibly separate them from God! Why is it we find it so hard to hold fellowship with God? A young minister once said to me, "Why is it I have so much more interest in study than in prayer, and how can you teach me the art of fellowship with God?" My answer was, "Oh, my brother, if we have any true conception of what God is, the art of fellowship with Him will come naturally, and will be a delight."

Yes, if we believed God to be only joy to everyone who comes to Him, just a fountain of unlimited blessing, how we should give up all for Him! Has not joy a far stronger attraction than anything in the world? Is it not in every beauty, or in every virtue, in every pursuit, the joy that is set before us that draws us? And if we believed that God is a fountain of joy, and sweetness, and power to bless, how our hearts would turn aside from everything and say, "Oh, the beauty of my God! I rejoice in Him alone." Unfortunately, to many the Kingdom of God looks like a burden, and as something unnatural. It looks like a strain, so we seek some relaxation in the world, and God is not our chief joy. I come to you with a message: It is right, it is our highest privilege, to listen to Christ's words, and to seek God and His Kingdom first and above everything.

—*Andrew Murray*

October 12

I have loved thee with an everlasting love; therefore with loving-kindness have I drawn thee.—Jeremiah 31:3

Underneath everything that revelation makes known to man is the fact of God's free sovereign love. It is the source of every other blessing. It is impossible to go back beyond the point of God's love to man. We can find nothing in man himself to answer the question of *why* God should love him. All we can do is recognize the fact that it is so.

The believer sees it as an unchanging love because it is

"everlasting." He may rely on this, that whatever circumstances of trial, of suffering, or of perplexity he may be called upon to pass through, that love remains the same.

Then, again, he sees that God's love individualizes His children. He says, "I have loved *thee*." As if there were no others on whom to bestow His loving-kindness. This personal aspect of God's love is not only very comforting; it is also very humbling. To live in the rays of that love is to have the natural hardness of our hearts melted and all the bitterness removed. But another thing—this divine love attracts the soul to Him who is the embodiment of love: "With loving-kindness have I *drawn* thee."   —*Evan H. Hopkins*

October 13

And the Lord said unto Moses . . . Go forward.—Exodus 14:15

God asks the impossible—and then He gives the power to do it. God doesn't waste power; He just gives His child enough strength to do whatever He asks of him. This is the lesson contained in this experience of Moses and the children of Israel.

This was the situation. The Israelites, led by Moses, had left Egypt and had come to the Red Sea, an impassible barrier, and an impossible impasse. The Egyptians were pressing close behind them, and there was just nowhere for them to go to escape certain death. The children of Israel were ready to turn back to Egypt. In verse 12 the writer records their words to Moses: "Is this not the word we did tell thee in Egypt, saying, Let us alone, that we may serve the Egyptians? For it had been better for us to serve the Egyptians than that we should die in the wilderness." To put it briefly, the Israelites were saying to Moses, "*Let's go back.*"

Moses counsels them, "Fear ye not, *stand still*, and see the salvation of the Lord" (v. 13). But God's command to Moses was: "Wherefore criest thou unto me? speak unto the children of Israel, that they *go forward.*"

There is a lesson here for the Christian today. Let's face it: God does sometimes ask the impossible of us, but He also supplies the needed strength to accomplish whatsoever He asks us to do. Humanly speaking, the Israelites should have just given up, and left to their own devices, that's exactly what they would have done. They would have turned around and gone back to their bondage in Egypt. Moses took them part way to the place where God would have them. At least he commanded them to "stand still, and see the salvation of the Lord." But even with his superior spiritual insight, he missed God's best; he failed to see the "big picture," God's divine plan for Israel, to pass through the Red Sea.

True, God does ask the impossible, but then He gives His child the power to do what He commands. Don't *dwell* on the impossibility of the task He has given you to do. *Depend* on the One who has called you to do it! Here is a rule for living that will pay dividends every day of your life.

October 14

He that putteth his trust in me shall possess the land, and shall inherit my holy mountain.—Isaiah 57:13

An awareness of the context within which the prophet is writing makes this striking passage even more meaningful. As God's spokesman to straying Israel, Isaiah is castigating the nation for its idolatrous ways, its blatant flaunting of God's will, its deliberate turning from the true God to worship idols. Pointing out the inability of idols to deliver the nation, even when the Israelites went so far as to sacrifice their children, Isaiah states flatly, "He that putteth his trust in me [God] shall possess the land, and shall inherit my holy mountain." The Living Bible renders the first part of this verse derisively, "Let's see if the whole collection of your idols can help you when you cry to them to save you! They are so weak that the wind can carry them off! A breath can puff them away."

God's promise of prosperity here is unconditional. There are no ifs, ands, or buts! The writer of the Proverbs makes a similar statement: "A greedy man stirs up strife, but he who trusts in the Lord will be enriched" (Prov. 28:25, RSV). The Living Bible says at this point, "Trusting God leads to prosperity."

There are no qualifications attached to this promise outside of an attitude of trust in God. But there are undoubtedly dark times in life when it is more difficult to trust than in the bright sunlight of His blessing. What about the dark nights of testing that come to all of us? That is when "the rubber meets the road." Trust in the daytime is a passive, sometimes pallid, faith. Trust in the darkness is a vigorous, active kind of faith. If we are trusting in the idols of materialism and worldly wealth, we will find them helpless as the idols in which the rebellious Israelites placed their faith. If, on the other hand, we accept God's measurement, we will find ourselves being led into the *real* prosperity of the Spirit. Our ultimate dwelling will thus be God's holy mountain where we can "enjoy Him forever."

October 15

Therefore I say unto you, Take no thought.—Matthew 6:25

Of course, we *are* to take thought in a true sense. Why were we made with brains if we are not to think with them? It would be as if God bade us not to walk after He had given us feet, or not to talk after giving us tongues. We are to train our minds, to think with them. We are to think about the future, too, laying plans with a long reach into the years before us. It is not forethought that is forbidden, but anxious thought, worry, fear. We will see as we go on just what we are to do instead of being anxious. The simple lesson here is that we are never to be anxious. This is not a rule with exceptions. It is not a bit of a creed that will not work in life. It is a lesson we are to strive to carry out in all our days, however full they may be of things calculated to distract us.

But why are we to take no thought? The "therefore" helps us to the answer: "Ye cannot serve God and mammon. Therefore take no thought." So, then, taking thought seems to be serving mammon. We say we are God's children, and yet when mammon seems in danger of failing us we get anxious. Practically, then, we trust mammon more than we trust our Father. We feel safer when mammon's abundance fills our hands than when mammon threatens to fail and we have only God. That is, we trust God *and* mammon. Anxiety about the supply of our needs is therefore distrust of our heavenly Father. If we serve God only, we should not worry, though we have not even bread for tomorrow; we should believe in our Father's love. Money we may lose any day, for "riches make themselves wings; they fly away as an eagle toward heaven"; but we never can lose God. Nothing can rob us of His love, nor rob Him of the abundance He possesses from which to meet our needs. So if we trust God we ought never to be anxious, though we have nothing else. —*J. R. Miller*

October 16

Therefore I say unto you, Take no thought for your life, what ye shall eat, or what ye shall drink; nor yet for your body, what ye shall put on. Is not the life more than meat, and the body [more] than raiment?—Matthew 6:25

If we can live in Christ and have His life in us, shall not the spiritual balance and proportion which were His become ours too? If He were really our Master and our Saviour, could it be that we could get so eager and excited over little things?

If we were His, could we possibly be so concerned over losing a little money we do not really need, or be exalted at the sound of a little praise which we know we only half deserve and the praiser only half intends?

A moment's disappointment, a moment's gratification, and then the ocean will be calm again and quite forgetful of the ripple which disturbed its bosom. Is this what Jesus is saying as He urges His disciples to "take no thought"?

—*Phillips Brooks*

October 17

I am the vine, ye are the branches: He that abideth in me, and I in him, the same bringeth forth much fruit; for without me ye can do nothing.—John 15:5

I need the Lord. What can a branch do apart from the vine? It may retain a certain momentary greenness, but death is advancing as soon as its connection with the vine is broken. And there are multitudes of professing Christians who are like detached branches; their spiritual life is ebbing away; they do not startle the beholder and cause him to exclaim: "How full of life!" They do not *strike* at all! They have no splendid *force* of character, and they therefore exercise no arresting witness for the King. Because they are not "abiding" in the Eternal, they therefore have no powerful pulse from the Infinite. Jesus said, "Apart from me ye can do nothing."

On the other hand, *my Lord needs me*—for the Vine has need of the branch! The vine expresses itself in the branch, and comes to manifestation in leaf, in flower, in fruit. My Lord would manifest himself in me and cause my branch to be heavy with the glorious fruits of His grace. If I deprive Him of the branch, and deny Him this means of expression, I am "limiting the Holy One of Israel."

"My son, give me thine heart."

Lord, help me to abide in you! Save me from the foolishness of a fatal independence. O Lord, *abide in me.*   —*J. H. Jowett*

October 18

The Lord God is a sun and shield.—Psalm 84:11

Notice what the Lord is ("a sun and shield"), what He gives ("grace and glory"), and then what He withholds ("no good thing . . . from them that walk uprightly"). First, "a sun and shield." Think of what the sun in the heaven is to all the inhabitants of the earth. The source of all light, heat, life, comfort, and every temporal blessing we possess. And all this, and much beside, God is to His children.

But there are times when the sun is so powerful that we are glad to find shelter from its rays, and so while God is a sun He is also a shield. As a sun He gives us life, comfort, and untold blessings, but as a shield He protects and preserves us from all real harm and danger. That is why He said to Abraham, "Fear not; I am thy shield," and the Psalmist said to Israel: "Trust thou in the Lord; he is their help and their shield." And when speaking to God himself he said, "Thou art my hiding place and my shield."

Think also of what this great God *gives*. First grace and then glory, the grace of pardon and the glory of sanctification, grace on earth and glory in heaven, with a goodly share of glory here while on the way to the fullness hereafter. And while He gives grace and glory He also *withholds no good thing* from them that walk uprightly. Those whose lives are straight, and holy, and wholly devoted to Him shall have no good thing withheld from them, for "they that seek the Lord shall not want any good thing." —*John Roberts*

October 19

I will lift up mine eyes unto the hills, from whence cometh my help.—Psalm 121:1

Many years ago the owner and editor of the *London Times*, the late Lord Northcliffe of England, was apparently going blind. His eyes were examined by specialists and nothing essentially wrong was discovered. The specialists concluded that he needed the far look. For too many years he had been using his eyes exclusively for reading and close observation.

Lord Northcliffe was advised to take days in the country away from the printed pages where he could look on the broad vistas of God's creation. This simple remedy corrected his eye trouble and he went on to many more years of fruitful service.

His lesson in life can be profitably applied to our lives today. Many of us are in danger of a form of spiritual blindness as we concentrate continually on the "fine print" nearby—the problems close at hand, the narrow interests of our small world. If our eyes are constantly occupied with the little things, we are very likely to suffer from a form of spiritual astigmatism. Our Lord warned of this when He urged: "Lift up your eyes and look on the fields; for they are white already to harvest" (John 4:35).

In our self-centeredness we endanger our spiritual health. As we take the broad view and look out across the harvest fields of the world, our spiritual selves will be enriched and our spiritual eyes will be refreshed. If we take the worldwide view, if we look to the hills, we will be renewed in the inner man, strengthened in our very heart. We need to pray, "Lord, open my eyes," that we may see life in its true relation to eternity. —*O. G. Wilson*

October 20

By faith Moses. . . .—Hebrews 11:24

His faith made Moses all he was. Why should we not have such faith? God's methods are never out of date. We make a profound mistake in attributing to Bible heroes extraordinary qualities of courage, and strength of body or soul. To do so is to miss the whole point of the reiterated teaching of Scripture. They were not different from ordinary men, except in their faith. In many respects it is most likely that they were inferior to ourselves. But there was one characteristic common to them all, which lifted them above ordinary men, and secured for them a niche in the temple of Scripture—that they had a marvelous faculty of faith; which indeed is but the capacity of the human heart for God. Four times over this is cited as the secret of all that Moses did for his people.

The same truth is repeatedly corroborated in the teaching of our Lord. He never stops to ask what may be the specific quantity of power, or wisdom, or enthusiasm, which exists in His disciples. But His incessant demand is for *faith.* If only there be faith, though it be but as a grain of mustard seed, sycamore trees can be uprooted, mountains cast into the midst of the sea; and demons exorcised from their victims. To a father He once said, "There is no *if* in My power; it is in thy faith. If thou canst believe, all things are possible to him that believeth."

And what is this faith? Is it not some inherent power or quality in certain men, by virtue of which they are able to accomplish special results unrealized by others? It is the attitude of heart which, having ascertained the will of God, and being desirous of becoming a conveyance for it, goes on to expect that God will work out His purposes through its medium.

It is, in brief, that capacity for God which appropriates Him to its uttermost limit, and becomes the channel, or vehicle, through which He passes forth to bless mankind. The believer is the God-filled, the God-moved, the God-possessed man; and the work which he effects in the world is not his, but God's through him. —*F. B. Meyer*

October 21

There was leaning on Jesus' bosom one of his disciples, whom Jesus loved.—John 13:23

We are not told the name of this disciple, but we know him by his place and posture. What were the traits in John's character which made him the beloved disciple? One was his humility; another was his love. Artists always paint his face in features of gentleness and affection. Another of his winning traits was his trust. He seems never to have doubted.

When was it he reclined on Jesus' bosom? It was in a time of great darkness. The Master was about to go away, and all the hopes of the disciples were being destroyed. But where was John in that darkness? Sorrow, instead of driving us to despair, should drive us nearer to Christ—to His very bosom.

> He's better to us than many mothers are,
> And children cannot wander beyond reach
> Of the sweep of His white garment.
> Touch and hold,
> And if you weep still, weep
> Where John was laid
> While Jesus loved him.

Where was it that John leaned? On Jesus' breast. Not merely on His arm, the place of strength; nor upon His shoulder, the place of upholding; but on His bosom, the place of love and tenderness. It is good to know that the divine omnipotence is underneath us in all our weakness; but mere omnipotence is cold. How much better when omnipotence has the heart of love within it!

But *what* did John do? He *leaned.* He rested his weight on the omnipotent love of his Lord. Christ wants all His friends to lean upon Him. He wants to carry our burdens for us— He wants us to lay upon Him our sins and all our cares; but more than this—*ourselves.* He wants to bear us as well as our loads. —*J. R. Miller*

October 22

Enoch walked with God.—Genesis 5:22, 24

Enoch was a family man. He lived many years after the birth of his eldest child, and had both "sons and daughters." But during the whole of this period he "walked with God," and he not only *walked* with God, but he also *pleased* God, and had the testimony or witness of the Spirit that he did so, "for before his translation he had this testimony that he pleased God" (Heb. 11:15).

He must, therefore, have been saved from all sin and kept by the power of God from sinning. Now, if Enoch was thus kept thousands of years ago, and long before the dispensation of the Holy Spirit, then surely we may have the same experience today, for God, and Christ, and faith are still the same.

Walking peacefully with a friend implies union, fellowship, and progress by interchange of thought. "Can two walk together, except they be agreed?" (Amos 3:3). We are exhorted in Rom. 6:13 to "yield ourselves unto God as those that are alive from the dead," and by doing so we manifest our oneness with Him. We live in fellowship with Him and so make real continual progress in the divine life. Oh, that we may this day and every day of this year thus "walk with God."

> Walk in the light! so shalt thou know
> That fellowship of love,
> His Spirit only can bestow
> Who reigns in heaven above.

> Walk in the light! and sin abhorred
> Shall ne'er defile again,
> The blood of Jesus Christ thy Lord
> Shall cleanse from every stain.

> Walk in the light! thy path shall be
> Peaceful, serene, and bright,
> For God, by grace, shall dwell in thee
> And God Himself is light.
>
> —*John Roberts*

October 23

God blessed the seventh day and declared it holy, because it was the day when he ceased this work of creation.—Genesis 2:3 (TLB)

God's finished work of creation was marred by sin, and our fellowship with Him in the blessing of His holy rest was cut off. The finished work of redemption opened for us a truer rest and a surer interest and entrance into the holiness of God. As He rested in His holy day, so He now rests in His holy Son. In Him we now can enter fully into the rest of God. "Made holy in Christ," let us rest in Him.

Let us rest, because we see that as wonderfully as God by His mighty power finished His work of creation, so will He complete and perfect His work of sanctification. Let us yield ourselves to God in Christ, to rest where He rested, to be made holy with His own holiness, and to be blessed with God's own blessing. God the Sanctifier is the name now inscribed upon the throne of God the Creator. At the threshold of the history of the human race there shines this word of infinite promise and hope: God blessed and sanctified the seventh day because in it He rested.   —*Andrew Murray*

October 24

And the very God of peace sanctify you wholly; and I pray God your whole spirit and soul and body be preserved blameless unto the coming of our Lord Jesus Christ. Faithful is he that calleth you, who also will do it. — 1 Thessalonians 5:23, 24

This is the glorious secret of sanctification. Underlying the commands of God is the promise that He will do it. The Christian life is not just a list of well-meaning religious exercises. It is a new full-time attitude of heart. It is, in the language of the Bible, a death-and-resurrection.

The story is told of Martin Luther one day answering a knock at his door. "Does Dr. Martin Luther live here?" the man asked. "No," Luther replied, "he died. Christ lives here now."

What expectancy, what a sense of adventure, this brings into one's Christian experience! Where before you looked to your own talents, abilities, and resources, now you look at the good work God has set before you, and you reckon upon the limitless resources of Christ Jesus!

This is the secret of sanctification, which includes gratitude, but goes beyond it. It makes of the Christian life not a duty but an adventure. Each day you can wake up and say, "Lord, what have You planned for today?" Not what am I going to do for the Lord, but what is He going to do with me?

—Larry Christenson

October 25

Who, when he was reviled, reviled not again; when he suffered, he threatened not. —1 Peter 2:23

Then I may be not only the betrayer, but the betrayed. In my inner circle there may be a friend who will play me false, and hand me over to the wolves. What then? Just this—I must imitate the grace of my Lord and "consider Him."

There must be no violent retaliation. "When he was reviled, he reviled not again." The fire of revenge may singe or even scorch my enemy, but it will do far more damage to the furniture of my soul. Every time I indulge in vengeful passion some precious personal possession has been destroyed. The fact of the matter is, this fire cannot be kept burning without making fuel of the priceless furnishings of the soul. "Heat not a furnace for your foe so hot that it singes yourself."

There must be a serene committal of the soul to the strong keeping of the Eternal God. "He committed himself to him that judgeth righteously." This is the way of peace, as this is the way of victory. If ever the enemy is to be conquered, this must be the mode of the conquest. When men persecute us, let us rest more implicitly in our God. —*J. H. Jowett*

October 26

Neither is there any daysman betwixt us, that might lay his hand upon us both.—Job 9:33

This was what Job desired, but what he felt was impossible to obtain. And he seems not to have been alone in this great want. Eli felt himself to be in the same difficulty. When reproving his unruly sons, he said to them: "If one man sin against another, the Judge shall judge him; but if a man sin against the Lord, who shall intreat for him?"

And here we have poor Job's complaint: "Neither is there any daysman betwixt us, that he might lay his hand upon us both." What a blessing that no man need utter this doleful complaint today! For in this gospel dispensation we may all have a "daysman," a mediator, between God and man, one who has already made atonement. He has, as it were, laid "His hand upon us both," so that, "being justified by faith, we have peace with God, through Jesus Christ our Lord." It is therefore recorded in 1 John 2:1, "My little children, these things I write unto you, that ye *sin not.*" But "if any man sin," as all are liable to, "we have an advocate with the Father —a daysman betwixt us—Jesus Christ the righteous."

> Not all the blood of beasts,
> On Jewish altars slain,
> Could give the guilty conscience peace
> Or wash away our stain.
>
> But Christ the heavenly Lamb
> Takes all our sins away,
> A sacrifice of nobler name
> And richer blood than they.
>
> Believing, we rejoice
> To see the curse remove;
> We bless the Lamb with cheerful voice
> And sing His dying Love.
> —*John Roberts*

October 27

The God of all comfort; who comforteth us in all our tribulation that we may be able to comfort them which are in any trouble, by the comfort wherewith we ourselves are comforted of God.—2 Corinthians 1:3, 4

"The God of all comfort"—what a wealth of rich meaning is wrapped up in that phrase. Indeed, it is one of the most meaningful names given the Godhead. The Holy Spirit, God's presence in the world, is called the "Comforter" (John 14:16, 26; 15:26; 16:7). Trace the theme throughout the Scriptures and you will find your heart strangely warmed as did Martin Luther when he first sensed the full impact of what it meant to be justified by faith.

Our God is not One who cannot be touched by the feeling of "our infirmities," but was in all points tempted like as we are, yet without sin. This is the crucial difference between Jesus Christ, our Saviour and Brother, and us. The characteristic or trait that makes Him worthy to be our Saviour, to be accepted by God, is His sinlessness. It is the same power over sin that makes Him able to be only the effective Comforter for His people. If He were subject to sin as we are, His comfort would be powerless and transitory. It would not help us, but would be as weak and limited as our own efforts to enter into the tragic experiences of those around us. Sure, we can sympathize and empathize, but can we really comfort? We are limited by our finiteness, but He is as infinite in His ability to comfort as He is in His ability to save!

> The Comforter has come,
> The Comforter has come!
> The Holy Ghost from heav'n—
> The Father's promise giv'n;
> O spread the tidings 'round,
> Wherever man is found—
> The Comforter has come!
> —*Frank Bottome*

October 28

God is my defence. —Psalm 59:9

The strength of the believer against his foes does not consist in what he is in himself, but in what God is for him. The believer, however, must avail himself of that strength; he must appropriate, by faith, what God is for him. When he can say, "God is my defence," it implies that he has forsaken all false confidences, and has retreated into his castle. "The name of the Lord is a strong tower" (Prov. 18:10).

But how am I to have the benefit of that strength? By "running into it." When the little child has the walls of an impregnable fort between himself and the enemy, he is as strong as the full-grown man who is within the same fortress. His strength is not a question of growth or attainment, but of position. So it is with the believer.

It is a question of relationship to Christ. Where do I stand? What is the ground that I occupy? Where do I live spiritually? "The Lord is my rock, and my fortress.... in him will I trust" (2 Sam. 22:2, 3).

The great lesson of life, when we have found our Refuge, is to know how to *abide* in Him. See Psalm 28:7; Isaiah 59:19; Hebrews 13:6.   —*Evan H. Hopkins*

October 29

Wherefore come out from among them, and be ye separate, saith the Lord, and touch not the unclean thing; and I will receive you.—2 Corinthians 6:17

When we turn away from the world and leave it, we ourselves are not left desolate and orphans. When we "come out from among them" the Lord receives us! He is waiting for us. The new companionship is ours the moment the old companionship is ended. "I will not leave you comfortless." What we have lost is compensated by infinite and eternal gain. We have lost "the whole world" and gained "the unsearchable riches of Christ."

Therefore separation is exaltation. We leave the muddy pleasures of Sodom and we "drink of the river of his pleasures." We leave "the garish day," and all the feverish life of Vanity Fair, and he causes us "to lie down in green pastures," "He leads us beside the still waters." We leave a transient sensation; we receive the bread of eternity. We forfeit fireworks; we gain the stars!

What fools we are, and blind! We prefer the scorched desert of Sodom to the garden of Eden. We prefer a loud reputation to noble character. We prefer delirium to joy. We prefer human applause to the praise of God. We prefer a fading garland to the crown of life. Lord, that we may receive our sight!
                                                            —*J. H. Jowett*

October 30

For thou, O God, hast proved us; thou hast tried us, as silver is tried.—Psalm 66:10

The greatest and most enviable form of power in human experience is staying power. The ability to keep going when every muscle is crying out for rest. The determination to keep climbing when there are those all about us who have quit.

The apostle Paul never uttered more triumphant words than, "I have finished my course." There had been many good reasons for quitting, but he never let up. Even when age stole away his physical forces he was still sustained by an invisible spiritual force superior to the combined forces arrayed against him.

Life seems peculiarly designed to test our ability to endure, to survive. It grows harder as the years multiply. The life of our Lord moved over a route of increasing difficulties from the manger to Golgotha's awful hour. Perhaps no more wonderful words were ever spoken by Him than when, while dying, He said, "It is finished." A glorious hour of consummation for Him and an exalted hour of salvation for our race.

Most lives begin in the shelter of a mother's love and the protection of a father's strong arms. As the years pass the experiences become harder and more complicated. Unexpected struggles appear. Then come increasing complications from failing health and loss of earning power, and the soul is gripped with the haunting fear of uncertainty. The question, What is to become of me? dogs his steps through the day and disturbs his sleeping hours. I have profound admiration for the heroism and fortitude and downright courage of the men and women who stand on the western slope of life and face the future with its loneliness, its pains, its separations, unafraid and uncomplaining.

"O bless our God, ye people, and make the voice of his praise to be heard: which holdeth our soul in life, and suffereth not our feet to be moved" (Ps. 66:8, 9). Happy is the soul that has something to look backward to with pride, and something to look forward to with hope. The heritage of old age is not whining despair, but a whisper of hope that another cannot hear. Its song is not a dirge but a praise. Its drink is not the bitter waters of Marah, but the gushing springs of eternal life which have their source in the hills of God's eternal country. —*O. G. Wilson*

October 31

Whether therefore ye eat, or drink, or whatsoever ye do, do all to the glory of God.—1 Corinthians 10:31
With good will doing service, as to the Lord, and not to men.—Ephesians 6:7

A SERVANT, with this clause,
Makes drudgery divine:
Who sweeps a room, as for Thy laws,
Makes that and th' action fine.
—*G. Herbert*

Surely the truth must be, that whatsoever in our daily life is lawful and right for us to be engaged in, is in itself a part of our obedience to God; a part, that is, of our very religion. Whensoever we hear people complaining of obstructions and hindrances put by the duties of life in the way of devoting themselves to God, we may be sure they are under some false view or other. They do not look upon their daily work as the task God has set them, and as obedience due to Him. We may go farther; and say, not only that the duties of life, be they never so toilsome and distracting, are no obstructions to a life of any degree of inward holiness; but that they are means, when rightly used, to promote our sanctification.

—*H. E. Manning*

With meekness, humility, and diligence, apply yourself to the duties of your condition. They are the seemingly little things which make no noise that do the business. —*Henry More*

Nothing is too little to be ordered by our Father; nothing too little in which to see His hand; nothing, which touches our souls, too little to accept from Him; nothing too little to be done to Him. —*E. B. Pusey*

November 1

Only be thou strong and very courageous.—Joshua 1:7

Our God's tender love for His servants makes Him concerned for the state of their inward feelings. He desires them to be of good courage. Some think it a small thing for a believer to be bothered by doubts and fears, but not God. From this text it is plain that our Master would not have us entangled with fears. He would have us without anxiety, without doubt, without cowardice.

Our Master does not take lightly our unbelief, as we do. When we are desponding we are subject to a grievous disease, not to be trifled with, but to be taken at once to the beloved Physician. Our Lord does not like to see us sad. It was the law of Ahasuerus that no one should come into the king's presence dressed in mourning: this is not the law of the King of Kings, for we may come mourning as we are; but still He would have us put on the garment of praise, for there is much reason to rejoice.

The Christian man ought to be of courageous spirit that he may glorify the Lord by enduring trials in a heroic manner. If he is fearful and fainthearted, it will dishonor his God. Besides, it is a bad example.

This disease of doubting and discouragement is an epidemic which soon spreads among the Lord's flock. One downcast believer makes twenty souls sad. Moreover, unless your courage is kept up Satan will be too much for you. Let your spirit be joyful in God your Savior; so the joy of the Lord will be your strength and no servant of Satan will make headway against you: but cowardice throws down the banner.

Moreover, labor is light to a man of cheerful spirit; and success waits upon cheerfulness. The man who toils, rejoicing in his God, believing with all his heart, has success guaranteed. He who sows in hope will reap in joy; therefore, dear reader, "be thou strong, and very courageous." —*C. H. Spurgeon*

November 2

My God shall supply all your need according to his riches in glory by Christ Jesus. —Philippians 4:19

The apostle leads the Philippian converts at once to the fountain of all blessing: "My God"! How great and glorious and all-sufficient God was to him. It is He who will look after them who had so lovingly been thinking of his necessities and ministering to his wants.

"All your need," no matter how great and how varying. He will fill them to the full. Let your need be as the empty vessel which is brought to the fountain to be filled. The greater your need, the larger the vessel, the deeper the capacity, and the richer and fuller the blessing.

And this He will do—not simply *out* of His riches in glory, but *according* to those riches. The first would indicate the *source* only, but the latter shows the *measure* of the supply.

It was in dependence on such a God that the apostle lived. He spoke of himself "as having nothing, and yet possessing all things." None of God's gifts, however rich and precious, could make him for a moment independent of God. His great fullness and our emptiness have continually to meet. And when they do, our emptiness is filled with His riches!

—*Evan H. Hopkins*

November 3

Thou hast put gladness in my heart. —Psalm 4:7

David was still a fugitive through the cruel treatment of his son Absalom, but instead of being filled with sadness and bitterness, his heart was running over with gladness. And what was his secret? The Lord his God was the fountain-head of this river of joy. "Thou hast put gladness in my *heart.*"

There are many with smiles upon their faces while experiencing feelings of wretchedness and loneliness within their hearts. Divine joy is the result of inward peace. Those who let "the peace of God rule in their hearts" know the experience of "the peace which passeth all understanding," keeping their "hearts and minds through Christ Jesus."

See also in our meditation today David's condition compared with that of his enemies. His worst experiences were superior to their greatest blessings. When exclaiming, "Thou hast put gladness in my heart," he was cut off from home and the sanctuary of his God. He was literally in a desert land where no water could be found, while they were in their home and their city, amid their harvest of plenty and apparent prosperity, for "their corn and their wine increased." But God's blessing was not with it, so that they felt sharp thorns within their feathered pillows.

David, it is true, was driven from his throne and from his home, but he could not be driven from his God, and so he had "gladness" put within his "heart," causing him afterwards to exclaim: "Happy is the people whose God is the Lord."

> Upon my heart, bestow'd by Thee,
> More gladness I have found
> Than they, ev'n then, when corn and wine
> Did most with them abound.
>
> —*John Roberts*

November 4

He shall give his angels charge over thee, to keep thee in all thy ways.—Psalm 91:11

We often talk about God's ability to help His child whatever that child's need. One of the reasons He can help you is that He has a host of angels waiting to do His bidding. It is comforting to remind ourselves that each one of us has his own guardian angel, but we're shortchanging ourselves! God is not limited, as some think, to one guardian angel for each of His children. No! A whole garrison of angels may surround you at God's command. There is no limit to God's protection of His loved ones.

The Psalmist goes on to point out that these angels will "keep thee in *all* thy ways." Generations have sung the hymn, "There's a wideness in God's mercy." God cannot be limited by geography or topography. We cannot go far enough or high enough to get beyond His care.

I don't think we'll know until eternity just *what* we have been spared in this life, just what we have been protected *from*. What terrible disasters could have come our way, what horrible diseases we have missed, what gruesome accidents we have been spared simply because of God's protective care, His ability to keep us in *all* our ways? How many angels has He employed to save us from the hand of the evil one? Job on the ash heap still acknowledged God's care and sovereignty over him. Daniel in the lions' den had a dramatic lesson in God's love, and credited God with saving his life. Can we do less as we contemplate His watch-care over us?

November 5

Blessed are they that keep judgment, and he that doeth righteousness at all times.—Psalm 106:3

There are three kinds of lives which make up the great majority of the human race: the other-directed life, the self-directed life, and the Christ-directed life. The other-directed life has a built-in radar apparatus that keeps the person lined up, not with what is right, but with what is preferred according to the majority. Conformity and adjustment are the two poles of life for the other-directed life. He hides in the herd, no matter what color the herd is. In Mecca, he would be a Moslem; in Moscow, a Communist.

The man who lives the self-directed life is unconcerned with the opinions of the crowd, so long as attention is focused on him. The welfare of others is secondary to him. He is religious because of what he expects to receive as benefit from his devotion. If he unites with a church, it is because of what it can do for him, not what he can do for it.

The man living the self-directed life is covetous, cruel, sensual. He serves no one, but would make all men serve his interests. He would exalt himself above God and would usurp His authority. He lives by the law of the jungle. Supreme examples of this kind of man are Nero, Hitler, Stalin.

The Christ-directed life is God-likeness. This man lives independent of the appeal of tradition, and scorns the control of the crowd or big majorities. The outflow of such a life is sympathy, compassion, generosity, tenderness in dealing with straying humanity, but as harsh as truth when dealing with sin. Jesus described this Christ-directed life in Matthew 5-7. Here we learn that such a life maintains an attitude of forgiveness (5:23), spurns a superiority attitude (7:4, 5), scorns the attitude of self-righteousness (7:21), avoids an attitude of anger and disdain (5:22).

In this age of confused values, the man for whom God is looking is one whose "righteousness exceeds the righteousness of the scribes and Pharisees." His influence is compared to salt, light, to a good tree which bears only good fruit. "Christ crowned within" produces the man for whom God is looking —the man with the Christ-directed life. —O. G. Wilson

November 6

There is therefore now no condemnation. —Romans 8:1

Come, my soul, think of this. Believing in Jesus, you are actually and effectually cleared from guilt; you are led out of your prison. You are no more bound as a bondslave; you are delivered *now* from the bondage of the law; you are free from sin, and can walk about as a freeman; your Savior's blood has purchased your full pardon.

You have a right now to approach your Father's throne. No flames of vengeance are there to harm you now; no fiery sword; justice cannot touch the innocent. Your disabilities are taken away; once you were unable to see your Father's face: you can see it now. Once you could not speak with Him, but now you have access with boldness. Once there was the fear of hell in you, but now your fear is gone, for how can the guiltless be punished? He who believed is not condemned and cannot be punished. And more than all, the privileges you might have enjoyed if you had never sinned, are yours now as if you had never sinned!

All the blessings which you would have had if you had kept the law, and more, are yours because Christ kept it for you. All the love and acceptance which perfect obedience could have obtained of God, belong to you because Christ was perfectly obedient on your behalf and has imputed His merits to your account that you may be exceedingly rich through Him, who for your sake became exceedingly poor.

Oh, how great the debt of love and gratitude we owe our Savior! —*C. H. Spurgeon*

November 7

The Lord of peace himself give you peace always by all means. The Lord be with you all.—2 Thessalonians 3:16

Notice the special title given in this passage: "The Lord of peace." It occurs again in 1 Thessalonians 5:23, "The God of peace himself sanctify you wholly"; and again in Hebrews 13:20, 21, "The God of peace who brought again from the dead the great Shepherd of the sheep . . . make you perfect in every good work." He has revealed himself as the God of peace in the gospel of His Son.

The message He has sent us is the word of peace—"preaching peace by Jesus Christ." The work He has accomplished is the work of peace, "having made peace by the blood of his cross." The path into which He leads us is the "way of peace."

In our text we have the apostolic prayer that the same Lord might himself continually bestow upon these Thessalonian Christians the gift of peace. A perpetual gift of peace! Not at certain times of special devotion only—but "always." Not when circumstances are favorable only—but "by all means." That is, "in all ways." In dark and trying ways, as well as in bright and smooth ways. —*Evan H. Hopkins*

November 8

The dogs eat of the crumbs which fall from their masters' table.—Matthew 15:27

Both the humility and the quick, eager faith of this woman appear in her response to Jesus. She was not offended by the figure our Lord had used. She was willing to be as a little dog under the Master's table. The children were first served, and then the pieces they let fall belonged to the dogs. All she asked was the portion that ordinarily went to the dogs. And even the crumbs from that table were enough for her, more than the richest dainties from any other table.

Thus both humility and faith were shown in her answer; and in both she is an example to us. We should come to Christ with a deep sense of our own unworthiness, ready to take the lowest place. It is such a precious thing to be permitted to take even the crumbs from the Master's table that we should exult in the privilege. The crumbs of His grace and love are better than the richest feasts of this world.

> Not worthy, Lord, to gather up the crumbs
> With trembling hand that from Thy table fall,
> A weary, heavy-laden sinner comes
> To plead Thy promise and obey Thy call.
>
> I am not worthy to be thought Thy child,
> Nor sit the last and lowest at Thy board;
> Too long a wanderer, and too oft beguiled,
> I only ask one reconciling word.

Yet we are not fed with crumbs; we are seated at the full table, with the richest provisions before us. The prodigal, returning, asked only to be made a servant, as he felt unworthy to be restored to a son's place. But father-love knew no such half-way restoration as that. The white robe, the ring, the shoes were given to him, insignia of sonship. God puts the lowliest and unworthiest at once into the children's place, and feeds them abundantly. —*J. R. Miller*

November 9

Praise ye the Lord. O give thanks unto the Lord; for he is good: for his mercy endureth forever.—Psalms 106:1; 107:1

David's thanks is a recurring note throughout the Psalms. Again and again he raises his voice and heart in a resounding and exultant shout of praise. This note of joy echoes down to our present day with its ringing declaration of worship and gladness. It should characterize our lives as well.

David uses almost identical words in the opening verses of Psalms 106 and 107, but prefaces his expression of thanksgiving in Psalm 106 with a hearty "Praise the Lord!" In the Modern Language Bible and the Living Bible, this thought is given as "Hallelujah." Interestingly enough, Psalm 106 stands at the very threshold of Book V in the Psalter, a section which includes Psalms 107 through 150. Psalm 106 is in fact the first of the so-called "Hallelujah" Psalms, so named because each begins with this joyful "hallelujah" to God for His goodness (the others are Psalms 111-113, 117, 135, 146-150). In all these Psalms the keynote is praise. Both Psalm 106 and 107 speak of Israel's experiences during the Exodus and the wilderness wanderings, tracing the people's unfaithfulness and recurring repentance for their evil ways.

We modern pilgrims are not immune to "wandering" from God's will. We, too, stray from the way God would have us to go, and we need to return to Him in repentance. When we do, the note of praise and thanksgiving for His goodness should not be missing from our worship, for praise is the key to true worship. As Annie Johnson Flint points out poetically:

> As we offer our small rejoicing
> For the love that surrounds our days,
> All the wonderful works of Thy goodness
> Shall open beyond our gaze;
> Through the gates of narrow thanksgiving
> We shall enter Thy courts of praise!

November 10

Consider how great things he hath done for you. —1 Samuel 12:24

A consideration of God's past mercies strengthens our faith in His future blessing, and deepens our sense of unworthiness. We lose much from a lack of thoughtful consideration. The remembrance of what He has already done for us, and prayerful meditation on those truths, will dispel our doubts and turn our days of clouds and darkness into sunshine.

There is a divine logic in the reasoning: "He that spared not his own Son, but delivered him up for us all, how shall he not with him also freely give us all things?" (Rom. 8:32).

It is impossible to grasp the extent or to estimate the value of those gifts God has already bestowed, but we may "consider" them. Let us cultivate this habit of holy and devout meditation on the "great things" that God has done for us. It will deepen our thankfulness and quicken the spirit of prayer.

"Bless the Lord, O my soul, and *forget not* all his benefits" (Ps. 103:1).
                                                    —*Evan H. Hopkins*

November 11

O give thanks unto the Lord, for he is good: for his mercy endureth forever. —Psalm 107:1

The soul is prone to feel in the day of calamity, sorrow, and loss that it is compelled to depend upon its own resources. The moment Satan starts us down that road he is certain of victory.

Turn your attention to Psalm 107 and see God working for us:

"He delivered them out of their distresses."

"He satisfieth the longing soul, and filleth the hungry with goodness."

"He brake their bands in sunder."

"He hath broken the gates of brass."

"He sent his word and healed them."

"He maketh the storm a calm."

"He bringeth them into their desired haven."

Look back through those statements and ponder the riches here promised.

Do you believe in God's goodness? Then step into the waters, advance into the furnace, be content to be thrown to the lions. His will, even His permissive will, is good. Do not look for signs or wonders. His Word is equal to His presence.

Many of us are reluctant to turn over our burdens and our griefs to Christ. We get a secret enjoyment from nursing them and taking them out for public display. Cast *all* your burdens upon the Lord. When you do you no longer have any burdens. You have not a single trial to bemoan, not a burden to complain of, not one slight over which to grow bitter.

This is the secret of victory. This is the life of glory and grace.

There is nothing more attractive in a world filled with God's wonders and beauty than a soul so filled with God, so committed to God that he is a perpetual well of praise. Let God work out your problem for you. You will discover that out of the chaos of your thought will come calm, and into your troubled soul will tiptoe peace. What concerns you is also His concern. An abiding trust in Him will dispel the shadows.

—*O. G. Wilson*

November 12

Praise ye the Lord from the heavens: praise him in the heights. . . . Praise him, ye heavens of heavens, and ye waters that be above the heavens.—Psalm 148:1, 4

"Praise ye the Lord." And the Psalmist calls upon the creation to join in the anthem. That is the gracious purpose of our God, that the world should be filled with harmonious praise.

It is His will that the character of man should harmonize with the flowers of the field; that the beauty of his habits should blend with the glories of the sunrise; and that his speech and laughter should blend with the songs of birds and with the melody of flowing streams. But man is too often in a discord with creation. The birds, by contrast, make his voice sound harsh and jarring. He is "out of tune" and "out of step."

What then? "Tune my heart to sing Thy praise." We must bring the broken strings, the jarring strings, to the repairer and tuner of the soul. It is the glad ministry of His grace to reawaken silent chords, to restore broken harps, to "put new songs" in our hearts and mouths. He will make us kin to all things bright and beautiful. We shall "go forth with joy," and "all the trees of the field shall clap their hands."

—*J. H. Jowett*

November 13

Fear not to go down into Egypt; for I will there make of thee a great nation: I will go down with thee into Egypt; and I will also surely bring thee up again. —Genesis 46:3, 4

Jacob must have shuddered at the thought of leaving the land of his fathers and dwelling among heathen strangers. It was a new scene, and likely to be a trying one. Who shall venture among strangers without anxiety? Yet the way was evidently appointed for him, and therefore he resolved to go.

This is frequently the position of believers today. They are called upon to change jobs, to face situations new and untried: at such times let them imitate Jacob's example by offering sacrifices of prayer to God, and seeking His direction; let them not take a step until they have waited upon the Lord for His blessing. Then they will have Jacob's Companion to be their friend and helper.

How blessed to feel assured that the Lord is with us in all our ways, to know that He condescends to go down into our humiliations and difficulties with us! Even beyond the ocean, our Father's love beams like the sun in its strength. We cannot hesitate to go where Jehovah promises His presence; even the valley of death grows bright with the radiance of this assurance.

Marching onwards with faith in their God, believers shall have Jacob's promise. They shall be brought up again, whether it be from troubles of life or chambers of death. Jacob's seed came out of Egypt in due time, and so shall all the faithful pass unscathed through the tribulation of life, and terror of death.

Let us exercise Jacob's confidence. "Fear not" is the Lord's command and His divine encouragement to those who at His bidding are launching upon new seas and new ways; the divine presence and preservation forbid so much as one unbelieving fear. Without our God we should fear to move; but when He bids us go, it would be dangerous to delay. Reader, go forward and fear not!

—*C. H. Spurgeon*

November 14

The God of all grace.—1 Peter 5:10

What an encouraging aspect of God's character is this! It is one of His names. The whole gospel is incorporated in the names of God. He is the God of peace—the God of hope—the God of all comfort. Here we have "the God of all grace."

Grace embraces our every need. "God is able to make all grace abound toward you" (2 Cor. 9:8). It is submission to His will and trust in His love and faithfulness that are needed on our part in order to live in the stream of His boundless, ceaseless, and victorious grace.

None of us know what grace means until we are brought to rely on God's pardoning love to us in Christ Jesus. Grace means unmerited favor—receiving what we do not deserve. Grace is the opposite of merit—we are saved by grace.

But grace also means the complement of our need—that which fills up our emptiness. It is on the ground of grace that God deals with us, not only when we first come to Him in our guilt and misery, but all along the way, and every day in our lives, when, as pardoned souls, and children in His family, we walk in the light of His countenance. We cannot, and we dare not, leave this ground of grace. —*Evan H. Hopkins*

November 15

Let patience have her perfect work, that ye may be perfect and entire, wanting nothing.—James 1:4

The apostle refers in the passage to the trial of faith. God, who gives the faith, appoints the trial. The purpose of the trial is the strengthening of faith. But this is not reached if the trial does not have its full course. The endurance, which the trial calls for, must continue. It must have its "perfect work."

The blessing hidden in the trial may never be realized, simply because the endurance did not last out. Therefore it is that in every trial our special need is that of patience. And the secret of this patience is a spirit of submission to the will of God, and an unquestioning faith in His love. Judged by outward surroundings, the believer may sometimes look very much like one forsaken of God and afflicted. But faith works through all adverse circumstances, and keeps steadily in view the unchanging love and faithfulness of God.

The grace of God can enable a man not only to submit to the trial that God appoints; it can enable him to rise higher—namely, to acquiesce in it, and still higher, to *rejoice* in it (see 2 Cor. 12:9). —*Evan H. Hopkins*

November 16

Continue in prayer, and watch in the same with thanks-giving.—Colossians 4:2

In John 11:41 Jesus sets a beautiful example for His followers in this matter of combining prayer and thanksgiving. In fact, here Jesus expresses His thanks to the Father for answering a prayer He had not even prayed. Looking at the passage, we cannot find His petition that Lazarus be raised even recorded. All we have is His eloquent expression of praise to the Father that His "unspoken request" was granted. After this, in verse 43, He commands Lazarus to come forth—and he does so dramatically, a startling example of death defeated at its own game. If Jesus, divine Son of God, expressed thanksgiving in prayer, shouldn't we? And our thanks is not to be a complacent expression of self-satisfaction as was the Pharisee's prayer, "I thank thee that I am not as other men—such as this publican"! No, our prayers are to be *humble* expressions of our praise, not arrogant demands on God's bounty, as if He owed us anything at all. Jesus here does not really *ask* for anything. He just thanks God for prayer already answered. Do you and I ever do that? In Matthew 11:25 Jesus gives us another capsule "model prayer": "I thank thee, O Father, Lord of heaven and earth, because thou hast hid these things from the wise and prudent, and hast revealed them unto babes." Let's follow His blessed example. With Christina Rosetti, recognize this truth: "Were there no God, we would be in this glorious world with grateful hearts: and no one to thank!"

November 17

Can the children of the bridechamber fast while the bride-groom is with them?—Mark 2:19

This was our Lord's answer to those who thought His religion too sunny and joyous—that it had not enough fast days in it. They thought that religion was genuine only when it made people sad, and that its quality was just in proportion to its gloom. But Christ's reply showed that mournful faces are no essential indicators of heart piety. Should His disciples be mournful and sad when He was with them, filling their lives with the gladness of His presence? Should Christians go around heavy-hearted, wearing the symbols of grief, when they are really filled with joy, and when there is no occasion for sorrow? Why should one who has been saved by the Lord Jesus, and who is rejoicing in full assurance of hope, go about in sackcloth and ashes? Is there any piety in a sad face?

Does God love to see His children always in mourning? Is human joy displeasing to our Father?

All these questions are answered here in our Lord's words. He does not wish His disciples to go mourning and fasting when they have no occasion for such action. His words are a defense of Christian joyfulness. Christ wants His friends to be glad. There is an utter incongruity in a sad and mournful Christian life. By its very nature true Christian faith is joyous. Our sins are forgiven. We are adopted into God's family. We are heirs of God; and joint-heirs with Christ. The covenant of love arches its shelter over us. All things in this world work together for our good, and then glory awaits us in the next world. With all this blessed heritage, why should we be mournful and sad? While we enjoy the smile of God, the consciousness of His love, the assurance of His forgiveness, and the hope of heaven and eternal life, what should make us sad? We "children of the bridechamber" should live this life with radiant faces. —*J. R. Miller*

November 18

God hath caused me to be fruitful in the land of my affliction.—Genesis 41:52

These were Joseph's words in reference to Ephraim. He had already spoken of his firstborn Manasseh. Joseph's true home, after all, was in Canaan. Egypt was the land of his affliction; but even there God had blessed him and made him fruitful. Joseph is thankful for the past with all its sorrow.

So the believer today may often look back to seasons of bitter trial and affliction, and see how God has made them times of special fruitfulness. Not that affliction necessarily sanctifies the heart or causes us to glorify God. After all, it is not our circumstances that are the secret of our spiritual progress; the true cause lies in something above all our surroundings. None can sanctify our souls or cause us to be fruitful but the Triune God. But He often uses our adversities to humble our hearts, subdue our pride, and make us submissive. Then it is that He causes us to be fruitful in the land of our affliction. Even there we may yield fruit unto God. God says to Ephraim, "O Ephraim, what have I to do with idols? It is I who answer and look after you. I am like an evergreen cypress, from me comes your fruit" (Hosea 14:8, RSV). —*Evan H. Hopkins*

November 19

When the poor and needy seek . . . , I the Lord will hear them, I the God of Israel will not forsake them. —Isaiah 41:17

A prominent psychiatrist, whose office was stormed daily with people whose souls were in distress, cried out in despair: "Doesn't the church have an office for the care of souls anymore?" Whether or not the church has such an office, the Almighty God has arranged such a place of help, and the waiting rooms are never overcrowded and appointments may be made at any time. Modern man sorely needs to close his ears to the clamoring voices of worry and distress all about him, and direct his cry for help to the very throne room of the universe where God has promised to hear. Make your appointment now and meet with God for counsel and guidance.

Are you perplexed as to which course to follow? God has promised to hear your cry, so at this moment direct your cry to Him. "But know that the Lord hath set apart him that is godly for himself; the Lord will hear when I call unto him" (Ps. 4:3).

Does your life seem an impossible jigsaw that, try as you may, you cannot properly place the parts? What have you done about it—worried, fretted yourself to illness? Why not try God? Remember, "I the Lord will hear."

A kettle of boiling water was simmering over the hunter's campfire. In the absence of the hunter, a bear wandered by and seized the kettle. Instead of dropping the scalding vessel, he hugged it to himself—his only known method of defense. Why not try dropping your kettle of boiling water, remembering God says, "Casting *all* your care upon him, for he careth for you"?

To the prophet Jeremiah, shut up in prison, forsaken by friends, and in serious danger of losing his life, came the message: "Call upon me and I will answer thee and show thee great and mighty things that thou knowest not." God is our present, living, available help. He will supply all our needs "according to his riches in glory by Christ Jesus."

—*O. G. Wilson*

November 20

O God, my heart is fixed: I will sing and give praise. Awake up, my glory; awake, psaltery and harp. —Psalm 57:7, 8

David was in a cave hiding from King Saul when he wrote this psalm. Yet instead of saying, "O God, my heart is frozen with fear," he declares, "O God, my heart is fixed"—calm, happy, resolute, firm, established. His soul is among lions, yet he cries as if to arouse himself to the spiritual joy that is beyond the reach of one's enemies, "Awake up, my glory; awake, psaltery and harp."

Many of us need at times to make this same call upon ourselves to awake. The harps are hanging silent on the walls. The figure of speech showing instruments of music sleeping is suggestive. They are capable of giving forth rich melodies, but not a note is heard from them. There are two thoughts suggested by this prayer. One is that life is meant to be glad, joyous. It is pictured as a harp. The other is the splendor of life—"Awake up, my glory."

It is to a life of joy and song we are called to awake. Life is a harp. There is a legend of an instrument that hung on a castle wall. Its strings were broken. It was covered with dust. No one understood it, and no fingers could bring music from it. One day a stranger saw the silent harp, took it into his hands, reverently brushed away the dust, tenderly replaced the broken strings, and then he played upon it, and the glad music filled all the castle.

This is a parable of everyday life, which is a harp, made to give out music, but broken and silent until Christ gets possession of it. Then the song awakes. We are called to joy and joy-giving. "Awake up, my glory."   —*J. R. Miller*

November 21

Daniel . . . went into his house; and his windows being open in his chamber toward Jerusalem, he kneeled upon his knees three times a day, and prayed, and gave thanks before his God, as he did aforetime.—Daniel 6:10

We have already looked at the life of our Lord as an example of thanksgiving in prayer. His Word is full of stories of His followers who were thankful to God, and expressed that thanksgiving in prayer. Daniel was an outstanding example of a prayer warrior who practiced good prayer habits. Our verse for today tells us prayer was his regular practice: "as he did aforetime" (KJV); "as he had done previously" (RSV); "just as he always had" (Living Bible).

The Psalms of David are full of exhortations to combine praise and prayer:

"Let us come before his presence with thanksgiving, and make a joyful noise unto him with psalms" (Ps. 95:2).

"I will praise the name of God with a song, and will magnify him with thanksgiving" (Ps. 69:30).

Thanksgiving expressed in prayer and singing is an inherent and integral part of the Christian's worship of God. Look in any church hymnal and you will find a wide selection of hymns expressing thanksgiving and praise to God for His goodness and faithfulness. Those who find time to praise God seldom find time to grumble! A spirit of thanksgiving should characterize every Christian. As J. H. Jowett once said: "Life without thankfulness is devoid of love and passion. Hope without thankfulness is lacking in fine perception. Faith without thankfulness lacks strength and fortitude. Every virtue divorced from thankfulness is maimed and limps along the spiritual road."

Which would you rather be along the road of life—a limper or a leaper?

November 22

Now therefore, our God, we thank thee, and praise thy glorious name.—1 Chronicles 29:13

Another of God's great men, David, was a man deeply committed to the concept of thankful prayer. As we have already noted, his writings are full of praise and expressions of thanksgiving. The words of our text lie right in the heart of his last recorded prayer. The aged king was expressing his "thanksgiving policy" one more time.

Even David's early life was a paean of praise to his heavenly Father. One of his first recorded psalms is found in 1 Chronicles 16. In verse 8 he begins: "Give thanks unto the Lord, call upon his name, make known his deeds among the people." At the triumphant conclusion (vv. 35 and 36) of this same prayer, David exults: "Save us, O God of our salvation, and gather us together, and deliver us from the heathen, that we may give thanks to thy holy name, and glory in thy praise. Blessed be the Lord God of Israel for ever and ever."

J. R. Miller puts it succinctly thus: "Thanksgiving is nothing if not a glad and reverent lifting of the heart to God in honour and praise for His goodness." The poet, John Oxenham, says:

> We thank Thee, Lord,
> That of Thy tender grace,
> In our distress
> Thou hast not left us wholly comfortless.
>
> We thank Thee, Lord,
> That of Thy wondrous might,
> Into our night
> Thou hast sent down the glory of the Light.
>
> We thank Thee, Lord,
> That all Thy wondrous ways,
> Through all our days
> Are wisdom, right, and ceaseless praise.

This should be our attitude as we contemplate God's great goodness and mercy to us, His chosen children.

November 23

Then he (Simeon) took him up in his arms, and blessed God. . . . And she (Anna) coming in that instant gave thanks likewise unto the Lord, and spake of him to all them that looked for redemption in Jerusalem.—Luke 2:28, 38

We have been looking at examples of thankful people in the Old Testament, as well as seeing the spirit of thanksgiving exemplified in our Lord. Now we take time to consider two dear old people whose lives were almost over, yet their lives give us a fragrance of thankfulness that remains to our modern day. Of Simeon we read: "There was a man in Jerusalem, whose name was Simeon; and the same man was just and devout, waiting for the consolation of Israel: and the Holy Ghost was upon him" (v. 25). Simeon's song when he took up the Christ-child in his arms is second only to Mary's in its insights and lofty spirit. His prayer of praise is a model for all of us as we contemplate God's goodness and greatness. His assessment of God's great gift in the person of the Christ-child: "Lord, now lettest thou thy servant depart in peace . . . for mine eyes have seen thy salvation" (vv. 29, 30).

Old Anna, too, has a striking spiritual pedigree as given in verses 36 and 37: "A prophetess . . . of great age . . . and she was a widow [who] departed not from the temple, but served God with fastings and prayers night and day." The natural outgrowth of her adoration of the Savior is given in verse 38: "She . . . gave thanks . . . and spake of him to all them that looked for redemption in Jerusalem."

Based on our look at Simeon and Anna, it is safe to say that the healthy Christian life demands a thankful spirit, praising God for His greatness in sending His Son to be our Savior. If old people like Simeon and Anna can be so outspoken in their Christian witness, how much more should we praise Him for His goodness to us today! As the great Plutarch said at the dawn of the Christian era: "The worship most acceptable to God comes from a thankful and cheerful heart."

November 24

I thank my God through Jesus Christ for you all, that your faith is spoken of throughout the whole world.
—Romans 1:8

For Paul, thanksgiving was "thanks-living." No matter what his circumstances, he was always ready to give thanks. If his thankfulness did not arise from his circumstances, where *did* it come from? We find the answer not only here in Romans, but more specifically in that "journal of joy," the epistle to the Philippians. Written while Paul was in prison, Philippians celebrates the joy the Christian has *despite* his circumstances, rather than *because* of them. The words "joy" and "rejoice" appear fourteen times in this brief epistle, and just two of the verses will reveal the source of Paul's joy and thanksgiving:

"Rejoice in the Lord alway" (4:4).

"I *thank* my God upon every remembrance of you, always in every prayer of mine for you all making request with joy" (1:3, 4).

Paul's joy did not come from material blessings or bounty. No, he had learned to rejoice without these. "I have learned in whatsoever state I am therewith to be content." His joy arose from his relationship *to* Christ and his position *in* Christ. And because of his rejoicing in Christ, he could not keep silent but had to share his joy with others. Even in jail, his joy in the Lord resulted in the salvation of the jailor (Acts 16:19ff.).

Paul had learned the lesson that the joyful life cannot center itself around self. The self-centered man measures himself against other men—and finds pride or discouragement in the comparison. The life of the Christian must revolve around Christ. When Paul states the principle in Philippians 1:21, he rounds it out in chapter 4, "Find your joy, your source of satisfaction, your state of contentment, in the Lord Jesus Christ." Along with Christ, Paul found his fellow Christians a cause for thanksgiving and rejoicing. We should follow his example and pattern our lives around this blueprint for successful living.

November 25

When Paul saw [the brethren coming to meet him], he thanked God, and took courage. —Acts 28:15

Of all the sacred writers, Pauls seems to exhort Christians to take on a thankful spirit more frequently than any other. Our verse today reveals that he practiced what he preached in his letters and sermons: In Colossians 1:3 he said of the Colossian Christians: "We give thanks to God and the Father of our Lord Jesus Christ, praying always for you," emphasizing again the close relationship of prayer and praise. Writing to his spiritual son Timothy he said: "I thank Christ Jesus our Lord, who hath enabled me, for that he counted me faithful, putting me into the ministry" (1:12).

We have quoted many of Paul's admonitions to praise elsewhere in this book, particularly in this series on thankfulness, but let me remind you here of some passages not usually quoted in a context of thankfulness:

"Or despisest thou the riches of his goodness and forbearance and longsuffering; not knowing that the goodness of God leadeth thee to repentance?" (Rom. 2:4).

"Rooted and built up in him, and stablished in the faith, as ye have been taught, abounding therein with thanksgiving" (Col. 2:7).

"I exhort therefore, that . . . giving of thanks, be made for all men" (1 Tim. 2:1).

"For every creature of God is good, and nothing to be refused, if it be received with thanksgiving" (1 Tim. 4:4).

Paul, the spiritual giant, who stands head and shoulders above most of those in the early Church, believed in thankful prayer. He would have echoed Annie Johnson Flint's words:

> As we offer our small rejoicing
> For the love that surrounds our days,
> All the wonderful works of Thy goodness
> Shall open before our gaze;
> Through the gates of our narrow thanksgiving
> We shall enter Thy courts of praise.

November 26
And let them sacrifice the sacrifices of thanksgiving, and declare his works with rejoicing.—Psalm 107:22

If our pilgrim forefathers could set foot on a rock, fell stout timbers for houses, and grind maize into meal, surely we can adjust our lives to new frontiers of peace and plenty.

We may have to sell our choice apples, but we will have enough of the second-grade apples even though we may need to cut out some spoiled spots.

We may need to sell our choice turkeys, but we have a nice fat hen for our Thanksgiving dinner.

We may not have the family home for Thanksgiving, but we have the Christ whose presence makes a cabin a palace and floods a dark day with radiance.

The apostle Paul, with a crippled and afflicted body, surrounded by hate, opposed by jealous rivals, and suffering from terrible and unjust treatment, could write: "In every thing give thanks, for this is the will of God in Christ Jesus concerning you" (1 Thess. 5:18). Paul gave us substantial ground for thanksgiving: "Giving thanks unto the Father, which hath made us meet to be partakers of the inheritance of the saints in light" (Col. 1:12).

Our thankfulness rests not upon possessions, and it is not destroyed by the loss of possessions. Our thankfulness rests not upon our health, our wealth, our position, or reputation. Our thankfulness rests upon the love of the eternal God in His work for us at Calvary and in His work in us in personal experience.

We are thankful for truth as it is revealed in Jesus Christ.

We are thankful for a hope which rests upon the work of Christ at Calvary. We are thankful for God's love with which we have been surrounded all our lives through.

We are thankful for the spiritual life, the sanctifying grace, the empowering of the Holy Spirit, and that with Him we may walk unafraid and victorious. "Enter into his gates with thanksgiving, and into his courts with praise; be thankful unto him, and bless his name" (Ps. 100:4).   —O. G. Wilson

November 27

Because that, when they knew God, they glorified him not as God, neither were thankful; but became vain in their imaginations, and their foolish heart was darkened.
—Romans 1:21

In following the theme of thankfulness through the Scriptures, we need to look at the negative side of the coin as well as the positive. Here, speaking to the Gentiles, Paul points out their problem—*unthankfulness.* In Ephesians 4:17, 18 he expands upon the reason for their spiritual blindness: "Walk not as other Gentiles walk, in the vanity of their mind, having the understanding darkened, being alienated from the life of God through the ignorance that is in them, because of the blindness of their heart." An ungrateful spirit is characteristic of a closed heart and mind—a closed soul. Ingratitude to God is an indication that one does not believe He is the source of everything we have. Basically, gratitude demonstrates faith, and ingratitude shows lack of faith. No faith—no promises from God except His judgment.

An unthankful spirit, says Paul, fails to honor God. Our refusal to thank God for His creation carries a companion with it—refusal to thank God for His Son. Creation and the Son go together, as is made abundantly clear by John 1 as well as the other New Testament writers. Jesus himself said, "If they hear not Moses and the prophets, neither will they be persuaded, though one rose from the dead" (Luke 16:31). By rejecting the Creation story, we are also denying God's gift of His Son. Jesus Christ is God's revelation of Himself, and in rejecting Him men are turning their backs on God, as God says: "What iniquity have your fathers found in me, that they are gone far from me, and have walked after vanity, and are become vain?" (Jer. 2:5).

A true spirit of thankfulness is the key to humility and wholeness. The opposite spirit is pride, and on that subject Henry Ward Beecher once said: "Pride slays thanksgiving, but an humble mind is the soil out of which thanks grow naturally. A proud man is seldom a grateful man, for he never thinks he gets as much as he deserves." Get on the positive side with God—forsake false pride and honor Him for His goodness and greatness.

November 28

I will never leave thee.—Hebrews 13:5

No promise is of private interpretation. Whatever God has said to one saint, He has said to all. When He opens a well for one, it is that all may drink. When He opens a granary door to give out food, there may be one starving man who is the occasion for its being opened, but all who are hungry may come and feed too. Whether He gave the word to Abraham or Moses does not matter. O believer, He has given it to you as one of the covenanted seed.

There is not a high blessing too lofty for you, nor a wide mercy too extensive for you. Lift up now your eyes to the north and to the south, to the east and to the west, for all this is yours. There is not a brook of living water from which you may not drink. If the land flows with living milk and honey, eat the honey and drink the milk, for both are yours. Be bold to believe, for He has said, "I will never leave *thee*, nor forsake *thee*." In this promise God gives to His people everything.

"*I* will never leave thee." Then no attribute of God can cease to be serving us. Is He mighty? He will show himself strong on behalf of them who trust Him. Is He love? Then with lovingkindness will He have mercy upon us. Whatever attributes may compose the character of God, every one of them to its fullest extent shall be engaged on our behalf.

To put everything in one, there is nothing you can want, there is nothing you can ask for, there is nothing you can need in time or in eternity, there is nothing living, nothing dying, there is nothing in this world, nothing in the next world, there is nothing now, nothing at the Resurrection morning, nothing in heaven which cannot be contained in this text: "I will never leave thee, nor forsake thee."

—*C. H. Spurgeon*

November 29

It is good for me to draw near to God.—Psalm 73:28

God is the center and source of all our happiness. We are privileged to draw near to Him in our unworthiness and sin, through His Son Jesus Christ. We draw nigh not merely for pardon and relief, but to find in Him our portion and in His presence our home. The first thing He would have us do is to "draw near" unto Him. He has opened the way and provided the sacrifice. Every barrier that stood in the way between the guilty sinner and the holy God, He himself has removed by the blood of His cross. The way into the holiest has now been made open and plain (Heb. 10:19, 20, 22).

The believer is one who not only came unto God at his conversion, but who is also in the habit of coming continually unto Him. It is to such that those words in Hebrews 7:25 primarily refer: "He is able to be saving to the very end, those that are in the habit of coming unto God by Jesus Christ." There can be no real act of worship without thus drawing near. We must enter into the *place* of worship— that is, into the holiest of all—if we would know what worship means. —*Evan H. Hopkins*

November 30

But thanks be to God, which giveth us the victory. —1 Corinthians 15:57

There is nothing more fundamentally Christian than a thankful spirit. To be oblivious of the benefits bestowed is the mark of a diseased, depraved soul.

To be thankful is to be gracious, happy, contented, and in possession of one of humanity's most noble characteristics. In the midst of the hurricane, when the storm-battered vessel was plunging at its four anchors off the coast of Malta, Paul "gave thanks to God in the presence of them all" (Acts 27:35). And he could do that because he had faith in the word and promise God had given him.

Despite hardships, toil, persecution, lonely hours, imprisonment, beatings, slander, there is a spirit of thanksgiving running through all Paul's epistles which shows his gratitude toward life:

"Now thanks be unto God, which always causeth us to triumph in Christ" (2 Cor. 2:14). "Thanks be unto God for his unspeakable gift" (2 Cor. 9:15).

"Giving thanks always for all things" (Eph. 5:20). "In everything give thanks" (1 Thess. 5:18).

How could he do it; what were the springs from which Paul drank that caused him to break forth into strains of thanksgiving and praise? The source of his life of praise was the indwelling presence—not the circumstances with which he was surrounded.

We find a beautiful Thanksgiving service, highly spontaneous, in 1 Chronicles 29:11-13: "Thine, O lord, is the greatness, and the power, and the glory, and the victory, and the majesty: for all that is in the heaven and the earth is thine; thine is the kingdom, O Lord, and thou art exalted as head above all. Both riches and honour come of thee, and thou reignest over all; and in thine hand is power and might; and in thine hand it is to make great, and to give strength unto all. Now therefore, our God, we thank and praise thy glorious name."

Let us join the saints of the ages in a paean of praise to our God!
—*O. G. Wilson*

December 1

The Word was made flesh, and dwelt among us. —John 1:14

We must notice that it is the same person who was in the beginning, who was God, and who made all things, who is here said to have become flesh. The Jesus of the gospel story is the God of eternity, the Jehovah of the Old Testament. The reason for the incarnation was the salvation of man.

The Good Shepherd came to seek and to save His sheep which were lost. He came in human form that He might get nearer to the sinner. A Moravian missionary went to preach the gospel to the slaves in the West Indies. Failing as a free man to reach them, he became a slave himself, and went with them to their field work, into all their hardships and sufferings, thus getting close to them.

This illustrates Christ's sacrifice to save the world. We could not understand God in His invisible glory; so Immanuel came, and in human form lived out the divine life, showing us God's grace and His love for sinners, His thoughts and character. This was one object of the incarnation—it revealed in a way which men could understand the invisible things of God.

Then Christ became man also that He might learn life by actual experience, and thus be fitted to become our Saviour, and to sympathize with us in all our experiences of temptation, struggle, sorrow. We are sure now, when we come to Christ in any need, that He understands our condition and knows how to help us. We have a high priest in heaven who can be touched with the feeling of our infirmities, because He was tried in all points as we are. Christ became man also that He might taste death for every man, thus abolishing death for His people. He remembers what He suffered being tempted; and when He sees His people in their struggles, He remembers when He endured the same, and is ready to sympathize with and help them.
—*J. R. Miller*

December 2

Watch, therefore, for ye know neither the day nor the hour wherein the Son of man cometh. —Matthew 25:13

"I remember," says a well-known writer, "once living at a place where a large number of people were constantly employed in keeping the walks, grounds, and gardens in order. The proprietor was absent, and everything had a sleepy, slovenly look. But when news came that he would soon return, all became awake, earnest, and active. The pruning, the rolling, the weeding, the sweeping that went on! No one rested 'til all was ready; and all were gratified by the look and word of approval when the master came."

Just so, if we constantly remembered the words, "Ye know neither the day nor the hour wherein the Son of man cometh," we would feel it is not the time to sleep. It is a time for watchfulness, for earnest diligence and unceasing activity. The time is short, and the day of the Lord's return is close at hand.

"What I say unto you," said our Lord to His disciples, "I say unto all, Watch" (Mark 13:37). The disciple who lives in the spirit of watchfulness will meditate on his Master's word, will live in the Master's presence, and will seek perpetually to be doing His Master's will. —*Evan H. Hopkins*

December 3

Come unto me . . . and I will give you rest.—Matthew 11:28

The needle in the compass never stands still till it comes right against the north pole. The wise men of the East never stood still till they were under the star which appeared unto them; and the star itself never stood still till it came right against that other Star, which shone more brightly in the manger than the sun did in the firmament. So the heart of man can find no rest till it comes to Christ.

This is a tired world! Multitudes tired of body or tired of mind or tired of soul! Every one has a burden to carry, if not on one shoulder, then on the other. In the Far East, water is so scarce that if a man owns a well, he is rich. . . . God is the rest of the soul that comes to Him. He rests us by removing the weight of our sin and by solacing our griefs with the thought that He knows what is best for His children.—*Talmage*

December 4

Go up into Gilead, and take balm.—Jeremiah 46:11

Time may wrinkle the skin but it cannot wrinkle the soul.

Manufacturers are spending their best energies, employing highly trained technicians to work out formulas to prevent wrinkles and to remove them from the face. Should they ever fully succeed they will have made a fortune indeed. All are interested. Every youth and adult would be a perpetual customer.

All of this has to do with a part of man that is to perish.

Wrinkles are sure signs of ultimate dissolution. Man's best efforts can never prevent them.

Jesus Christ stands in the midst of the ages and promises life without a wrinkle. What an announcement!

"Christ ... loved the church, and gave himself for it: that he might sanctify and cleanse it with the washing of water by the word, that he might present it to himself a glorious church, not having spot or wrinkle, or any such thing" (Eph. 5:25-27).

Grace is the great wrinkle remover. It will not take the wrinkles from the face, but it will from the soul. This is the part we should particularly be concerned about. Grace will take away the ugly wrinkles of hate which scar the soul so deeply, and in their place engraft the beautiful spirit of love.

The wrinkles of care, worry, and distrust may be displaced by a song of contentment, gladness and peace. Soul wrinkles are inexcusable. The remedy may be had for the asking. It has worked effectively across the millenniums, in all climates, and upon every race.

As the ancient Israelite in the wilderness was compelled to look in faith to the brazen serpent, just so must wrinkled souls look in faith to Christ. There is a balm in Gilead (Jer. 8:22). There is a cure for soul wrinkles. Look and gain soul beauty.

—O. G. Wilson

December 5

For I know that my redeemer liveth, and that he shall stand at the latter day upon the earth: and though after my skin worms destroy this body, yet in my flesh shall I see God. ...—Job 19:25-27

When a man is agitated by the Spirit of God, he utters words from which he takes comfort for himself, and others can do the same, but the treasure contained in the words can never be exhausted. Job did not understand all the meaning of these words, yet he took a meaning of great preciousness to himself out of them. So with us, it is never possible for us to understand what we utter when we get a glimpse of God, or to express the rapture that sweeps our soul at such times. If a man's words spoken in the power of the Spirit have such inexhaustible value, who can estimate the value of the Word of God, our Lord Jesus Christ himself, who expresses to us the very thoughts of God?

For I know that my redeemer liveth. ... Job is assured that his Redeemer (his Vindicator) will arise and will put right the wrong; and every upright soul will likewise one day be vindicated, never fear. But Job's words convey to us as Christians a deeper, more glorious truth; they mean that our Redeemer, the Lord Jesus Christ, will one day stand upon this earth and will clear *His* name from reproach and slander! The people of God cry, "O Lord, how long shall the adversary reproach? shall the enemy blaspheme thy name for ever?" The enemies of Christ are triumphant, Christianity is a failure, they say; and the Church of God herself looks on in pain at the short-comings in her midst. But lo, at length from the very heart of the shadows appears the majestic figure of Jesus; His countenance is as the sun shineth in his strength, around those wounds in brow and side and hands and feet—those wounds which shelter countless thousands of broken hearts—are healing rays; in that glorious figure meets every beauty inconceivable to the imagination of man.

O Christians, dry your eyes! Be not downcast, for I know that my Redeemer liveth! He is nearer than you think. Oh, the speechless rapture of it, that suddenly He will appear to us! "Yea: I come quickly. Amen: come Lord Jesus."

—Oswald Chambers

December 6

Beloved, be not ignorant of this one thing, that one day is with the Lord as a thousand years, and a thousand years as one day. The Lord is not slack concerning his promise, as some men count slackness.—2 Peter 3:8, 9

Why does God delay in fulfilling His promise? It is not because of inability or fickleness, as is the case with men. He delays because He is "longsuffering to usward, not willing that any should perish."

Peter views God's eternity in relation to the last day. It seems to us, short-lived human beings, long in coming; but *with the Lord* the interval is irrespective of the idea of long or short. His eternity exceeds all measures of time. To His divine knowledge future things are present. His power requires not long delays for performing His work. His longsuffering excludes men's impatient expectation. He can do the work of a thousand years in one day.

But what is the promise here referred to? It is the promise of His coming—His Second Advent. It was at this that men scoffed. It was so then; it is so now. But the believer expects what the Lord has promised (2 Pet. 3:13).   *—Evan H. Hopkins*

December 7

And when Zacharias saw him, he was troubled, and fear fell upon him.—Luke 1:12

Yet the angel had come on an errand of love—had come to announce to Zacharias tidings which would fill his heart with great joy. It is often so. All through the Bible we find people were afraid of God's angels. Their very glory startled and terrified those to whom they appeared.

It is often the same with us. When God's messengers come to us on errands of grace and peace, we are terrified as if they were messengers of wrath. Angels do not appear to us in these days in their heavenly garb. They come no less really and no less frequently than in the Bible days; but they wear other and various forms. Sometimes they appear in robes of gladness and light, but often they come in dark garments. Yet our faith in our Father's love should make us confident that every messenger He sends to us, whatever his garb, brings something good to us.

> All God's angels come to us disguised—
> Sorrow and sickness, poverty and death,
> One after other lift their frowning masks,
> And behold the seraph's face beneath,
> All radiant with the glory and the calm
> Of having looked upon the face of God.

The things we call trials and adversities are really God's angels, though they seem terrible to us; and if we will only quiet our hearts and wait, we will find that they are messengers from heaven, and that they brought blessing to us from God. They have come to tell us of some new joy that is to be granted—some spiritual joy, perhaps to be born of earthly sorrow, some strange and sweet surprise of love waiting for us. We want to learn to trust God so perfectly that no messenger He ever sends shall alarm us. —*J. R. Miller*

December 8

Yet once, it is a little while, and I will shake the heavens, and the earth and the sea, and the dry land; and I will shake all nations, and the desire of all nations shall come.
—Haggai 2:6, 7

What a graphic description of this present day is given in this brief excerpt from the prophet Haggai. The heavens, earth and sea are constantly being shaken, sometimes as a result of man's weapons and mistakes, but more often by God's cosmic activity. Earthquakes, tornadoes, and other disturbances were never more prevalent. This shaking is somehow symbolic of many things happening in our world: politically, economically, morally, in every way.

God is getting everything ready for the second coming of His Son. These shakings in the world around us are His warning signs of His soon return, that great event for which the Christian waits. For the Christian, these signs are not alarming but are rather comforting and assuring, for we know that His coming is certain and imminent. For the worldling, the unbeliever, these signs of His return are man's last opportunity to repent and accept the Savior and the solution to his sin problem, the solution God has provided.

As I contemplate the events of these last days, I am reminded that it is God who does the shaking—or allows it to happen. And it is God who provides the way of escape from the terrible consequences of this cosmic upset. That way of escape, that answer to life's greatest question, is "the desire of all nations," or as the Living Bible states it, "the Desire of All Nations."

Jesus Christ is coming again; the ominous "shakings" we see occurring around us, are sure signs of His soon return. Believe it and rejoice, Christian; recognize it and make ready for His return, unbeliever!

December 9

Behold, I come quickly. . . . The Lord direct your hearts into the love of God, and into the patient waiting for Christ.—Revelation 22:7, 12, 20; 2 Thessalonians 3:5

The last message the risen Christ gave His people was the promise of His soon return. Couple this with Paul's admonition to the Thessalonian Christians and you get a good rule for life: Live both expectantly and patiently, and you will be fulfilling the Lord's will until He returns.

What are some of the blessings awaiting the believer when Jesus Christ comes back? First of all, the faithful ones can confidently expect to be rewarded for their faithfulness. This is a matter of scriptural record, for in foretelling His return in Matthew 16:27 (RSV), Jesus promised, "For the Son of man is to come with his angels in the glory of the Father, and then he will repay every man for what he has done."

There is also a clear-cut promise of reward to the obedient Christian, "And being made perfect, he became the source of eternal salvation to all who obey him" (Heb. 5:9, RSV). Besides these promises of reward for faithfulness and obedience, Jesus has also promised to deliver His followers from the great tribulation awaiting the world at the end time. Paul told the Thessalonian believers "to wait for his [God's] Son from heaven, whom he raised from the dead, Jesus who delivers from the wrath to come."

In the light of such promises, our response should be, "Even so, come, Lord Jesus!"

But in addition to waiting expectantly, we are also admonished to wait patiently, to "occupy 'til he comes." And while we are waiting, we are to be yielded to the "love of God" operative in our lives. If the love of God flows through us, we will find ourselves sharing that love with those around us, for God is love, and that love is bigger than its container, the Christian, so it must overflow. Those around us long for love, for our world is full of hate, Satan's legacy since the Garden of Eden episode. Let us as Christians share God's love as we await the return of "His Son from heaven."

December 10

Watch therefore: for ye know not what hour your Lord doth come. —Matthew 24:42

May I give you a searching test to find what is your relationship to Christ? Jesus says to you, dear child of His love, "Behold, I come quickly." What do you reply? If you say: "Yes, Lord, I want Thee to come, but not just yet; there are a few things I want to do first," then you are not as near to Christ as He wants you to be. Oh, the bright light that falls upon our pathway if we understand that He is coming—and long to see Him! —*G. Campbell Morgan*

Paul's teaching ranges, just as did the teaching of Jesus, about two great points of time: "today," which is the day of salvation, and "that day," which is the consummation of all hope and faith. He writes regarding the Lord's Supper: "As oft as ye do this, ye do shew forth the Lord's death till he come." Again he says, "He that hath begun in you a good work will perfect it until the day of Jesus Christ." And, "When Christ who is our life shall appear, ye also shall appear with him in glory." —*J. Stuart Holden*

We who are His at His coming shall "meet the Lord in the air: and so shall we ever be with the Lord" (1 Thess. 4:17). A. B. Simpson wrote, "I see two races of men, the one marching to the grave, the other marching to the sky; the one going down to the cemetery, the other looking up to the ascension. Beloved, to which do you belong?"

December 11

Behold, he cometh with clouds. —Revelation 1:7

In the Bible clouds are always connected with God. They are those sorrows or sufferings, or providences without or within our lives which seem to dispute the empire of God. If there were no clouds we would not need faith. Seen apart from God, they are accidents or difficulties, but by those very clouds the Spirit of God teaches us to walk by faith. Faith must be an autobiography; until we know God, we have no faith. Faith is the spontaneous outgoing of my person to another person whom I know.

The clouds are the very sign that God is there. What a revelation it is to know that sorrow, bereavement and suffering are clouds that come along with God! God does not come near in clear shining; He comes in the clouds.

It is not true to say that God wants to teach us something in our trials. In every cloud He brings, God wants us to *un*-learn something. God's purpose in the cloud is to simplify our belief until our relationship to Him is exactly that of a child. God uses every cloud which comes in our physical life, in our moral or spiritual life, or in our circumstances, to bring us nearer to Him, until we come to the place where our Lord Jesus Christ lived, and we do not allow our hearts to be troubled.

Christianity does not add to our difficulties, it brings them to a focus, and in the difficulties we find Jesus himself. Is your relationship to God becoming simpler? The proof that it is, is that you do not bother God about yourself so much as you used to because you know Him better.

What is your cloud just now? Is it something you cannot see through, something foggy and indefinite and perplexing? Are there clouds of thinking which make you afraid as you enter them? The revelation in God's Book is that the clouds are but "the dust of his feet." Then thank Him for them.

"They feared as they entered the cloud," and suddenly ... "they saw no man save Jesus only." Have you anyone save Jesus only in your cloud? If you have, it will get darker. You must come to the place where there is "no man, save Jesus only." All others are shadows. Spiritual education is to know God, and nothing simplifies our life more than learning to see in the clouds the goings of His feet.   —*Oswald Chambers*

December 12

I will dwell in the midst of them for ever.—Ezekiel 43:9

This is the Lord's proper place, and it is where He ever desires to remain. When He appeared to Moses in the wilderness, it was in the midst of a burning bush. To Israel afterwards, Moses said: "The Lord thy God walketh in the midst ... to deliver thee." Of Zion the Psalmist said: "God is in the midst of her; she shall not be moved."

Isaiah said: "Cry out and shout, thou inhabitant of Zion, for great is the Holy One of Israel in the midst of thee." Jeremiah exclaimed: "Thou, O Lord, art in the midst of us!" Zephaniah called Jehovah "the King of Israel," and said He was "in the midst" of His people.

When God the Son visited this earth as our Redeemer, His position was still "in the midst." At the age of twelve He was found in the Temple, "sitting in the midst of the doctors." At Calvary two thieves were crucified, and "Jesus in the midst." When His disciples were conversing together after His resurrection, "Jesus himself stood in the midst of them," and said, "Peace be unto you."

When John had a vision of "the seven churches," he saw "in the midst one like unto the Son of Man," and when he looked into heaven he saw the throne and the elders, but "in the midst . . . stood a Lamb" who was slain "before the foundation of the world." So that is why I say our Lord's proper place is "in the midst." May He therefore have His place in my heart, home, and life, and so fulfill His ancient prophecy: "I will dwell in the midst." —*John Roberts*

December 13

To wait for his Son from heaven. —1 Thessalonians 1:10

Dogmatic people are often criticized, especially dogmatic Christians! They are cautioned to make allowances for the differing views of others, and not to offend others by taking a firm stand on a particular doctrine or creed. The apostle Paul would have been considered a *very* dogmatic Christian indeed, for his statement here concerning the second coming of Jesus Christ leaves no room for opposing views or differing interpretations. Jesus *is* coming and we Christians are to patiently wait for that coming.

Jesus Christ *will* return for His own, His bride, the Church. Granted, many generations of believers have watched expectantly for that return in their lifetime—only to be disappointed. Indeed, Jesus anticipated their impatience when He cautioned in Acts 1:7, "It is not for you to know the times or the seasons, which the Father hath put in his own power." The Living Bible emphasizes, "The Father sets those dates, and they are not for you to know." So what if Jesus has not yet returned for His own? Does that alter the fact that He *is* coming again?

"Now is our salvation nearer than when we first believed," Paul says in Romans 13:11, reminding us that every day that passes brings us closer to that great and glorious event so central to the Christian faith, the Second Coming. Today, all eyes are riveted on the Middle East where the time clock of eternity is winding down to the final hour. We have been waiting for centuries, but our waiting will soon be over!

December 14

Good will toward men. —Luke 2:14

This sums it all up! It tells of the good will of God toward all men. A legend that comes down to us from medieval times illustrates this truth: An infidel knight, almost mad in his hatred of all things godly, determined to test by the only means he knew the reality and power of the God whose existence he denied. Going out into the field, armed as if for combat, he cast his glove down upon the ground, after the manner of ancient challengers, and cried out to heaven: "God—if there be a God—I defy You here and now to mortal combat! If You indeed exist, put forth Your might, of which Your pretended priests make such boasts."

As he spoke his eye was caught by a piece of parchment fluttering in the air just above his head. It fell at his feet, and he stooped to pick it up. On it were inscribed the words, "God is love!" Overcome by this unexpected response, he broke his sword in token of his surrender, and kneeling upon the fragments, he consecrated his life to the service of the God he had just before denied.

Thus to all men's defiance, to the rebellion of the world, to the godlessness of the nations, the answer falling from heaven is: "God is love!" This was the message that wafted down that night on the silent Bethlehem air in this sweet note of the angels' song. Cold was the world; shut were men's hearts to God; defiant was the attitude of the nations. Yet to this coldness, this defiance, this revolt, the answer was not swift judgment, but the gift of the Son of God as Saviour—"On earth peace, good will toward men." Wherever the gospel goes today, it breathes the same loving message. God does not hate us; He loves us with a love tender and everlasting.—*J. R. Miller*

December 15

They shall be mine, saith the Lord of hosts, in that day when I make up my jewels.—Malachi 3:17

It is not humility to say, "I am too unworthy to be precious unto the Lord; I cannot believe I can be one of His jewels." For this is God's own testimony concerning those who love to dwell upon His name. He regards them as His own "peculiar treasure" (RV). At "that day" the Lord will gather together all the members of His completed Church. Already we are His; but then it shall be seen and known that we belong to Him. "That day" was always before the mind of the apostle Paul. All that he endured, all that he tried to accomplish, had reference to "that day."

This remembrance of our preciousness to the Lord will not foster pride. It will produce the very opposite effect. It will humble us, while it fills us with surprise that creatures so sinful and unprofitable can ever be regarded by the Lord as His "jewels." It will make us watchful and prayerful that we should walk worthy of so high a distinction.   —*Evan H. Hopkins*

December 16

In that day shall the Lord defend the inhabitants of Jerusalem.—Zechariah 12:8

The Revised Standard Version of this verse promises that "the Lord will put a shield about the inhabitants of Jerusalem so that the feeblest among them on that day shall be like David." Jerusalem means "city of peace" and peace is the promise Zechariah is making to God's people in this richly rewarding passage. Do you feel that you stand alone against the world? That no one really cares about you? Child of God, remember that "if God be for us, who can be against us?" (Rom. 8:31). This is no idle boast of a feeble intellect, "whistling in the dark," but it is the triumphant conclusion of one of the greatest intellects this world has ever known, Paul the apostle. And this concept of God came to him after a lifetime of serving God in the most difficult places, carrying out the most dangerous assignments.

I like the additional emphasis the RSV places here in Zechariah 12:8. Not only will the Lord "defend" us, but He will put a "shield" about us. His defense of me includes the dimension of protection illustrated by a shield. The enemy may be firing his darts of wickedness at me, but I stand beneath the protective shield provided by God himself, so none of these things can touch me, none of these dangers can reach me even though they are falling all around me.

This reminds me of the story of the painting captioned "Serenity." It pictures a tiny bird sitting peacefully on a branch, sheltered from the raging storm by the leaves above its head. The child of God may be in the midst of a chaotic world, but sheltered by God's care, he remains tranquil in spite of the turmoil around him.

As an inhabitant of God's "city of peace," Jerusalem, I can confidently rest in the shelter of His shield, knowing that He holds me in His mighty hands, that His plan for me includes protection and provision—everything I need He will supply. In fact, this is more than the promise of a passive peace, for He will make me "like David," God's mighty warrior king!

December 17

My spirit [soul] hath rejoiced in God my Saviour.
—Luke 1:47

What is the joy of Christmas? Is it the giving of gifts, the family gatherings and the return to old familiar surroundings, the singing of carols and the dramatizing of the scenes of the nativity? Yes, and more.

The joy of Christmas is more than the combined joy of all these blessings. Mary expressed it correctly when she said, "My spirit hath rejoiced in God my Saviour." True Christmas joy is in the right relationship with God through Jesus Christ the Lord. It flows from a security gained by faith in God's protecting love.

The joy of Christmas is the joy of a new hope. Christ's birth caused a new song to be heard, a new life to be seen, and a new venture to be undertaken.

The joy of Christmas is the joy that touches earth and sky. Shepherds and wise men, angels and maidens unite in glorious celebration of a most glorious event—Christ Jesus was born.

The joy of Christmas is the joy of liberty, the joy of deliverance, the joy of God's approval in pardoning mercy and in sanctifying grace. Charles Wells says: "Men always have a hope for a better world when they see the miracle of Christmas. All the selfishness, bitterness and hatred pause and for a day surrender to the sweet charm of a little divine Prince who cast a spell over the earth two thousand years ago, a spell that has not been broken, a charm that has increased to become a spiritual dominion stretching around the earth from pole to pole."

—O. G. Wilson

December 18

And Mary said, My soul doth magnify the Lord.—Luke 1:46

No wonder Mary sang that day. At the shut gate of the garden of Eden there was a promise given of a Saviour—a Saviour who should be "the seed of the woman." Ever after that, all along the line of the covenant, each woman hoped that she might be the mother of this Saviour.

Centuries passed, and generations of disappointed hearts saw their hopes fade. At length one day a heavenly messenger came to this lowly Nazarite maiden, and announced to her that she should be the mother of this long-expected Messiah. What a glorious honor! No wonder she rejoiced.

One strain of her song was, "My soul doth magnify the Lord." We cannot make God any greater; He needs nothing from us. Can the candle add to the glory of the sun's noonday splendor? Yet we can so tell others of God that He will seem greater to them. It was said in praise of a distinguished preacher that in his sermons he made God appear very great. We can declare God's goodness and grace. Then we can so live ourselves as to honor Him, and thus magnify His name.

Retzsch, a German sculptor, made a wonderful statue of the Redeemer. For eight years it was his dream by night, his thought by day. He first made a clay model, and set it before a child five or six years old. There were none of the usual emblematical marks about the figure—no cross, no crown, nothing by which to identify it. Yet when the child saw it he said, "The Redeemer! the Redeemer!" This was a wonderful triumph of art. We should exhibit in our life and character such a reproduction of the nobleness and beauty of Christ that everyone who looks upon us may instinctively recognize the features, and say, "Behold the image of our Redeemer!" There is no other way of magnifying the Lord that so impresses the world.   —J. R. Miller

December 19

My spirit hath rejoiced in God.—Luke 1:47

This is another strain of Mary's song, and it has for us the secret of all deep Christian joy. We have no real and lasting joy till we are in God's family, and in God as the refuge of our souls. One of the old prophets says, "Let the inhabitants of the rocks sing!" None can sing with lasting gladness but the inhabitants of the Rock—those who are in the shelter of the Rock of Ages. The world's songs soon change to cries of terror.

During the battle of Gettysburg there was a little bird on a tree that would sing a few notes every time there was a lull in the awful roar of battle; but when the crash began again, its song would cease. That is the way with this world's joy. It sings a few strains now and then in the pauses of life's struggle and discontent. When the waves of sorrow break, its voice is drowned; it cannot sing in loss, in bereavement, in the hour of dying.

But one who rejoices in God has a joy that sings on through all the roar of battle, through all the darkness of night. Troubles come to the Christian, but they do not rob him of his joy. He may be in deep sorrow, but all the while there is a fountain of joy welling up in his heart. Sometimes there is a freshwater spring by the seashore. Twice every day the salt tides roll over it, but the spring never ceases to flow; and when the brackish waves have rolled back, the waters of the spring are still sweet as ever.

That is the way with the Christian's joy. It is a living well in his heart. Even in his sorrow he has a deep peace in his soul. Then when the sorrow is past, the joy springs fresh as ever. The permanence of all joy depends upon the source from which it comes. If it be in God that we rejoice, then earth has no power to take from us the gladness.   —J. R. Miller

December 20

My Saviour.—Luke 1:47

It is a great thing when anyone can say, "My Saviour!" Many people can talk about Christ very beautifully and eloquently. They can linger upon the story of His life, and speak with tender accents of His sufferings and death. They can paint the beauties of His character, and tell of the salvation which He has provided. Yet they cannot say, "He is my Saviour." And what good does all this knowledge of Christ do them if they are not saved by Him?

I saw a picture of two little beggar children standing on the pavement before a beautiful house, looking in at the windows, where they beheld a happy family gathered around the table at their evening meal. There were evidences of luxury and great comfort within the house. It was winter, and the night without was bleak, and the snow was falling. The poor children outside saw all the brightness and beauty that were within; they could describe it, but they could not call it their own. And while they looked in upon the happy scene, the storm swept about them, and they shivered in their thin rags, and felt the gnawings of unsatisfied hunger.

So it is with those who know of Christ and His salvation by the hearing of the ear, but who cannot say, "He is my Saviour." They see the deep joy of others in time of trouble, but around them the storm still breaks. They look at others feeding upon Christ, and witness their satisfaction, but they themselves stand shivering in the winter of sorrow, and their hungry hearts find no bread to eat.

All our study about Christ will do us no good if we do not take Him as our own personal Saviour, and learn to call Him, "My Jesus." But when we can say of Him, "He is my Saviour," all life is bright and full of joy for us. He is ready to be ours, to give himself to us with all His blessed life, and all the privileges of heirship in the Father's family, the moment we will accept Him   —*J. R. Miller*

December 21

He hath visited and redeemed his people.—Luke 1:68

What a beautiful thought it is that God pays visits to His people in this world! We remember a number of visits He made in the olden times—to Adam and Eve, to Abraham, to Jacob, to Moses, to Joshua, and to others. But the most wonderful visit He ever made was when Christ came and stayed so long, and did so much to bless the world.

After a while He went away; yet we must not think that He went away to stay, and that He never pays visits to this world anymore. Every time any of His children are in trouble He comes to help them. They do not always know it; for He comes unseen, and often so softly and silently that people do not know they have such a glorious visitor within their doors.

He visits those who are not saved, to try to persuade them to accept salvation. When we are in great danger, He visits us to deliver us. When we are sick or suffering, He visits us to give us grace to bear our suffering.

Then there are times He comes and knocks at our doors, and wants to visit us and give us some rich blessing, and we will not open the door. There was an old Scotch woman who could not pay her rent, and the landlord said he would seize her goods. A good friend heard of it and went to her house to give her money to save her property. He knocked, but could not get in. Next day he met her and told her of his visit. "Was that you?" she asked with amazement; "I thought it was the officer coming to take my goods, and I had all the doors and windows barred, and would not let him in." So Christ comes and knocks. He knows of our need, and wants to bless or help us; and we bar our doors and keep Him out, not knowing who He is nor why He comes. We must remember that when Christ comes it is always to do us good, and that we shall rob ourselves if we ever keep Him out or refuse His visit. —*J. R. Miller*

December 22

To give light to them that sit in darkness and in the shadow of death.—Luke 1:79

Suppose the sun were never to rise again, and the light of every star were put out, what a gloomy world this would be! This is the picture of the world, in a moral and spiritual sense, without Christ, as it is painted in these words, "darkness and the shadow of death!"—no light to guide, to cheer, to produce joy and beauty.

A world without Christ would be utter blackness, unil lumined by a single ray of sun, or even by a single burning faraway star. Christ is light. Only think what light does for us! It makes our days very bright; it shows us all the beautiful things that are around us. But it does far more. It produces all the life of the earth, and then nourishes it. There would not be a bud or a root or a leaf were it not for the sun. Nor would there be any beauty, for every lovely thing in nature the sun paints.

Think of Christ, then, as light. His love brooding over us causes us to live, and nourishes in us every spiritual grace. Every beam of hope is a ray of light. What the coming of light is to a prisoner in a darkened dungeon, that is the bursting of mercy over the guilty soul. Light gives cheer; and what cheer the gospel gives to the mourner, to the poor, to the troubled! Is it not strange that any will refuse to receive this light? If anyone would persist in living in a dark cave, far away from the light of the sun, with only dim candles of his own making to pour a few feeble, flickering beams upon the gloom, we should consider him insane.

What shall we say of those who persist in living in the darkness of sin, with no light but the candles of earth's false hopes to shine upon their souls? There are many such, too. They turn to every "will-o'-the-wisp" that flashes a little beam —anywhere rather than to Christ. It is like preferring a tallow candle to the sun.   —J. R. Miller

December 23

To guide our feet into the way of peace.—Luke 1:79

First Jesus made the way of peace for us. Sin had destroyed the road to heaven, leaving only a rough and thorny way for human feet to go upon. There never would have been a path of peace had not Jesus himself made it. All ways in life save that one which He has opened for us are full of pain and trouble, and lead only to sorrow, despair, and death. But Christ prepared a highway that is beautiful and blessed, and that leads to eternal joy and glory.

It was not easy work building this road. In the construction of some of this world's great thoroughfares thousands of human lives were sacrificed. We forget sometimes, as we move on in the highway of redemption, amid peaceful scenes, with soft music in our ears, and rich comforts in our hearts, and heavenly hopes to woo us forward, what it cost our blessed Lord, what toil and tears and blood, to prepare the way for us, to bridge over the chasms and level down the mountains. But now the way is open, and from beginning to end it is a way of peace.

A great many people think that the Christian life is hard and unpleasant, that it is a rough and steep road; but truly it is a way of pleasantness and peace. The only really happy people in this world are those who are following Christ along the way of redemption. They have their share of troubles, disappointments, sorrows; but all the time in the midst of these they have a secret peace of which the world knows nothing. There are paths in the low valleys, among the great mountains, which are sweet pictures of the Christian's way of peace. High up among the peaks and crags the storms sweep in wild fury, but on these valley paths no breath of tempest ever blows. Flowers bloom and springs of water gurgle along the wayside, and trees cast their grateful shadow, and bird-songs fill the air. Such is Christ's "way of peace" in this world.   —*J. R. Miller*

December 24

Unto you is born this day in the city of David a Saviour, which is Christ the Lord.—Luke 2:11

How wonderful this was! We must remember who it was that was thus born. The birth of another child in this world was nothing unusual, for thousands of children are born every day. But this baby was the Lord of glory. This was not the beginning of His life. He had lived from all eternity in heaven. His hands made the universe. All glory was His. All the crowns of power flashed upon His head. All the mighty angels called Him Lord. We must remember this if we would understand how great was His coming to earth.

Peter the Great of Russia left his throne and in the lowly disguise of a shipwright he apprenticed himself at Zaandam and Amsterdam. He worked among the common laborers dressed in the same kind of clothing, living in a hut, preparing his own food, making his own bed. Yet in so doing he never ceased to be the ruler of Russia. His royal splendor was laid aside for a time; his regal power and majesty were temporarily hidden beneath the disguise he wore; but there was never an hour when he was not the emperor.

So Christ's glory was folded away under robes of human flesh. He never ceased to be the Son of God; yet He assumed all the conditions of humanity. He veiled His power, and became a helpless infant, unable to walk, to speak, to think, lying dependently upon His mother's breast. He veiled His knowledge, and learned as other children do. He laid aside His sovereignty, His majesty. What humility! And it was all for our sake that He might lift us up to glory. It was as a Saviour that He came into the world. He became the Son of Man that He might make us the sons of God. He came down to earth and lived among men, entering into their experiences of humiliation that He might lift them up to glory to share His exaltation.   —*J. R. Miller*

December 25

They presented unto him gifts.—Matthew 2:11

THE CHRISTMAS PARTY

I have many friends. When they arranged to have a celebration in honor of my birthday, I was greatly pleased. One likes to be remembered by one's friends, and celebrations are gratifying events. Moreover, it was intimated to me that extensive preparations were being made for gifts to be given. This made me especially happy, for my needs are great, or rather, the needs of others to whom I am giving my life are many, and in my present circumstances are wholly dependent on what my friends are doing. You may be sure that it was with kindling emotions and welling gratitude that I looked forward to the day when I was to be so signally honored with a great party and with gifts.

The great day came. A vast number had remembered it, and my name was on every tongue. Gifts also came in such profusion that I was almost overwhelmed at the sight of them. But when I looked at the cards on which the names were written, indicating those to whom the gifts were given, I was astonished and amazed. I could not find my name on one card!

My friends were giving gifts back and forth to one another in hectic complexity! But I, whose birthday was the occasion for the party, was strangely forgotten. I walked about, enjoying the occasion as best I could, watching the happiness of others. But what a lonesomeness I felt, and how I wondered how I would meet those needs which I had thought the gifts would supply.

I am the Christ whose birthday people celebrate by giving gifts to each other but not to Me.   —*Author Unknown*

December 26

Sir, we would see Jesus.—John 12:21

Keeping Christmas

Are you willing to stoop down and consider
    the needs and desires of little children;
And remember the weakness, the loneliness of
    people who are growing old;
To stop asking how much your friends love you
    and ask yourself whether you love them enough;
To bear in mind the things that other people
    have to bear in their hearts;
To try to understand what those who live in the
    same house with you really want, without
    waiting for them to tell you;
To trim your lamp so that it will give more light
    and less smoke, and to carry it in front so
    that your shadow will fall behind you;
To make a grave for your ugly thoughts—and a
    garden for your kindly feelings with the gate
    open—are you willing to do these things,
    even for a day?

Then you can keep Christmas.
Are you willing to believe that love is the
    strongest thing in the world—stronger than
    hate, stronger than evil, stronger than
    death, and that the blessed life that began
    in Bethlehem nineteen hundred years ago is
    the image and brightness of the eternal Love?
Then you can keep Christmas.
And if you keep it for a day, why not always?
But you can never keep it alone.

—Henry Van Dyke

December 27

The days of thy mourning shall be ended.—Isaiah 60:20

These are prophetic words concerning Israel. But they have a voice for God's children today. The passage describes the transition from a state of "violence" and "wasting"—of darkness and gloom—into a condition of light, and joy, and boundless prosperity.

The soul may read in the history of God's dealings with His ancient people the counterpart of his own existence and experience. The great principles on which He dealt with them in relation to their backsliding and sin are precisely those on which He deals with His spiritual Israel today.

So the apostle Paul declares: "Now all these things happened unto them for ensamples; and they are written for our admonition, upon whom the ends of the world are come" (1 Cor. 10:11). There is a time coming when the day of our mourning shall cease, and God shall wipe away all tears from all faces. But we need not wait until glory for a fulfillment of these words in our own experience. We may have a foretaste, in a measure at least, of the joy and blessing contained in these words. Fullness of joy is a privilege our Lord speaks of as belonging to His chidren even now (John 15:11).

—Evan H. Hopkins

December 28

Be thou faithful unto death, and I will give thee a crown of life.—Revelation 2:10

These words are taken from the very last message Christ uttered directly to His people. They are most precious, for they are spoken to a church persecuted unto death, yet holy in the midst of tribulation.

Nothing is said of any special works or achievements credited to the praise of this church, yet a poor persecuted church suffering for Christ cannot be expected to do much. To endure steadfastly, then, is all that can be expected, and such perseverance is worthy of highest commendation.

Look carefully at the words of Christ: "I know thy works, and tribulation, and poverty." No one else may think you are doing anything. All may think your life a failure so far as spiritual accomplishments are concerned. But the Master knows the pressure under which you live, the day-by-day irritations and frustrations you must endure. He knows it all, and He rewards your faithfulness. Note what He says: "Fear none of these things" (v. 10) but "Be thou faithful."

Note carefully: He did not say, "Be brilliant." No, "Be faithful." Not "Be popular," but "Be faithful," knowing you will be anything but popular. He did not say, "Be successful. Produce a large harvest. Greatly impress your generation." No, He said, "Be faithful."

In Luke 16:10, the Master said, "He that is faithful in that which is least is faithful also in much." Our lives are made up of little things—"that which is least." Life can be a drudgery, monotonous, deadening. But the Christian course is to be a faithful branch and produce only good fruit; be a faithful light. Your light may not dazzle the world, but keep it burning.

The crowns of this world are studded with valuable gems, but even the most valuable are of only finite worth. Only one crown is eternal and infinite in value—the crown of life.

—*O. G. Wilson*

December 29

Behold, I come quickly: blessed is he that keepeth the sayings of this book.—Revelation 22:7

The quality of a life becomes increasingly important as one nears the end of it. At least that has been my experience. Look at our text for the day and then reflect on the caliber of your life as you are living it right now. In the light of the suddenness—and the imminence—of the return of Jesus Christ, how are you living?

In another part of the Word we are warned, "Prepare to meet thy God" (Amos 4:12). This admonition applies particularly to the unbeliever, but I think Christians, too, need to examine their lives to see whether they are truly living them in the light of the Lord's soon return.

He *is* coming again—and soon. Elsewhere in the book of Revelation John emphasizes that fact. At the very beginning of his treatise he states, "Blessed is he that readeth, and they that hear the words of this prophecy, and keep these things which are written therein: for the time [of His return] is at hand." In chapter 3, verse 11, he writes, "Behold, I come quickly," and again in chapter 22, verse 12, he reminds the readers of Revelation one final time, "Behold, I come quickly; and my reward is with me, to give every man according as his work shall be."

What is the significance of the word "quickly"? I think it simply means without advance warning, a shocking event in a split-second of time, making it impossible for the unready to do their house-cleaning, to get their tangled affairs in order. How is it with you, Christian? Would you be ready if He returned at this very moment?

And how is it with you, unbeliever? Are you still sitting on the fence of vacillation? Oh, get ready for His return today, for it is coming soon!

December 30

As sorrowful, yet alway rejoicing; as poor, yet making many rich; as having nothing, and yet possessing all things. —2 Corinthians 6:10

Is the Christian life a sad or joyous one? In one sense it is both. The Lord Jesus was "the Man of Sorrows," and yet one of the most precious gifts He leaves to His people is His peace (John 14:27).

To be sorrowful and yet alway rejoicing is a paradox that cannot be understood intellectually, but is perfectly intelligible when we experience it practically. There may be much around us to occasion sorrow, but if within, His peace guards the heart and mind, and His Spirit fills with love and joy and peace, the life will not be a sorrowful one. No, in spite of trying circumstances we shall then know what it is to "rejoice with joy unspeakable and full of glory" (1 Pet. 1:8).

In the same way the other two statements of this paradox may be understood. The apostle was poor, and yet he was rich; he had nothing, and yet he possessed all things. Every child of God has the same inheritance in Christ. It is as he uses what God has bestowed that he brings others into the same riches. —*Evan H. Hopkins*

December 31

The Lord thy God bare thee, as a man doth bear his son, in all the way that ye went, until ye came into this place. —Deuteronomy 1:31

Who were they of them whom this blessed fact is declared? They were a chosen people, a redeemed people, a delivered people. The Lord who had brought them out of the house of bondage did not set them free that they might be a self-guided self-governed people. Bondage, misery, and perplexity would inevitably have followed had they been left to their own resources. The Lord had redeemed and delivered them for himself.

They were to be a people for His possession. We see here how God's gracious upholding follows immediately His work of redemption. And is this not the history of His dealings with His people today?

He bears us as a man bears his son, in all the way that we go. As we meekly follow His guidance and confide in His keeping power, we have the comfort of knowing that it is divine Wisdom who plans our future and leads us into the unknown future. He thinks of us and provides for us as a father pities and cares for his children.

Let this blessed fact assure our hearts as we enter another year.   —*Evan H. Hopkins*